THE CONCERT SONG COMPANION

THE CONCERT SONG COMPANION

A Guide to the Classical Repertoire

by

CHARLES OSBORNE

LONDON
VICTOR GOLLANCZ LTD
1974

784.3009
O52c
97488
June 1976

To

Lotte Lehmann

in friendship and admiration

MADE AND PRINTED IN GREAT BRITAIN BY
THE GARDEN CITY PRESS LIMITED
LETCHWORTH, HERTFORDSHIRE
SG6 1JS

ACKNOWLEDGEMENTS

During the course of writing this book, I have received valuable assistance from too many people, libraries and other institutions to be listed here. My thanks are also due to the authors and publishers of those books from which I have quoted, and to Mr Kenneth Thomson for his help with proof-reading.

C.O.

CONTENTS

INTRODUCTION

WHAT I HAVE attempted in this book is a survey of song; the kind of song which one finds variously described as 'concert', 'art', or sometimes even 'classical song'. 'Concert song' seems the most useful, certainly the least inexact or misleading, of some descriptions, especially since 'art song' sounds primly off-putting, and 'classical song' really ought to be used only to refer to songs written during the classical period, i.e. the 18th century. Concert song clearly means the kind of songs one hears sung at concerts or recitals.

Addressing myself to the general music-lover who, though he possesses no special knowledge of the song literature, is never-theless interested enough in songs and their singers to attend recitals of *Lieder* or of songs in various languages, I have naturally confined myself to that period of time in which the vast majority of these songs was composed, though not necessarily only to those composers whose songs have survived to be remembered in recital programmes today. I suppose this to be roughly the three centuries covered by the years 1650–1950, though most of the songs we, as audiences, know and love were composed in the middle of this period, in other words in the 19th century. The heart of this survey, understandably, as it is the heart of the song repertoire as we know it, is the great period of the German *Lied*, the century which gave us the songs of Schubert, Schumann, Brahms, Wolf and Strauss. Almost as important are the English and Italian forerunners of the German *Lied*, the song literatures of other countries in the 19th century, such as Russia, Scandinavia and France, and, in the present century, the re-emergence, to some extent, of the English language in the world of serious or concert song.

In arbitrarily suggesting the year 1950 to end the period under survey, it is not my intention to be too rigidly dogmatic. There are several composers mentioned in the following pages who are now, in the mid 1970s, making important contributions to song; among them, to confine one's examples to English-language song, are Benjamin Britten, Michael Tippett and Ned Rorem. There are many younger composers as well whom I have not mentioned. But it takes a certain amount of time nowadays for new music (even songs, which are, in general, perhaps more easily assimilable than pieces of orchestral or chamber music) to familiarize itself, and the most popular songs of today to be encountered in song recitals will usually, on closer scrutiny, turn out to be those which singers have been letting us hear and re-hear for the past ten or twenty years.

Also, to many lovers of song, a great era seemed symbolically, if not actually, to end with the *Vier Letzte Lieder* of the great *Lieder* composer, Richard Strauss. That several masterpieces of song in a more modern musical idiom than that favoured by Strauss were composed much earlier than the *Vier Letzte Lieder*, by Alban Berg amongst others, does not invalidate the symbol. Of course, the *Vier Letzte Lieder* are, in wider terms, not a full stop but merely a semi-colon. Nevertheless, it does seem to us at this particular period in musical history, while we mark time, waiting for the next movement to begin, that a clearly defined period has recently drawn to a close, or perhaps a half-close; a period in which communication from creator to appreciator was always of primary importance, and in which composers addressed themselves to a wide intelligent audience, non-specialist in knowledge, but receptive in tendency. My aim in this book has been to provide a broad historical survey of the period covered by modern performing practice, to comment on its highways and even to draw attention to the more interesting of its byways.

C.O.

THE CONCERT SONG COMPANION

I

THE GERMAN LANGUAGE

IN GERMANY, THE development of solo song was rapid throughout the 18th century, although no major composer's output of songs could be called voluminous. Although Johann Sebastian Bach (1685–1750), for example, wrote a good deal for the voice (more than 300 cantatas, several of them for solo voice and orchestra), he composed no more than five songs for solo voice and clavier. But it is from this trickle, increasing in size and importance with Haydn, Mozart and Beethoven, that the great broad stream of Schubertian song derives. Bach's five songs, transcribed in his second wife Anna Magdalena Bach's *Notenbuch*, date from 1725. Their titles are: (1) 'So oft ich meine Tabakspfeife'; (2) 'Bist du bei mir'; (3) 'Gedenke doch'; (4) 'Gieb dich zufrieden'; (5) 'Willst du dein Herz mir schenken?' The last song is sentimental, domestic; the first is heavily north Germanic in its philosophizing about the joys of smoking. The second, 'Bist du bei mir', a deceptively simple tune in which passion and spiritual power curiously combine, is the first great German *Lied*. 'If thou art with me, then will I go joyfully to my death.' The rapt ecstasy of the vocal line brings something of sensuousness to the religious fervour of the words. Everything is in the voice part, of course. The accompaniment is formal. It was to remain so until Mozart.

Song played hardly a more important part in the *œuvre* of Bach's great contemporary, George Frideric Handel (1685–1759), though it ranged over three languages, thus reflecting the composer's cosmopolitanism and the geographical aspects of his career. In addition to twelve German songs, Handel's output contains seven *Airs français* which he wrote in his twenties, and *A Collection of English Songs*, written at various times and published in 1731. The English songs are also known as 'Minuet Songs', and some of them may well be vocal arrangements of instrumental minuets. The Arcadian pastoral air of many of them is reflected in their individual titles: 'Chloe, when I view thee'; 'Strephon, in vain'; 'Ye winds to whom Collin complains'. But these and the seven French songs which are of a similar type ('Petite fleur brunette', 'Vous qui m'aviez procuré un amour éternel' . . .) are very slight. Of more interest are the twelve songs which Handel wrote to German texts. Three are juvenile pieces to words which may well be by the thirteen-year-old composer himself. The remaining nine, dating from around 1729, are mature works, settings of poems by Barthold Heinrich Brockes, to continuo accompaniment with a violin obbligato. These beautiful, reflective pieces are large in scale, pre-figuring the concert aria, perhaps, rather than the concert song. Numbers 4 ('Süsse Stille, sanfte Quelle') and 6 ('Meine Seele hört im Sehen') are particularly to be admired for their confidence and poise.

For many years, almost the only Handel song at all well-known was 'Dank sei dir, Herr', thought to be composed about 1739. It now seems most likely, however, that this was a 19th-century forgery by a German composer and conductor Siegfried Ochs (1858–1929).

The songs of Carl Philipp Emanuel Bach (1714–1788), the second son of Johann Sebastian, are of interest not only as a link between his father and Haydn but also in their own right. C. P. E. Bach was a fluent and prolific composer who turned his back on the contrapuntal style of his father, and wrote pleasantly agreeable music, much of it for keyboard instruments, in which his themes are usually treated homophonically. He produced a large number of songs, both secular and spiritual, which share the qualities of his instrumental music. Generally plain of texture, they are nevertheless accomplished, and always give evidence of a real lyric gift. Even the smaller secular songs are usually rescued from triviality by their melodic charm, as often as not supported simply by an Alberti bass; but the spiritual songs are much finer, deeply expressive and harmonically more interesting. The accompaniments are usually quite formal and unadventurous, but as early as the *Geistliche Oden und Lieder* of 1754, settings of poems from the volume of that name produced by Christian Fürchtegott Gellert in 1737, C. P. E. Bach can be seen to strive for some degree of independence in his keyboard parts. Gellert's verse, moral rather than deeply religious, and born of the Enlightenment, appealed to the younger Bach's temperament, and inspired some of his finest songs, of which 'Wider den Übermut' from the *Geistliche Oden und Lieder* is a particularly remarkable example with its relatively free accompaniment and individual melodic line. A later example of C. P. E. Bach's style in devotional song is the collection, *Christian Christoph Sturms geistliche Gesänge mit Melodien* (1780–1).

C. P. E. Bach's younger brother, Johann Christian Bach (1735–1782) settled in London in his twenties, so is it not surprising that his thirty or so songs are to English texts, many of them written to be performed at the pleasure gardens at Vauxhall, and therefore with accompaniments for small orchestra. Though pleasant, they lack the distinction and individuality of the other Bachs.

As the 18th century progressed, the main stream of German song became noticeably broader, although, until Mozart, not very noticeably deeper. Several minor composers contributed to it in various ways. Johann Friedrich Agricola (1720–1774), a pupil of Johann Sebastian Bach, settled in Berlin as organist and teacher of singing. His songs are a reflection of his other interests, music for the church and, in somewhat Italianate style, for the theatre. Johann Philipp Kirnberger (1721–1783), another Bach pupil, wrote songs and also, more importantly, edited and helped to make known vocal music of earlier composers such as Hans Leo Hassler (1564–1612). Johann Adam Hiller (1728–1804) is important mainly as one of the earliest composers of the *Singspiel*, but he also helped in the development of the *Lied* or German classical song by moving away from the simple strophic song in the direction of a freer, more dramatic utterance. Johann Abraham Schulz (1747–1800), a favourite pupil of Kirnberger, wrote a number of songs, mostly in the style and spirit of folk song. He was perhaps the first composer to raise the simple folk song to the level of art, which he did in part by choosing with great care the poems he set. He was fortunate in that German poetry at that time was undergoing a healthy revival : Goethe apart, there were such excellent lyric talents as those of Burger, Claudius, Hölty and Overbeck to choose from. Three volumes of Schulz's *Lieder in Volkston bei dem Clavier zu singen* appeared between 1782 and 1790.

With Christoph Willibald Gluck (1714–1787), German song took on a new dimension. It would be as idle to pretend that Gluck's songs are as important a part of his *œuvre* as his operas, as it would be to assert the reverse for Schubert; nevertheless

Gluck's intentions in the field of song were as serious as they were in opera, and they are very well realized in the few songs, at once ambitious and simple, which he wrote towards the end of his life. These are all settings of Friedrich Gottlieb Klopstock (1724–1803), Goethe's great predecessor and the precursor of the *Sturm und Drang* school of German poetry. A pietistic strain runs through Klopstock's work : indeed he made his name with a huge religious epic, *Messias*. But his finest and purest poetry is to be found in his unrhymed odes and songs, to which Gluck was strongly attracted.

Virtually all of Gluck's songs are to be found in the volume published in Vienna in 1785 as Klopstock's *Oden und Lieder beim Clavier zu singen*. The volume contains seven songs, the last of which, 'Die Neigung', is not a Klopstock poem. An eighth, 'Ode an den Tod', another Klopstock setting, although written at the same time was published five years after Gluck's death. By the time he came to compose these songs, Gluck had behind him a lifetime's experience in the setting of words to music. But whereas, in the operas, his concern was to heighten and to extend the emotion expressed in his librettists' words, his intention in song was quite different. It is the simplicity and straightforwardness of his Klopstock settings which impress us today. His melody never becomes florid, and for the most part is content to move syllable for syllable with the poem. The rightness of his declamation, a deceptively plain arioso, is equally striking. Goethe, whose poetry Gluck never set, wrote to his own 'official' composer Kayser,* '. . . I found [Gluck's] settings of poems by Klopstock, which he had conjured into a musical rhythm, remarkable.'†

Even the simpler of these *Oden und Lieder*, for instance no. 4, 'Der Jüngling', have a breadth and spaciousness which set them apart from the songs of Gluck's predecessors. And in 'Die frühen Gräber', the unity of mood between voice and piano, so quietly yet surely achieved, anticipates the melodically more prodigal Schubert. Only in no. 7, 'Die Neigung', does one sense that the composer is looking back to the more formalized arias of his operas.

With Joseph Hayden (1732–1809), song begins to assume more

* Philipp Christoph Kayser (1755–1823), a friend of Goethe's youth, set a few of the poet's lyrics, and also wrote incidental music for one or two of the plays
† Alfred Einstein *Gluck* J. M. Dent London 1936

importance in the complete *œuvre*. Not only did Haydn write considerably more songs than Gluck, he also integrated them more fully into his working life as a composer, though this is not to say, of course, that he necessarily brought to solo song the individuality that is the hallmark of his symphonies and quartets. Although Haydn, too, could write a simple and tender melody, unlike Gluck he inclined in his songs towards the same floridity of expression as is to be found in his arias for the stage.

It was not until he was well into his forties that Haydn began to turn his attention to solo song. His twenty-four German songs were published in two parts: twelve *Lieder für das Klavier* in 1781, and a further twelve songs three years later. Together with twelve English songs which appeared in 1794–5, and a handful of miscellaneous pieces, these constitute the bulk of his writing for the solo voice. The German songs are remarkable for the splendour and detail of their keyboard writing as much as for their melodic charm. In many of them, for instance 'Das Leben ist ein Traum', Haydn's treatment of the words is so broad as to suggest something of the operatic aria. Others are slight and trifling, but there are some which, in their interfusion of voice and keyboard part, anticipate Schubert; notably the delicate and tender 'Trost unglücklicher Liebe' and the deeply felt 'O fliess, ja wallend fliess in Zahren'. 'Gebet zu Gott' is interesting for its free declamation, as well as for its elaborately stately piano part. At least one of the slighter songs, 'Gegenliebe', fulfils a more useful purpose later by being used in the Symphony No. 73 ('La Chasse'). Attempts at humour, in 'Lob der Faulheit' and 'Die zu späte Ankunft der Mutter' are less than completely successful, though the latter song is interesting for the manner in which the melody is shared by voice and keyboard. The former celebrates sloth in an extended, two stanza yawn whose heaviness is self-defeating.

The twelve English songs, or canzonettas as they were originally called, are both superior and inferior to Haydn's German settings: superior in that the accompaniments have become more independent and therefore interesting in their own right, inferior in that, understandably, the composer's feeling for the English language is superficial in comparison with his setting of texts in his own tongue. 'A Pastoral Song' ('My mother bids me bind my hair') is quite charming, but would be equally so as an instrumental melody. The tune nowhere suggests that it has been called into being by the poem. The well-known 'She never told her love', a setting of Viola's lines from Shakespeare's *Twelfth Night*, achieves a greater fusion of voice and words. Indeed, behind its touching formality there lurks a minor masterpiece. A song which should be better known is 'The Wanderer', finely romantic in the grand manner. 'The Mermaid' is pleasant and lively, though the music seems inappropriate to the words. 'The Sailor's Song' is a rousing patriotic ditty, with a graphic piano part, illustrative of the 'rattling ropes and rolling seas' which the seaman grapples with as he strives to maintain Britain's glory. Other canzonettas of particularly graceful charm include 'Sympathy' with its sweet melody and calmly classical accompaniment, the cheerful 'Piercing Eyes', and the serene, leisurely 'Content'. In addition to the twelve canzonettas, two English songs were published separately, 'O Tuneful Voice' and 'The Spirit's Song', the former a tender cry of farewell, the latter perhaps the finest of all Haydn's songs, poised yet emotionally charged. The words of many of these English songs are by Anne Hunter, wife of the famous surgeon Dr John Hunter, who befriended Haydn on his London visits. Haydn, like Beethoven after him, also made hundreds of arrangements of British folk songs, mainly Scottish and Welsh, with *ad lib* violin and cello parts as well as piano. Though not admired by folk-song experts, Haydn's accompaniments usually dress up the tunes quite prettily.

Among the few German songs by Haydn published individually are 'Der schlaue und dienstfertige Pudel' which deserves to be better known, and the famous hymn, 'Gott, erhalte Franz den Kaiser', whose noble and affecting melody Haydn used again in his 'Emperor' Quartet in C op. 76 no. 3. The composer intended his hymn as a national anthem, having written it in 1797 after his second visit to England where he had been greatly impressed by 'God save the King'. Haydn's hymn did, in fact, become the first Austrian national anthem.

Writers on Wolfgang Amadeus Mozart (1756–1791) have frequently expressed surprise that a composer with his genius for lyrical melody should have written no more than thirty-five or so solo songs. But possibly it is because he cared deeply about song that Mozart was not more profuse in this form. Certainly, each one of his songs, though not all are equally good, is worthy of consideration. None of them are hastily written trifles, not even those he composed in childhood and adolescence, and several are minor masterpieces. One does not seek in these songs the genius in word-setting and declamation of a Hugo Wolf; one finds rather a rare poetic impulse and, on occasion, dramatic intensity in miniature.

The early Salzburg songs that Mozart wrote in his teens are simple in manner, and possess piano parts that do not stray very far from the vocal line, though the earliest song of all, 'An die Freude', which the eleven-year-old Mozart composed at Olmütz, has a charming gravity all its own. The finest of the Salzburg songs is 'Ridente la calma', with an Italian text, a stately yet gracious arietta. Two songs to French texts, written in Mannheim in 1777 and 1778, are even more interesting: they are 'Oiseau si tous les ans' and 'Dans un bois solitaire'. The latter has a pleasantly flowing piano part, anticipating the future independence the accompanying instrument was to achieve. An unfairly neglected group of three simple but very beautiful songs (1780) consists of 'An die Bescheidenheit', 'An die Einsamkeit' and 'Ich wurd' auf meinem Pfad', to poems from the novel *Sophiens Reisen* by J. T. Hermes. These, like the majority of Mozart's songs, are strophic. So, too, is 'Komm, liebe Zither', whose accompaniment is not for zither, but for mandolin. Another song whose beauty is born of simplicity is 'Gesellenreise', written for the initiation of the composer's father into the Viennese masonic lodge 'Zur wahren Eintracht'.

It has been said that Mozart's songs are flawed by the mundane quality of their words. True, Mozart usually chose poems of innocuous piety and impeccable sentiment without much regard to their literary quality. Even Goethe's 'Das Veilchen' can hardly be called one of the poet's finer lyrics. But Mozart's settings magically enhance the frequently mediocre verses which inspired them. The songs composed in Vienna in the 1780s to verses of the minor, not very talented, Christian Felix Weisse (1726–1804) are striking examples of this: 'Der Zauberer' and 'Die Zufriedenheit' are both excellent. 'Die betrogene Welt' may be less good, but 'Die Verschweigung' is a gem, whose melody could be by no one but Mozart.

The poem 'Das Veilchen' by Goethe (1749–1832) has been mentioned. Mozart's setting of this early lyric is one of his finest songs, this time *durchkomponiert*, composed throughout. C. P. E. Bach has been called the father of the *durchkomponiertes Lied*, but it was Mozart who, in a handful of songs, wrote the first masterpieces in this form, and 'Das Veilchen' is the earliest of them. The apparent lightness and ease of Mozart's writing mask a depth of feeling which is revealed only at the end of the song, in the little postlude which the composer added using his own words, sentimental but real and unaffected : 'Das arme Veilchen! Es war ein herzigs Veilchen.'

'Die Alte', a comic character-song is directed to be sung 'ein bisschen durch die Nase' ('somewhat nasally'). Dating from the same year, 1787, are the touching lament, 'Das Lied der Trennung' which has the pathos of a Mozartian instrumental slow movement, and the magnificently passionate 'Als Luise die Briefe ihres ungetreuen Liebhabers verbrannte', sung by the heartbroken Luise as she burns the letters of her faithless lover. This last is a fine dramatic scena in miniature. The short poem, three four-line stanzas, by Gabriele von Baumberg (d. 1839), is worthy of its setting. 'Abendempfindung', whose verses by Joachim Heinrich Campe (1746–1818) are somewhat mannered, is perhaps the loveliest of Mozart's songs, its bitter-sweet mood expressed in hauntingly memorable phrases. In lighter vein is the charming 'An Chloe', whose poem is by Johann Georg Jacobi (1740–1814). 'Meine Wünsche', a mock patriotic, anti-Turkish war song, has begun to figure in recital programmes in recent years—the writer has heard Elisabeth Schwarzkopf sing it to great effect on more than one occasion; but originally it was an aria for baritone voice and orchestra, which Mozart composed in 1788 for a Viennese actor called Baumann.

'Sehnsucht nach dem Frühlinge', a five stanza strophic song must not be overlooked. It was to be Mozart's last Frühling, for he wrote the song in Vienna on 14 January 1791 and died the following winter; curiously, something of the sad transience of things can be heard in the melody, whose feeling is, on the surface, one of serene anticipation. The modestly pleasant verses are by C. A. Overbeck (1755–1821). The tune, which has its basis in folk song, is also heard in the last movement of the B flat piano concerto K. 595, which Mozart had finished composing earlier in January. Mozart's last composition for voice and piano, composed in July 1791, is not, strickly speaking, a song, since it is cast in the form of recitative and aria. This is 'Die ihr des unermesslichen Weltalls Schöpfer ehrt', described as 'a little German cantata'. Formal and public in utterance, it is nevertheless a thing of beauty.

There remains to be mentioned, and this is as good a place as any to do so, the famous cradle song, 'Schlafe, mein Prinzchen, schlaf ein', which was for many years thought to be by Mozart, and is still known to many as Mozart's 'Wiegenlied'. It was, in fact, written by a younger contemporary of Mozart, a German amateur composer named Bernhard Flies, born in Berlin around 1770. It is a sweet and innocuous little song, but Mozart surely would not have written so square a tune.

Of Mozart's contemporaries, three names are worthy of mention, not only because of the excellence of some of the songs they wrote but also because they all, to some degree, were to exert an influence upon the young Schubert. The senior of the three is Johann Reichardt (1752–1814) who is more important as a composer of *Singspiele*, but who nevertheless wrote a great many pleasantly unpretentious songs, including several settings of Goethe. His 'Heidenröslein', for instance, which was later to be included by Brahms in his collection of *Volkskinderlieder*, is as charming in its way as Schubert's famous song. Both Reichardt and Carl Zelter (1758–1832) set Goethe's 'Erlkönig', though both were generally more successful with less dramatic subjects. Zelter was a great admirer of Goethe, many of whose poems he set, and with whom he corresponded for many years. Johann Zumsteeg (1760–1802) is sometimes referred to as the father of the ballad, and it is true that his often quite long narrative songs left their mark on Schubert. They are not, in themselves, however, of much intrinsic value, the majority of them being rambling and of little melodic or harmonic individuality.

With Beethoven (1770–1827), song can hardly be said to have continued its development. The greatest composer of his time was really not a writer for the voice. It is, in fact, somewhat surprising that he wrote so many songs, more than eighty, as well as nearly 200 arrangements of folk songs, mainly Scottish, Irish and Welsh. Beethoven thought instrumentally, and it is probably no more than a happy accident that some of his songs lie gratefully for the voice: most of them betray their instrumental inspiration. This generalization will, however, be contradicted on particular occasions as we consider the songs in closer detail. The influence of Haydn can more clearly and easily be discerned in them than that of Mozart, for Beethoven, and not only in his *Lieder*, is part of a line of development from Haydn to Schubert. Mozart was somehow already closer to Schubert. His songs, as a whole, sound as though they came after Beethoven. Beethoven's, on the contrary, seem to look back to the classical melody of Haydn, and, in keeping with this, his accompaniments tend to know their place and stay in it. This is not to say that Beethoven's songs are mere exercises in composition, for many of them are deeply felt and affecting pieces of music. But they are, for the most part, the by-products of genius, a genius which reached its proper fulfilment in the quartet, the symphony and the sonata.

Beethoven was certainly attracted to song at an early age; he wrote his first one when he was thirteen : 'Schilderung eines Mädchens', an innocuous trifle in one swift stanza. The eight songs of op. 52 were written at different times during the composer's adolescence, to texts of various poets, and they include the first two of Beethoven's Goethe settings, of which there were to be another five in due course. These two, 'Mailied' and 'Marmotte', are square and undistinguished little pieces, though the high-spirited 'Mailied', whose tune was originally set to different words, has always been popular with singers. The finest of the op. 52 songs are the graceful 'Die Liebe' (poem by Lessing) and the quietly reflective 'Das Liedchen von der Ruhe' (Wilhelm Ueltzen). The oddest is the fourteen-stanza 'Urians Reise um die Welt' in which Mr Urian tediously recounts his non-adventures all over the world to a recurring choral refrain of 'Tell us more, Herr Urian', which changes at the end to 'Don't tell us any more, Herr Urian'. The poem obviously appealed to the thirteen-year-old composer, whose song is an extended, cheerful, but dogged joke.

One of the most attractive of Beethoven's early songs is 'Elegie auf den Tod eines Pudels', a sentimental yet affecting lament which is oddly neglected by singers. In 1793 and 1794, Beethoven studied with the Italian opera composer Antonio Salieri, from whom he learned a great amount about the setting of words. Not surprisingly, therefore, the vocal works he composed in the mid 1790s bear strong traces of Italian influence. 'Seufzer eines Ungeliebten' and ' Gegenliebe', for instance, two poems by Gottfried Burger welded into a miniature scena consisting of recitative, andantino and allegretto, sound like part of an Italian opera deprived of its orchestral accompaniment. The allegretto section was used again by Beethoven thirteen years later as the theme of the variations in his Choral Fantasy. Equally Italianate in style is the beautiful 'Adelaide', a love song composed in 1795. This, too, is really a *bel canto* aria in disguise, with its gentle opening theme and ecstatic cabaletta-like conclusion.

In addition to Italianate songs to German texts, Beethoven at this time also tried his hand at setting Italian verses by

Pietro Metastasio and others. The majority of these attempts resulted in purely formal pieces, lacking in individuality. Even when the composer produces two settings of the same poem about an impatient lover, 'L'amante impaziente', first as a comic arietta and then seriously, they are virtually interchangeable. By far the most successful of the Italian songs is 'In questa tomba oscura' (Giuseppe Carpani), a sombre reproach from beyond the tomb, written in 1807 as an entry in a competition.

The *Six Songs to poems by Christian Gellert,* which appeared in 1803, comprise a unified group of songs to religious texts, and are highly impressive both collectively and individually. These poems, which C. P. E. Bach had already set half a century earlier, inspired Beethoven to his first real expression in song of the spiritual aspect of his nature. The finest of them are, perhaps, the solemnly hortatory 'Vom Tode' and the hymn to God in nature, 'Die Ehre Gottes aus der Natur'. Two separate songs also written in 1803 are both among the composer's finest. 'Zärtliche Liebe', a tender love song, almost anticipates Schubert in the charm and simplicity of its melody, and 'Der Wachtelschlag' improves and elevates Samuel Sauter's poem about the cry of the quail, by virtue of its unusually free-ranging accompaniment as much as by its interesting vocal line.

'An die Hoffnung' (poem by Christopher August Tiedge) exists in two versions, the first of which (1804) is both more spontaneous and, as a lyrical reflection, more effective. The second, 1813, version is more extended, and preceded by a verse set to recitative, a verse which was not set at all in 1804. This second version sounds less like a private reflection than a public utterance.

Strophic songs pose their own problems of word setting. When the same music is being used for a number of verses, it is useless to look for miracles of declamation and stress. On the other hand, it is reasonable to expect a tune which expresses the general feeling of the poem. Beethoven never disappoints in this respect, though sometimes, as in 'Als die Geliebte sich trennen wollte', a setting of a poem by Stephan von Breuning, his music can sound pedestrian, and even contrived.

Beethoven's settings of the great poet who seems closest to him in spirit, Johann Wolfgang von Goethe, are remarkably few : especially when one recalls that the composer once wrote '. . . Goethe—he lives and wants us all to live with him. That is the reason he can be composed. Nobody else can be so easily composed as he.'* Apart from the cantata 'Meeresstille und glückliche Fahrt' and Clärchen's two superb songs with orchestra in the incidental music for *Egmont*, Beethoven's Goethe songs consist of the following: four settings of 'Nur wer die Sehnsucht kennt', none of them a match for Schubert, Wolf or Tchaikovsky; the two songs mentioned earlier; three of the six songs that comprise op. 75, and the three songs of op. 83. The Goethe settings of op. 75 include an unsuccessful attempt at Mignon's 'Kennst du das Land?', the attractive, restlessly lively 'Neue Liebe, neues Leben', and 'Der Floh', the satirical 'Song of the Flea' sung by Mephistopheles in *Faust*: 'Es war einmal ein König', a tuneful song which calls for a chorus in the final bars. The non-Goethe songs of op. 75, to poems by Halem and Reissig, are pleasant but undistinguished. Beethoven's most fruitful encounter with Goethe is the first song of op. 83, 'Wonne der Wehmut', a deeply felt lyrical sermon on Goethe's gentle text about sensibility. The other two songs are slighter. 'Sehnsucht' is, in fact, about a longing that is fairly easily dispelled, while 'Mit einem Gemalten Band' is a gentle little picture of contented love.

Some of Beethoven's finest songs date from 1809, the year of such middle-period masterpieces as the Piano Concerto op. 73 (The 'Emperor'), the String Quartet op. 74 (The 'Harp') and the Piano Sonata op. 81a (Les Adieux), all, incidentally, in E flat major. One of the most attractive of these songs of 1809 is 'Andenken', an amiable and gentle expression of love. Haydnesque formality and Beethovenian high spirits are engagingly blended in 'Lied aus der ferne'; 'Die laute Klage' takes itself and Johann Gottfried Herder's love-sick poem a trifle too solemnly; a more suitable lightness of touch is found for Reissig's poem 'Der Liebende'; and another of Reissig's unhappy lovers, 'Der Jüngling in der Fremde' is delicately portrayed. A poem by Josef Ludwig Stoll, 'An die Geliebte', was set twice by Beethoven: the charming melody remains the same in each setting, but the accompaniments differ. Beethoven's first thoughts in this instance seem the happier ones.

Of the remaining solo songs written between 1811 and 1820, many, such as 'Der Bardengeist', 'Das Geheimnis' and 'Ruf vom Berge' are disappointing in that, though competently and sensitively put together, the spark of life is missing from them. The little arietta, 'Der Kuss', which was not published until

* Marion M. Scott *Beethoven* J. M. Dent London 1934

1825, was in fact written much earlier, when Beethoven was still in his twenties; despite its 18th-century formality it remains popular by virtue of its graceful and witty melody. If Beethoven's final decade of song contains too many dull pieces, however, it redeems itself with *An die ferne Geliebte*, for, with the six songs published under this title, the composer can be said to have invented the song-cycle.

The poems of *An die ferne Geliebte* are by an amateur poet, Aloys Jeitteles (1794–1858), a Jewish doctor who wrote them during his student days in Vienna, and presented Beethoven with a copy of them. In the first poem, the young lover sits on a hill-top gazing into the distance and thinking of his far-off beloved. He resolves to sing songs to her, and the following four poems are the songs he sings. In the sixth poem, he asks her to accept his songs, to sing them herself, and so help to lessen the pain of separation. Beethoven has woven all six poems into one complete whole, linking the individual songs together by the continuous piano part, and returning in the last song to material used in the first one. In fact, this is not only the first real song-cycle; it is almost, with the possible exception of Schumann's *Dichterliebe*, the only real cycle of any distinction, for both Schubert's two great cycles and Schumann's *Frauenliebe und -Leben* are collections of songs which combine to tell a story but which also each exist as a separate entity. 'Der Lindenbaum' makes perfect and beautiful sense on its own, but it would be impossible to extract a song from *An die ferne Geliebte* for separate performance, and highly inappropriate to do so with *Dichterliebe*.

If its musical content were as slight as that of some of his other songs, Beethoven's cycle would be no more than a historical curiosity. Fortunately, it is a work of sheer loveliness which owes nothing to Haydn or Mozart, but which springs from Beethoven's own deepest and tenderest feelings. The variations of mood, tempo and key from song to song are subtly and unobtrusively managed, and the effect of a fine performance of this cycle is out of all proportion to the apparently miniature scale of the work. Beethoven's delight in nature, and his ability to take solace from its beauty, are evident in every page of this outpouring of song.

Beethoven's folk song settings are numerous. In addition to occasional arrangements of German and Austrian folk songs, he completed nearly two hundred settings of English, Scottish,

Welsh and Irish songs, for the Scottish music publisher George
Thomson. Thomson, an enthusiastic collector of folk songs, was
embarrassed by the plainness or crudity of what he collected,
and therefore engaged eminent poets to write new and decorous
words for the melodies, and famous composers to provide dressed-
up accompaniments. Beethoven, ever ready to earn a reasonably
honest penny, provided the violin, cello and piano accompaniments that Thomson required. Although the results are not what
the puritans of the folk song movement of today would regard
with favour, many of these Beethovenized songs are quite charming. They range from such well-known titles as 'Charlie is my
Darling', 'Robin Adair' and 'Sally in our Alley' to more obscure
ones like 'Cease your funning' and 'English bulls'.

In his day, the composer and violin virtuoso Louis Spohr
(1784–1859) achieved considerable success with his songs, which
he usually published in groups of six. But his idiom was an
extremely conservative one, and, although one or two of the
songs might perhaps pass for Mozart, the majority of them,
though pleasant, are somewhat stiff and self-conscious. Those
of Carl Maria von Weber (1786–1826), by contrast, are more
vigorous, even popular in style, which is not surprising when
one considers Weber's great interest in German folk song. His
output consists of about eighty German songs for solo voice,
many of them with accompaniments for guitar instead of piano,
as well as a handful of Italian, French and English settings.
Several of the German songs are, in fact, modelled on folk song,
while a few are actually arrangements of existing folk tunes.
In addition to these *volkstümlich* pieces, Weber, who in his
operas was as much influenced by Italian vocal melody as by
German, also produced more ambitious songs, some of which
are stepping stones on the way from Beethoven to Schubert.
And, like Beethoven, he too tried his hand at arranging Scottish
songs: ten such arrangements were published in 1825.

Friedrich Silcher (1789–1860) must at least be mentioned
here, although he is far from being a major composer of the
Lied. For most of his life, Silcher held the post of Conductor to
the University of Tübingen. He composed a number of hymns,
and, more importantly, published a collection of German folk
songs, many of which have earned their place as folk
songs only through the years since Silcher's death, for he composed several of them himself, including the universally known
'Lorelei', a setting of Heine's 'Ich weiss nicht was soll es

bedeuten'. More than one famous German 'folk song' turns out on closer inspection, to be the work of Silcher: for example, 'Ännchen von Tharau', 'Morgen muss ich fort von hier', and 'Zu Strassburg auf der Schanz'.

The Viennese Franz Schubert (1797–1828) is not only indisputably the greatest master of the *Lied*, for reasons we shall attempt to discuss; he is also by far the most prolific. So apparently endless was his flow of melody that he was at one time in danger of being considered a kind of mindless songster, pouring forth his tunes 'in profuse strains of unpremeditated art'. No picture of this composer could be more false. He was by nature a convivial and amiable soul, but he was also a highly conscious artist who knew what he was doing at every step along the path of his tragically brief life. Before his death at the age of thirty-one, he had achieved a mastery so complete that it seemed casual, in symphonic and in chamber music. For song, although he developed surely and excitingly, his spontaneous gifts were remarkable from the very beginning. It was only in the field of opera that he appears to have been a comparative failure, and even that is by no means certain. Until more of his mature operas are given their chance in stage performance today, it would be wise to reserve judgment in that direction.

As a song composer, the young Schubert was influenced not by the great symphonists who preceded him—Haydn, Mozart, Beethoven—but by several minor Viennese specialists in the *Lied*. The names of such industrious local composers as Steffan, Ruprecht, Friberth, Kozeluch, Holzer and others are virtually unknown to us today, yet it is they to whom the young Schubert listened. That he also knew and was influenced by various German writers of song, including the three mentioned earlier, Reichardt, Zelter and Zumsteeg, can hardly be doubted. But Schubert's Viennese predecessors differed from the German school in their greater reliance on, indeed their more certain possession of, a melodic charm and facility which anticipate the melodic genius of Schubert. What the North German composers bequeathed to Schubert was their sense of the dramatic. In mature Schubert, North German drama and Viennese lyricism combine most productively—and Schubert was mature, in that sense, well before he was twenty-one—but the dramatic element in his songs was something he had to learn how to handle. His earliest ballads, in the manner of Zumsteeg, moving uneasily from melody to recitative and back again, are frequently astonishing, but they are the works of a remarkable apprentice. The Viennese lyricism in the early songs came to him easily and almost, as it were, without call.

From his fourteenth year, when he astonished his teacher Salieri with the cantata-like 'Hagars Klage', to within a few weeks of his death seventeen years later, when he composed 'Die Taubenpost', Schubert wrote more than 600 songs, so many of them of such beauty and power that he sometimes seems to us today to have been the fount of all song. It is occasionally claimed that his literary taste was poor, because he set some extremely bad poems to music. But he also set a great many masterpieces of German poetry. We cannot, in these pages, stop to examine every one of 603 songs, but it is likely that, after we have surveyed his *œuvre* in some detail, we shall realize that there simply were not enough great poems in existence to soak up all the music that Franz Schubert carried in his heart.

The earliest song, 'Hagars Klage', is a fifteen-page epic, very obviously derived from Zumsteeg. A setting of a ballad by a minor Münster poet, Schücking, it was written by the fourteen-year-old Schubert early in 1811. This elaborate composition is usually dismissed after a brief glance, even by lovers of Schubert, as being not only derivative but also rambling, repetitive, too long, and over-elaborate. True, it does not contain any feature that we would now consider to be distinctly Schubertian, but it is more, much more than simply a *tour de force* by a promising youngster. More a dramatic cantata than a song, this lament of the Old Testament Hagar contains some bold harmonies and unexpected key changes, but it is the confidence and quality of the writing for the voice which make it worth consideration today by singers with a mastery of the grand manner.

Many of Schubert's very early works for voice and piano are similar in style to 'Hagars Klage'. 'Eine Leichenphantasie' for example, is an even longer exercise on a Zumsteegian subject. The poem, this time, is by Schiller, but it is a dull and creaking one. The schoolboy Schubert found obvious enjoyment in these graveyard fantasies; 'Der Vatermörder' is a more concise essay in the same vein. But the first real Schubert song, as distinct from dramatic scena or cantata, is his setting, written when he was twelve, of Schiller's poem, 'Der Jüngling am Bache'. It was a poem the composer was to return to seven years later as an adolescent, but this first setting, fresh and youthful, occasionally

a trifle awkward, possesses a most engaging and typically Schubertian charm. It is basically a strophic song, but Schubert has
varied the melody from verse to verse. A simpler strophic song,
but one of tenderness and great appeal, is 'Klaglied'. In neither
of these songs has Schubert yet found a way to give the piano
its own interest and individuality. His writing for the piano is
still mere accompaniment.

One of the 1813 songs is interesting, if only because it introduces us to the poet, Ludwig Hölty, many of whose delicate
verses Schubert was to set in future years. This first poem, however, is a mournfully self-pitying outburst called 'Totengräber-
lied' which Schubert curiously lightens in his unaccountably
merry, if ironic, setting. Schubert's first setting of Schiller's
'Sehnsucht' also dates from 1813, his sixteenth year, though the
composer revised and improved it six years later.

A curiosity, but more than that, a splendid song as well, is
'Verklärung' which is a translation of Alexander Pope's 'Vital
spark of heav'nly flame', with its famous last lines, 'O Grave!
where is thy victory?/O Death! where is thy sting?'

The best known of the early Schubertian bloated ballads, if
one may coin so disrespectful a phrase, is 'Der Taucher' which
is thirty pages long, and takes nearly twenty-five minutes to
sing. Schiller's ballad is about a mediaeval king who tosses a
golden chalice into a whirlpool, daring any one of his courtiers
to retrieve it. It is theirs for the diving. A noble youth accepts
the challenge, and is successful. The wonders he describes when
he emerges so intrigue the king that he asks the youth to return
and explore further, this time offering his daughter in marriage
as reward. The foolhardy youth dives into the whirlpool a second
time, but never returns. Schubert's setting is determined, and not
uninteresting, but it cannot be claimed that he really succeeds
in bringing the exceedingly intractable material to life.

With 'Andenken', in 1814, we meet the first of the settings
of Friedrich Matthisson, a minor poet and a rather poor one,
to whom Schubert seems as an adolescent to have been attracted.
He set twenty-four of Matthisson's poems, thirteen of them in
1814. Not at all deterred by the fact that Beethoven had composed popular songs to two of the poems, 'Adelaide' and
'Andenken', some years earlier, Schubert made his own versions.
Both have a gentle charm, though neither stays in the memory
as do the Beethoven songs. Some of the other Matthisson songs,
however, are very attractive in their modest way, especially

'Lied aus der Ferne', 'Todtenopfer' and 'Trost an Elisa'. This last named song is especially interesting, consisting as it does entirely of accompanied recitative; an early lyrical equivalent of the dramatic recitative of 'Der Doppelgänger' which Schubert was to write years later.

Two Schiller settings date from 1814, 'An Emma' and 'Das Mädchen aus der Fremde'; simple, solemn music for poems, one of which is pompous, the other obscure. Then, on 19 October 1814, the seventeen-year-old composer wrote the first of his countless masterpieces, a song of sheer genius, 'Gretchen am Spinnrade', from Goethe's *Faust*. In the play, the virgin Gretchen has succumbed to the charms of Faust. She sits at her spinning-wheel, her disconnected thoughts only of him. 'Meine Ruh ist hin,/Mein Herz ist schwer;/Ich finde sie nimmer/Und nim-mermehr.' ('My peace is disturbed, my heart is heavy. I shall never again find rest.') The poem, simple in expression and form, matching the girl's artlessness, is touching in its portrayal of lost innocence. Schubert responded to the poem and the situa-tion with an intuitive flash of empathetic genius, and created a song which has so delicately yet firmly etched Gretchen's words into music that one would have to be determinedly wilful to imagine them in any other setting. (There *are* other settings, however, written before and after Schubert's.) At the same stroke, Schubert freed the piano part for once and all from subservience to the voice. In his piano, the treadle of the wheel is heard, transformed into musical image. As the girl's thoughts become more agitated, the pitch rises: from D minor up to E minor, to F. And then, as the phrase 'Meine Ruh ist hin' recurs, back to the plaintive D minor.

After 'Gretchen am Spinnrade', there could be no doubting the lyrical genius of the adolescent composer. Some weeks later, he composed his second Goethe song, 'Nachtgesang', a gentle serenade for which he provided a sensitive and graceful melody of no more than fifteen bars. If it is sung to three of the poem's five stanzas, the song can be made to sound a perfect little gem, but whether the melody can stand up to being heard five times is debatable. This is a problem thrown up by Schubert's many strophic settings. Did he always intend all the stanzas of a poem to be sung? Did he care? It would seem prudent to suggest that the singer has a responsibility to be selective.

Schubert had a tendency, though by no means so pronounced a one as Hugo Wolf was to display, to concentrate on a poet for a certain time, perhaps a few weeks. The autumn of 1814 brought other Goethe settings from him, among them the sweetly melancholy 'Schäfers Klagelied'. Before one accuses Schubert of lack of poetic judgment, one ought to remember that he set more poems by Goethe than by any other poet. But then, to be fair, one should admit that Johann Mayrhofer (1787–1836) runs Goethe a close second. 'Admit' is too hard a word : Mayrhofer was not a great poet, but he had a real, if facile talent for versification. His personality, however, clouded as it was in *Weltschmerz*, was far too portentously gloomy and pessimistic for his talent. He was a Viennese civil servant, and a friend of Schubert. He and the composer shared rooms for two years in 1819–20, and it was probably out of affection for his friend, rather than admiration for his friend's verses, that Schubert set forty-seven of them to music. Genius and friendship, he bowed to them both. In any case, we must be grateful to Mayrhofer, as to other minor poets of Schubert's circle, for having caused him to compose some very beautiful songs. The first Mayrhofer setting, 'Am See', though pleasant, is not one of the more successful of Schubert's attempts to find musical form for his friend's musings.

The songs of the following two or three years include several of Schubert's greatest. They also include a good many of comparatively slight interest, though to the devoted Schubertian there is hardly a song which does not contain something of interest. Some of the lesser known songs are, in fact, just as fine as the popular favourites. This is particularly true of certain of the simpler lyrics, rather than of the more dramatic pieces. 'Als ich sie erröten sah', for instance, is a song of great lyrical beauty. Its tessitura is high : though the voice part does not go above the tenor's A, it hovers around G for much of the time. Transposition from the key of G down to F would not harm it, or dispel its charm. A fugitive song from 1815 that deserves to be better known is 'Das Bild', which is not even mentioned in Richard Capell's standard work on Schubert's songs. To a poem on the portrait of a girl, by an unidentified poet, the young composer has added a graceful though quirky little melody.

The Zumsteegian ballads of 1815, some of them settings of Schiller, contain comparatively little of interest. At their best— 'Die Erwartung' or 'Die Bürgschaft' for example—they are pleasantly dull. Schubert even took on James MacPherson's 'Ossian', and produced nine songs to Ossian poems, five of them in 1815. These over-inflated, operatic scenas with piano accompaniment do no more than match the empty, grandiose quality of the verse. More attractive to contemplate is Schubert's encounter with the poems of Theodor Körner, twelve of which he used as texts. 'Sängers Morgenlied', the earliest of them, is a first-rate example of the kind of exalted nature-poetry to which Schubert's romantic nature responded so warmly. After describing daybreak in a mountain landscape, the poem ends

> Dürft' ich nur auf goldnen Hohen
> Mich im Morgenduft ergehen!
> Sehnsucht zieht mich himmelwärts.

(If only I could walk on the golden heights in the haze of morning! Yearning draws me towards the heavens.)

This is a mood, familiar in German romantic poetry, which Schubert was invariably able to adopt without effort.

In the same year, 1815, the young composer set thirty of Goethe's poems, and in doing so created some of his finest and best-known songs. The great poet more often than not inspired him to rare and exalted heights. Not always, however. Schubert's first Goethe setting of 1815, 'Der Sänger', is a rather conventional piece in his early manner, melodic passages alternating with arioso, though it is important in that it marks the composer's first encounter with the characters of Goethe's *Wilhelm Meister* whose passions he was to portray so unerringly in music. 'Der Sänger' is one of the Harper's songs from the novel. The next Goethe settings are not *Wilhelm Meister* poems, though one of them is of a poem called 'An Mignon'. In it, Schubert misses the poet's irony, and provides a sweetly romantic, immensely attractive melody whose beginning anticipates 'Am Feierabend' in *Die Schöne Müllerin*. 'Am Flusse', composed on the same day, is a minor masterpiece. Goethe's hurt and bitter little poem about derided love has drawn a powerfully compressed song of deep feeling from Schubert. 'Nähe des Geliebten' is gentler, and an even lovelier song about an all-pervading love.

After these first Goethe settings of 1815, the composer turned his attention again to Körner, the best of the resulting songs being a long ballad 'Amphiaraos' which he composed on 1 March 'in 5 Stunden' ('in five hours') as he noted on his manuscript. This evocation of a classical Greek hero in battle is dramatic, and more of a piece than most of Schubert's early ballads. 'Die

• •

Sterne', whose pallid verses are by one Johann Georg Fellinger, typifies the pleasant, not very demanding song for domestic use which Schubert was always able to produce for his friends to perform. This could be said, too, of several of the Körner songs, such as 'Sehnsucht der Liebe', 'Das gestörte Glück' and 'Wiegenlied'.

Among the Schiller settings of 1815 is 'An die Freude', the 'Ode to Joy' which Beethoven was to use eight years later for his Ninth Symphony. Schubert's tune is, in fact, more joyful, less thumping than Beethoven's theme, and his strophic song calls for a chorus to conclude each stanza. 'Amalie', an extended recitative and arietta whose words are the heroine's song in Schiller's play Die Räuber, is one of the most attractive of the Schiller settings of 1815. Nearly half of the songs to poems of Hölty also date from this year. Some of them are of great beauty, none more so than 'An den Mond' in which the poet begs the moon to illuminate the spot where his former sweetheart once sat. Schubert's tender, sorrowful melody is given added atmosphere by the delicately woven accompaniment. On the same day that he composed 'An den Mond', Schubert also wrote his setting of Hölty's 'Die Mainacht': a pretty tune, but not to be compared with Brahms's romantic outpouring to the same poem half a century later. Curiously, in the following week Schubert again set a Hölty poem which was to be more impressively handled by Brahms: 'An die Nachtigall'. Almost unknown is 'Liebeständelei'. Without being important, this is almost quintessential Schubert in its relaxed and unpretentious gaiety. The poem is by Theodor Körner. Similar in their homeliness and their suitability for informal music-making amongst friends are the simple settings of L. T. Kosegarten which Schubert composed in 1815. Other commentators have heard in the solemn harmonies of the most interesting of them, 'Nachtgesang', an adumbration of the mood and texture of the 'Wanderers Nachtlied' which was soon to follow.

Mention of the 'Wanderers Nachtlied' brings one back to the Goethe songs which Schubert composed in 1815, the earliest of which have already been mentioned. The challenge of matching the verse of Germany's greatest poet drew from the composer some of his most profoundly beautiful music: a further proof that he was not impervious to the literary merit of his poets. Fine feelings occasionally inspired him to great things; fine words invariably did. 'Meeres Stille' in which Goethe depicts a becalmed, serene seascape beautiful in itself, but, for the seaman, dangerous, is carried over into music which magically renders stillness and silence audible. The slow-moving yet tense voice part is supported simply by thirty-two semibreve chords. Similar in its brevity and calm, and even more moving by virtue of the controlled yearning of its melody, is 'Wanderers Nachtlied I', a setting of Goethe's quiet sigh of *Weltschmerz*, 'Der du von dem Himmel bist'. Schubert was to set another of Goethe's perfect little lyric verses seven years later under the same title ('Wanderers Nachtlied II'). But on the day that he set 'Der du von dem Himmel bist', he wrote music for two more Goethe poems 'Erster Verlust' and 'Der Fischer'. Neither is the equal of 'Der du von dem Himmel bist', though 'Erster Verlust' is a touching lament, and 'Der Fischer' a lighthearted strophic narrative of a fisherman lured into the stream by a water nymph. Of the several songs written in 1815 to verses by the minor poet Ludwig Kosegarten, 'Die Mondnacht' and 'Abends unter der Linde' are the most attractive.

Schubert was frequently able to compose a number of beautiful songs in one day. On 19 August 1815, for instance, he produced five Goethe songs: 'Der Rattenfänger', 'Der Schatzgräber', 'Bundeslied', 'An den Mond' and the popular 'Heidenröslein'. 'Heidenröslein' displays to perfection Schubert's extraordinary gift of apparently spontaneous melody. The tune, now jaunty, now sad, is so right and inevitable that one feels it has sprung, ready-made, from the soil in which the rose itself grew.

There is, of course, a price to be paid for facility, and that price is occasional failure. The day after these five gems, Schubert wrote only one song, a setting of Goethe's 'Wonne der Wehmut', and it is nowhere near the equal of Beethoven's great song. Schubert appears not to have been very deeply touched by the poem, and one wonders why he troubled to compose it. But 'Wer kauft Liebesgötter?', again a Goethe setting and composed the day after 'Wonne der Wehmut', is delicious, and perplexingly ignored by singers.

Schubert's tendency to concentrate on one poet for several weeks has been earlier remarked upon. In the autumn of 1815, the still only eighteen-year-old composer turned his attention to Friedrich Gottlieb Klopstock (1724–1803). Klopstock's reputation had been made with his huge religious epic, *Messias*, but some of his finest writing is to be found in his poems and

unrhymed odes. Though a variable and uneven poet, he is one
of the most important forerunners of the *Sturm und Drang*
period. Nine of Schubert's thirteen Klopstock songs were composed in the autumn of 1815, and of these the finest is undoubtedly 'Dem Unendlichen'. The poem is one of Klopstock's
more impressive pietistic outbursts. 'How uplifted is the heart
when it thinks of Thee, eternal one' it begins. And the last two
stanzas, with their deliberate repetition of 'Posaunen Chor' are,
of their kind, magnificent :

> Welten donnert, im feierlichen Gang,
> Welten donnert in der Posaunen Chor !
> Tönt, all' ihr Sonnen
> Auf der Strasse voll Glanz,
> In der Posaunen Chor !
>
> Ihr Welten, ihr donnert,
> Du, der Posaunen Chor,
> Hallest nie es ganz !
> Gott ! Gott ! Gott ist es, den ihr preist.

(Worlds, thunder, on your solemn way, to the choir of
trumpets. Resound, all you suns, on the path of splendour,
to the choir of trumpets. Your thunder, your worlds, and your
choir of trumpets, are scarcely heard at all. God, God, God
it is whom you praise.)
Schubert has matched the religious ecstasy of the poem with
a vocal line of majestic nobility, preceded by solemn recitative
for the opening lines, and a soaring, almost Wagnerian fervour
for the climactic vision of 'Gott, Gott ist es, den ihr preist'. The
piano part, though on the page it looks conventional, adroitly
follows the changing emphases of the words. 'Dem Unendlichen'
is a fine example of Schubert in his exalted vein.

Of the other Klopstock settings of 1815, the only one especially
worthy of note is 'Das Rosenband', a tender little love song. If
I draw attention now to another slight but charming little song
from the autumn of 1815—'Mein Gruss an den Mai'—it is
principally to indicate how many very agreeable Schubert songs
remain neglected simply because there are so many of them.
'Mein Gruss an den Mai', for instance, is not even mentioned
in Capell's valuable book* on Schubert's songs, and understandably so : Schubert was so prodigal with his riches.

* Richard Capell *Schubert's Songs* Ernest Benn London 1928

It was in Schubert's rich year of 1815 that he first grappled with the poems in Goethe's strange novel, *Wilhelm Meisters Lehrjahre*, which had been published in four volumes in 1795 and 1796. The poems are songs sung by a mysterious character, the Harper, and by Mignon the Italian waif who turns out to be the Harper's child, offspring of an incestuous love. 'Der Sänger' was the first of the Harper's songs to be set by Schubert. In this year, he also made a first attempt at 'Wer sich der Einsamkeit ergibt', which he was to set again the following year together with a further two of the Harper's songs, and composed his only setting of Mignon's 'Kennst du das Land wo die Citronen blühn?', the most famous lyrical poem not only in Goethe, but in all German literature, a poem whose resonances extend far beyond its apparent meaning in the context of the novel. It is a poem which speaks of a northerner's *Sehnsucht* for the south, of a child's desire for a dream world, of an adult's despairing cry after a vanished golden childhood. It has the truth, relevance and beauty of great poetry, and is so complete in itself that one sees both how and why composers were lured into setting it, and how and why they could not but fail. Schubert's setting is not insensitive, and indeed it is an attractive song, but it does not match Goethe's imaginative sweep, any more than that great poet could have found words to parallel the sound of Schubert's C major Quintet. We shall encounter this poem again when we arrive at discussion of later 19th-century composers. Meanwhile, if he failed with 'Kennst du das Land?', Schubert succeeded gloriously with his last two Goethe songs of 1815 : 'Rastlose Liebe' and 'Der Erlkönig', both of them absolute masterpieces.

Goethe's tempestuous young lyric, 'Rastlose Liebe', affected Schubert immediately and vividly, and wrung from him a song different from anything he had previously composed. The composer's violent depth of feeling provides the perfect musical response to Goethe's exultant cry of urgent young love. Of the composition of 'Der Erlkönig' one of Schubert's friends, Josef von Spaun, has left a valuable account :

One afternoon I went with Mayrhofer to see Schubert, who was then living with his father on the Himmelpfortgrund; we found Schubert all aglow, reading the 'Erlkönig' aloud from the book. He paced up and down several times with the book, suddenly he sat down and in no time at all (just as quickly as one can write) there was the glorious ballad finished on the paper. We ran with it to the Seminary, for there was no pianoforte at Schubert's and there, on the very same evening, the 'Erlkönig' was sung and enthusiastically received. The old organist, Ruzicka,* then sat down and, with the greatest interest, played it through himself in all its sections, but without the voice, and was most moved by the composition. When some people wished to point out a dissonance, which recurred several times, Ruzicka explained, sounding it on the piano, how it was necessary here, in order to correspond with the words, how beautiful it was on the contrary, and how happily it was resolved.'*

How those notes of Schubert's must have seared the pages. They still do. His 'Erlkönig' challenges and equals Goethe's, whereas Loewe's later setting merely interprets the poem. At that first performance in the Seminary, it was the minor ninths at the words 'Mein Vater' which startled some hearers. The song was performed three times in succession. After the first time, Schubert, who was at the piano, simplified the accompaniment which was too difficult for him to play, remarking, 'The triplets are too difficult for me; you need to be a virtuoso to play them'.

'Der Erlkönig' and a number of other Schubert Goethe settings were sent to the great poet at Weimar; he failed to acknowledge receipt of them. It was six years before the song was to achieve publication, as Schubert's op. 1, the first of his works to appear in print. We have seen just how much had been written prior to that op. 1. But now, having achieved such an astonishing maturity at the age of eighteen, Schubert did not develop in the conventional sense throughout the remaining thirteen years of his heartrendingly brief life. He was already a master, and embarked upon his finest and final creative phase while barely out of his adolescence.

One of the minor contemporary poets whom Schubert concentrated upon in March and April of 1816 was the Swiss, Johann Georg von Salis (1762–1834), but the dozen or so songs which resulted are only minor Schubert, with the exception of 'Die Einsiedelei', a pretty little nature piece. Five years later,

---

* Schubert's old teacher
* Josef von Spaun, *Notes on my association with Franz Schubert*. Written in 1858, published in Der Merker, Vienna, Feb.-Mar. 1912

Schubert came back to von Salis, and set 'Der Jüngling an der Quelle', one of his loveliest and most graceful songs. The six Schiller songs of 1816 are not among Schubert's finest, which is not surprising, for some of the poems seem quite intractable; the two most successful are 'Laura am Clavier' and 'Die Entzückung an Laura', especially the latter with its gentle infatuated melody. Also belonging to 1816 are the five settings of Johann Peter Uz (1720–1796). Again these are minor : charming little songs which, though only slightly, improve upon the rather stilted rococo quality of the poet's words. By far the best of them is 'Die Liebesgötter'. 'Der gute Hirt', which paraphrases the twenty-third Psalm is also quietly effective. Ludwig Hölty, the 18th-century poet (1747–1776) who died of consumption at the age of twenty-eight, had been first set by Schubert in 1815, and in 1816 the composer returned to Hölty, setting a further thirteen poems. While not a great or even a consistently good poet, Hölty had a quality which not only appealed to Schubert but also inspired him to some of his best essays in the slight, more often than not pathetic, vein which came so easily to him. Many of these songs, neglected by singers, are worth studying and singing : 'Auf den Tod einer Nachtigall', 'Die frühe Liebe' and 'Der Leidende' for example. One of them, the delightful 'Seligkeit' is already deservedly popular with concert audiences. It was used for many years by Irmgard Seefried as an encore.

Christian Schubart (1739–1791), the 18th-century poet who spent ten years in a German prison for his political opinions, provided Schubert with some sweet and unpolitical poems, which resulted in two splendid songs, the delightfully spontaneous 'Die Forelle' of 1817, and, in 1816, 'An mein Clavier' which Schubert made into a touching and heartfelt tribute to the instrument on which he worked.

Kosegarten appears for the last time in 1816, when Schubert composed a noble and beautiful setting of 'An die untergehende Sonne'. This is a song that is unaccountably neglected. A Schubertian poet encountered for the first—and last—time in 1816 is Johann Georg Jacobi, from whose verses Schubert fashioned seven songs, all except one of them pleasant but inconsequential. The exception is 'Litanei', one of the masterpieces of *Lieder*. This is not so much a prayer for the souls of the dead as a song of consolation to those who mourn them, and Schubert's calm and noble strophic melody is indeed sweetly consoling in its effect. There are nine stanzas to Jacobi's poem, too many to be sung. The song is heard to best effect when two or three stanzas only are performed.

The three great settings of the Harper's songs from Goethe's *Wilhelm Meister* belong to this year : 'Wer sich der Einsamkeit ergibt', 'Wer nie sein Brot mit Tränen ass' and 'An die Türen will ich schleichen', as well as two further settings of the second song, and two more of 'Nur wer die Sehnsucht kennt'. The three songs of the Harper, sorrow distilled into music, defy description in words, and do not always render up their secrets easily in performance. But, performed by a singer whose technique is secure enough for him to do no more than merely to enunciate the words sensitively and clearly, they can be almost unbearably moving to hear.

Another Goethe-Schubert masterpiece of 1816 is 'An Schwager Chronos'. The young Goethe's wildly imaginative address to Time, which he sees as a reckless postilion rushing him towards death, is superb poetry. Once one has heard Schubert's exhilarated and careless setting, it is difficult to contemplate the poem deprived of it.

The text of one of Schubert's most famous songs, 'Der Wanderer', is by a very minor poet indeed, one Georg Philipp Schmidt (1766–1849) of Lübeck, and Schubert is said to have come across the poem in an almanac. Schmidt's poem is, however, almost the perfect expression of the romantic *Sehnsucht* and *Weltschmerz* which were such prominent features of the *Sturm und Drang* movement. The wanderer has come from far away. To him the sun seems cold, the flowers faded. He continually hears the whisper 'Where?', and seeks in vain the land which speaks his own language. A ghostly voice tells him 'There, where you are not, that is where fortune resides'. A poem of splendid gesture, and Schubert responded to it by composing a scena, but not too elaborate a one, and by providing a slightly self-pitying but nevertheless beautiful tune for 'Ich wandle still, bin wenig froh'. The C sharp minor adagio tune of 'Die Sonne dünkt mich hier so kalt' was used again by the composer six years later in his Wanderer Fantasy for piano. This 1816 song was enthusiastically taken up by Viennese domestic amateurs, and soon became, after 'Der Erlkönig', Schubert's most popular song. Critics today tend to despise it, mistakenly in the present writer's view.

Would that there had been a literary genius in Schubert's

amiable band of Viennese friends. Johann Mayrhofer's poems
are rather poor, but they brought forth a few fine songs from
Schubert, some of them classical in subject and manner, some
curiously Wagnerian, and a few of them nature pieces that
would have been even better than they are, had not the gloom
of Mayrhofer's sentiment occasionally toppled over into
absurdity. 'Lied eines Schiffers an die Dioscuren' stands out
from the 1816 Mayrhofer songs, a noble hymn to his guiding
stars sung by a boatman. The following year brought a rich
crop, including the finest of them, 'Memnon'. Under the guise
of writing about the world of the past, the poet produced an unbearably painful *cri de coeur* which Schubert translated into
music which is at once noble and moving. Of the lighter songs,
the water music, 'Erlafsee', 'Auf der Donau' and 'Am Strome' are
all attractive examples.

The nine settings of Matthias Claudius (1740–1815) include
the famous 'Wiegenlied' which Richard Strauss unconsciously
borrowed for the music of Naiad, Dryad and Echo in *Ariadne
auf Naxos*, and 'Der Tod und das Mädchen' which is also justly
celebrated, its simplicity masking a resonance and depth which
even Schubert rarely achieved. The D minor 'Death' theme was
used again by the composer in the D minor Quartet of 1826.

Though the poems of Schubert's friend Franz von Schober
(1798–1883) are distinctly weak, they brought into being some
charming songs, including 'Am Bach im Frühling', and one
which is held dear by all lovers of Schubert, 'An die Musik'.
In this song, Schubert offers his thanks to the art of music itself.
It is one of his most deeply felt pages, its melody natural and
graceful, its chordal accompaniment simple and deeply affecting: a very beautiful prayer of gratitude to the art which
sustained Schubert and to which he contributed so prolifically
and to such immense effect.

The masterpieces of song, as we continue our journey through
the pages of Schubert, loom up with increasing frequency. In
March 1817, the month of 'An die Musik', we also find 'Ganymed', Goethe's great poem taken in by the composer and
breathed out again upon rapturous phrases, and 'Der Jüngling
und der Tod', a pendant to 'Der Tod und das Mädchen' from
which it quotes. Its poem is by Josef von Spaun (1788–1865),
Schubert's life-long friend from his schooldays. Later in 1817
came the popular and engaging 'Die Forelle' on Schubart's
poem. Its theme was used for the variations of the fourth move-

ment of the A major Piano Quintet two years later. In the autumn of 1817, Schubert composed the greatest of his Schiller settings, 'Gruppe aus dem Tartarus', in which he gives tumultuous musical life to the poet's wild vision of hell and damnation.

It is curious that the leading Viennese poet and dramatist of Schubert's time, Franz Grillparzer (1791–1872), whom the composer knew personally, is represented in his *Lieder* by only one solo song, 'Berthas Lied in der Nacht', which was written for inclusion in Grillparzer's play, *Die Ahnfrau*. The song is a compelling evocation of night and sleep.

Again and again, when one considers Schubert's vast output of song, one is struck most of all by the immense breadth of his range. The adjective 'Schubertian' has come unfairly to denote certain of his qualities only : his charm, his gentleness, his cosy Biedermeier *Gemütlichkeit*; but, as the later symphonies and piano sonatas remind us, he was a composer of more than graceful trifles. And we have already seen evidence of great power in many of the songs we have so far examined. In October 1819, Schubert tackled Goethe's 'Prometheus'. This great monologue of defiance is an extract from an unfinished drama, and in it Goethe used the classical myth to make an essentially modern utterance. His 'Prometheus' is the voice of 18th-century reason :

> Ich kenne nichts Ärmeres
> Unter der Sonn', als euch, Götter !
> Ihr nähret kümmerlich
> Von Opfersteuern
> Und Gebetshauch
> Eure Majestät
> Und darbtet, wären
> Nicht Kinder und Bettler
> Hoffnungsvolle Toren.

(I know nothing more pitiable under the sun than you, Gods ! Miserably, your majesty feeds upon offerings and the breath of prayer, and you would starve if children and beggars were not hopeful fools.)

Schubert seems to have been really and totally gripped by Goethe's proud monologue, which he has set as a dramatic scena of such force that one cannot help thinking he might well, in different circumstances, have become an opera composer of Wagnerian stature. Nevertheless, the comment, occasionally encountered, that the piano part of 'Prometheus' cries out for an orchestral sound, is not really to the point. This accompaniment is no substitute for an orchestra, but superb writing for the piano.

There is only one setting of the excellent poet Ludwig Uhland (1787–1862), but it is a setting of great beauty: the lyrical 'Frühlingsglaube' in which Schubert softly whispers his heart's secrets, as the season of renewal comes round again. The following year, 1821, we find the composer discovering Friedrich Rückert (1788–1866). No more than five songs came into being as a result, but they are all first-rate Schubert. The first of them was 'Sei mir gegrüsst' a wonderfully sensuous serenade. The other four Rückert songs followed two years later. 'Dass sie hier gewesen' is a remarkable love song in which Schubert's music is made to fit perfectly the syntax of the poem; 'Du bist die Ruh' is quite simply one of the most purely beautiful songs ever written; 'Lachen und weinen' is deceptively slight, graceful and bitter-sweet; and 'Greisengesang' the least well known of the five, is a pleasant reverie in which old age remembers youth and love.

An unfamiliar song from 1822 which deserves to be more widely known is 'Ihr Grab' (poem by Richard Roos), in which mawkishness is avoided by the gravity and poise of Schubert's melody. The opening phrase, to the words 'Dort ist ihr Grab' ('There is her grave'), repeated with slight variations throughout the song, is one of those which Richard Strauss was to borrow from Schubert. He turned it into an important motif in *Arabella*. 'Ihr Grab' is the only Roos poem Schubert set, and there are only two settings of August, Count Platen (1796–1835). These are not the only instances where, though Schubert appears not to have been sufficiently attracted by a poet to explore further, the one or two poems set to music have resulted in extraordinarily fine songs. The two from Platen, who is generally thought of as a classically-minded writer of sonnets, are passionate outbursts of betrayed love: 'Du liebst mich nicht' and, even more emotionally intense behind its controlled, slow tempo, 'Die Liebe hat gelogen'.

Of the Goethe settings of 1822, the earliest, and one of the finest, is 'Der Musensohn', its five gay and dancing stanzas set to alternating but closely related melodies in G and in B. This entrancing song is so similar to the German folk song, 'Im Wald und auf der Heide', that clearly one must derive from the other.

Since so many German folk songs turn out on close inspection to be the work of minor but known 19th-century composers, it is quite probable that Schubert's song came first.

The last song Schubert wrote in 1822 was that which has come to be known as 'Wanderers Nachtlied II', a companion piece to 'Der du von den Himmel bist'. The poem is Goethe's 'Ein Gleiches,' perhaps the most famous short lyric in the German language, of a startling simplicity yet vibrant with poetry:

Über allen Gipfeln	Over all the mountains
Ist Ruh,	is peace,
In allen Wipfeln	in all the tree-tops
Spürest du	you feel
Kaum einen Hauch.	hardly a breath.
Die Vögelein schweigen	The little birds are silent
im Walde.	in the woods.
Warte nur; balde	Wait awhile: soon
Ruhest du auch.	You too will rest.

The lines were written by the thirty-year-old Goethe on the walls of his bedroom in a lonely hunters' lodge called the Gickelhahn, near Ilmenau in the Thuringian hills. Many years later, ten years after Schubert had set the words to music, the eighty-three-year-old poet revisited Ilmenau, within a few months of his death. He walked up the hillside to the little hunting lodge, looked again at the writing on the wall, now preserved under glass, and pondered on the lines 'Warte nur; balde / Ruhest du auch'. In Schubert's wonderful B flat setting, as simple, direct and poetic as the words, all the stillness and peace of the world seem to reside, and music and words are completely fused into one statement. A calm resignation and acceptance of life's terms steals into the music at 'balde/Ruhest du auch'. (Although we are not examining the songs in bar-to-bar detail, I cannot refrain from remarking that the turn which the Mandyczewski edition prints as optional on 'balde' ought, in my view, not to be sung, as it is out of place in this otherwise pure and unadorned line. It would be appropriate, at least condonable, if added high-spiritedly by a singer to, say, the celebrated 'Ständchen'. But not here.)

In 'Auf dem Wasser zu singen', Schubert attempted to make something of one of the weakest of Count Stolberg's lyrical effusions, and, magically, he succeeded, for this is one of his most lovable water pieces, the accompaniment suggesting a rippling brook rather than a placid lake.

1823 is an important Schubert year, for it was in the summer of that year that the composer glanced at a copy of a new book of verse which he found in a friend's house, was at once seized with the desire to make many of the poems into songs, and began to write his first song-cycle. The poems he chose, a sequence of twenty-five called *Die schöne Müllerin, im Winter zu lesen* ('The beautiful mill-girl; to be read in winter') were by Wilhelm Müller (1794–1827), a German romantic poet whose verses were mostly in the folkish style affected by several of the nature poets of the period. The *Schöne Müllerin* sequence told the story of the unhappy love of a young apprentice for a country miller's daughter, who rejects him for a huntsman. Schubert's cycle utilizes twenty of Müller's twenty-five poems, tracing the apprentice's story from the time he sets out on his wanderings ('Das Wandern'), through his coming to work at the rustic mill ('Am Feierabend'), his growing love for the miller's daughter ('Ungeduld'), his conviction that his love is returned ('Mein'), and the arrival on the scene of a hunter ('Der Jäger') whom the girl clearly prefers ('Die liebe Farbe'), to the apprentice's despair ('Trockne Blumen') and his suicide in the brook to which he had been wont to confide his hopes and fears ('Der Müller und der Bach').

In his book on Schubert's songs, Richard Capell* made the shrewd and sympathetic suggestion that, despite the absurd *fausse naïveté* of these poems, 'we cannot be Schubertians without being a little Müllerian also'. It is true : real lovers of Schubert can probably never succeed in seeing Müller other than through Schubert's eyes, which is the best and kindest way of looking at him. The poems are, after all, period pieces, lifted out of their period and given a wider life by the composer's lyric genius. Müller's apprentice is at best a pathetic figure, if he is a figure at all. Schubert's is sweetly touching. No more than that, perhaps, until he reappears later in *Die Winterreise*, older, sadder, embittered, and on the way to despair. The death he dies in *Die schöne Müllerin* is simply a physical death, and perhaps we do not even really believe in it. The spiritual journey the mature lover makes in *Die Winterreise* is one to madness and the void, and it is terrifyingly believable.

The two cycles, then, should be seen as related, and not

* Richard Capell *Schubert's Songs* Ernest Benn London 1928

merely by the fact that the poet in both instances is Müller. But each cycle is, nevertheless, self-contained, and, for all its sadness, there is an air of spring, of lightness, of youth in the earlier cycle, for which Schubert wrote some of his loveliest strophic songs, songs with gentle, beguiling melodies, redolent of the kind of country outside Vienna through which the composer himself loved to wander. In *Die schöne Müllerin*, Schubert gave a new dimension to the song-cycle. He cannot be said to have extended or enlarged in any way the formal implications of the cycle as such; Beethoven's *An die ferne Geliebte* remains unique and unimproved upon. But he invented the unified collection of songs around a theme, which is what we have since come to understand by the term 'song-cycle', and he did this without forethought, simply by reacting to Müller's poem-cycles and making of them two large-scale masterpieces. The 1823 *Schöne Müllerin* is as dearly loved by Schubertians as the greater cycle, *Die Winterreise*, of 1827.

The year 1824 was not rich in songs, but to that and the following year belong the two settings of Carl von Lappe (1773–1843), a schoolmaster and minor romantic poet, whose 'Im Abendrot' and 'Der Einsame' Schubert has immortalized. 'Im Abendrot' is a flawless example of Schubert's religious music; religious because nature was the closest thing to a God that he worshipped. His solitary man in the second song is not lonely, but contented and even cheerful in his solitude. 'Der Einsame' is an entrancing song, with its jaunty repeated phrase in the piano part echoing a cadence in the voice part.

Of the three poems by Jakob Nikolaus Craigher de Jachelutta (1797–1855) which Schubert set (one of them Craigher's translation of Colly Cibber's 'Blind Boy' whose slight and sentimental melody is no better than the text deserves), the 1825 'Die junge Nonne' is the finest : a superb dramatic landscape of the soul. The tempest raging outside is but a reflection, it seems, of the storm raging in the young nun's mind and heart. At the end, the nun's repeated 'Alleluja' asserts that the conflict has been resolved and that she is at peace, though the bass octaves in the piano part suggest otherwise. 'Die junge Nonne' is only one of several masterpieces of these last years between the two great cycles. Another is 'Nacht und Träume' whose poem is by one of the members of Schubert's Viennese circle, Matthaus von Collin (1779–1824); a beautiful adagio greeting to night, repose, and respite from the turgid day, and one of the best-loved of all

Lieder. Two more which must be mentioned are 'Die Allmacht' (1825) and 'Im Frühling' (1826). 'Die Allmacht' is a setting of a poem by one of Schubert's grander friends, Bishop Johann Ladislav Pyrker von Felsö-Eör, who, at the period of the song's composition, was Patriarch of Venice and was soon to become Archbishop of Erlau. The song was written while Schubert and his friend Vogl, the singer, were holidaying at Bad Gastein, where Bishop Pyrker was supervising a hospital which he had founded for invalid soldiers. Both poem and song are born of a love for the magnificent Austrian mountain landscape around Gastein. God in nature always brought a rapturous response from Schubert (as from the later Austrian romantics Bruckner and Mahler), and 'Die Allmacht' is noble, harmonically rich, and exhilarating in its effect. 'Im Frühling', whose verses are by Ernst Schulze (1789–1817), is quite different : an enchanting little set of variations on a spring theme.

To these last years belong the Shakespeare and Walter Scott songs. The best of the Scott settings are the five from *The Lady of the Lake* (in German translations by P. A. Storck), which include the celebrated 'Ave Maria'. This song may be a trifle too sweet for some tastes, but it is, in its way, quite beautiful. The three Shakespeare songs were all written in July 1826. 'Trinklied' from *Anthony and Cleopatra* is 'Come, thou monarch of the vine', a jolly but unremarkable C major shout. Far better, in fact delicious, though perhaps more Viennese than Shakespearian, are the 'Ständchen' from *Cymbeline*, which is a joyous Ländler to the words of 'Hark, hark, the lark at heaven's gate sings', and 'Gesang an Sylvia' from *The Two Gentlemen of Verona.* This latter is, of course, 'Who is Sylvia?', the most graceful and endearing of pastoral songs.

Schubert's cycle, *Die Winterreise*, was written in 1827, the year before his death. Müller's sequence of twenty-four poems had been published in two parts in 1823 and 1824, and this time the composer decided to set all the poems, not merely, as with *Die schöne Müllerin*, a selection. He completed the first twelve songs in February, the rest in October. These new poems were much more deeply felt and tragic in their import than the earlier, gentle lyrics of the miller's apprentice. This wanderer is not the comparatively healthy young man of *Die schöne Müllerin*, but a saddened, disillusioned figure of despair. In Schubert's *Winterreise* one does not find the spring-sadness of the *Müllerin* but the chronic melancholy and deep resignation of a mind at the end of its tether. Schubert has journeyed in the waste land and brought back a moving and heart-searching account of human loneliness. Listening to these songs we over-hear the voice of sorrow itself.

The first performance of *Die Winterreise* was given in the autumn of 1827 by Schubert himself, before an audience of his friends, but the general gloom of the songs caused them not to be well received. Schober, the poet of 'An die Musik', liked only one song, 'Der Lindenbaum', with its folk-like melody. However, when the composer's friend, Vogl, sang the songs, a much more enthusiastic reception was accorded them, and, some months later, after the publication of the first part of the cycle (Schubert corrected the proofs of the second part on his death-bed), the critic of the *Wiener Allgemeine Theaterzeitung** wrote : 'Schubert has understood his poet with the kind of genius that is his own. His music is as naïve as the poet's ex-pression; the emotions contained in the poems are as deeply reflected in the composer's own feelings, and these are so brought out in sound that none can sing or hear them without being touched to the heart'.

This winter journey deep into the human heart cannot be made lightly, and the singer who attempts *Die Winterreise* must be armed with much more than a good voice and a fine tech-nique. I once heard the singer Elena Gerhardt, say, in a lecture, 'You have to be haunted by this cycle to be able to sing it'. You have also to be able to project simplicity, spontaneity and, above all, sincerity. Throughout the cycle, the accompaniments depict much of the narrative. Often the voice is given a lovely legato line above a piano part descriptive of the barking of dogs, the swiftly-flowing river, or the wind in the trees. Most of the songs are in minor keys. Some of them are expressions of quiet despair; some, like 'Gefror'ne Tränen', 'Irrlicht' or 'Einsamkeit', have great heart-felt climaxes. Schubert's state-ments on love, commitment and death are those of an artist of genius. Space does not allow discussion here of the individual beauties of each song in the cycle, but one can hardly fail to note, or to feel, for instance the wonderful consoling effect of the change into the major key for the last stanza of 'Gute Nacht' at the words, 'Will dich in Traum nicht stören' ('I will not dis-turb your dreams'), or the great broad phrases, so splendidly singable, in the middle section of 'Erstarrung', or the sense of

* Issue of 29 March 1828

yearning so accurately placed and identified as at the end of
'Irrlicht', at the words 'Jedes Leiden auch sein Grab' ('And
every sorrow its grave'). But there are so many landmarks to
marvel at on this journey : the sinister accompaniment of 'Die
Krähe' over which the tense legato of the vocal line circles like
the crow itself, the meltingly lovely melody of 'Täuschung'
(already used five years earlier in the opera *alfanso und Estrella*),
or the hypnotic fascination of 'Der Wegweiser'. The terrifying
final song, 'Der Leiermann', is not an end, not a beginning, but
a gaze into the void. We are not to know what becomes of the
betrayed lover; we take our leave of him because we have
exhausted him.

There remains one more Schubert cycle, which is not a cycle.
The title, *Schwanengesang*, was given by Schubert's publishers,
who issued them six months after the composer's death, to the
fourteen songs of the summer and autumn of 1828. These are
the last solo songs Schubert wrote. He did not think of them
as a cycle, but as groups of six songs on poems by Ludwig
Rellstab (1799–1860) and seven on poems by Heinrich Heine
(1797–1856) (both of them poets Schubert encountered for the
first time in this last year of his life), both groups composed in
August, plus a final song, 'Die Taubenpost', written in October.
With hardly an exception, these are magnificent songs. The six
Rellstab settings include the amiable 'Liebesbotschaft'; the
romantic 'Ständchen' which is, without question, the most
widely-known Schubert song, and which has suffered countless
transcriptions and arrangements; and an outburst of wrathful
despair, 'Aufenthalt'.

Schubert's Heine songs are all such masterpieces that one
cannot help regretting that the composer had not been able to
read Heine earlier than 1828. But the poet's 'Buch der Lieder'
was not published until 1827 so we must be grateful that
Schubert seized on some of these poems so quickly. Heine's
sentiment, tempered with irony, has been beautifully translated
into music in these seven songs. 'Der Atlas' is powerful and
bitter, compressed yet implacable. 'Ihr Bild' is a gentle portrait
of grief; 'Das Fischermädchen' a charming barcarolle which
perhaps ignores the note of sophistication in Heine's poem—if
so, it is Schubert's only lapse in complete understanding
throughout this group; 'Die Stadt', a masterly impressionistic
landscape. 'Am Meer' is another of Schubert's extraordinary
seascapes, in which nature's moods mirror the emotions suffered

by humans. It is also ineffably sad music. The final Heine song, 'Der Doppelgänger', is the greatest of all, written throughout as a kind of heightened recitative or arioso, the drama presented as importantly by the piano as by the voice, the total effect dramatic and heartbreaking.

The remaining *Schwanengesang* item is 'Die Taubenpost', sweet and gentle, Schubert at his most engaging. The poem is by Johann Gabriel Seidl (1804–1875), an Austrian country school-teacher who won a prize for the best set of verses for Haydn's 'Hymn to the Emperor'. This is probably Schubert's last song. If it is not, then that distinction passes to 'Der Hirt auf dem Felsen', also written in October 1828, a few weeks before the composer's untimely death. 'Der Hirt auf dem Felsen' is a rather long song, really a scena, with a clarinet part as well as piano, and was intended as a display piece for the Berlin soprano, Anna Milder-Hauptmann, who had repeatedly asked Schubert to write something spectacular for her. The clarinet part is well conceived for the instrument, and the entire song has a certain pastoral charm. Its final allegro calls for a wide range as well as a coloratura agility. The text, an innocuous piece of romantic verse in praise of spring, is concocted from two separate poems, one by Müller and the other by Wilhelmine von Chézy (1783–1856) for whose play *Rosamunde* Schubert had earlier written instrumental music.

Our survey of Schubert's songs has confirmed that, in addition to bringing his own lyric genius to the song form, he also developed the form in several ways, particularly in the direction of a more freely imaginative use of the piano as accompanying instrument. We shall find further development of this kind in Schumann, but must first glance at the songs of Johann Carl Gottfried Loewe (1796–1869) who, though he was Schubert's senior by a few months, outlived the younger composer by over forty years. At one time, there was a great vogue for Loewe in Germany, particularly on the level of domestic music-making, but his work is not today very frequently encountered in recital programmes. Loewe was no Schubert, but he was certainly gifted, though his gift was a somewhat specialized one. Of his songs—and there are nearly 400 of them—the majority are ballads, sometimes referred to in English as 'art ballads', presumably to distinguish them from the commercial publisher's ballad of Victorian and Edwardian England.

Like Schubert, Loewe derives from the earlier ballad writers :

Reichardt, Zumsteeg and Zelter. The ballad-poems which inspired these composers in turn derive from the Scottish and
English narrative ballads, many of which were translated into
German. The form was eagerly taken up in the 18th century,
even by poets of the stature of Goethe and Schiller, and the
subject-matter tended, as often as not, to involve the supernatural in some way (e.g. Goethe's 'Erlkonig'). Goethe, in fact,
said of the ballad that it required 'a mystical touch, by which
the mind of the reader is brought into that frame of undefined
sympathy and awe which men unavoidably feel when face to
face with the miraculous or with the mighty forces of nature'.
The English and Scottish ballads published in 1765 in Percy's
Reliques of English Poetry were translated into German by
such poets as J. G. Herder and G. A. Burger, and many of
them were set by German composers. Generally speaking, the
music tends to follow the mood and form of the words in a
fairly simple and subservient way in these ballads, underlining
and thus emphasizing the form's narrative importance. Loewe's
setting of Goethe's 'Erlkönig', for instance, obeys these unwritten
rules in a way that Schubert's does not. In Schubert, the over-
riding musical imagination sweeps subject, form and plot along
on its own, purely musical impetus. Loewe, as we shall see,
follows Goethe's words more closely and more faithfully. By
doing so, in this and other ballads, he found himself developing
his own musical narrative style, which is sufficiently distinctive to
set him apart from Zumsteeg and company, though not to
raise him to the stature of Schubert.

Loewe's op. 1 no. 1 is 'Edward', the Scottish ballad in
Herder's translation, which he composed in 1818. Its dramatic
force and power are typical of the best of his songs, for Loewe
is at his weakest and most anonymous in lyrical vein, though
some of his lyrical melodies are undeniably pretty. 'Der Erlkönig',
op. 1 no. 3, also dates from 1818, only three years after
Schubert's masterpiece. Loewe knew Schubert's song, was not
inhibited by it but encouraged 'to do it another way'. His other
way has not the onward rush and inevitability of Schubert, but
it is certainly effective in the dramatic quality of its declamation
and its remarkable sense of atmosphere. Its formal qualities are,
in fact, more impressive than those of Schubert's 'Erlkönig'. One
of the finest of these early ballads of Loewe is 'Herr Oluf'. The
poem, a version by Johann Gottfried von Herder of a 16th-
century Danish legend, tells of another encounter with the

family of the 'elfking'. (Both Herder and Goethe, incidentlly, misunderstand the Danish 'Ellerkonge', king of the elves, and translated it as 'Erlkönig', or king of the alder trees, thus inventing a new supernatural being.) Wagner, who not surprisingly preferred the German Loewe's 'Erlkönig' to the Austrian Schubert's, referred to 'Herr Oluf' as 'one of the most important works of musical literature'. This is somewhat of an over-statement, although Loewe does make a first-rate miniature drama from the not particularly original or compelling poem. The dancing of the elves in the marshes is depicted brilliantly in the piano part, and the various characters—Oluf, his mother, his bride-to-be and the elfking's daughter—are all strongly characterized.

Some of Loewe's early settings of Goethe are more successful than others. Of 'Gutmann und Gutweib', Goethe's lighthearted adaptation of a Scottish ballad, he made somewhat heavy weather, but some of his more lyrical settings are, of their kind, remarkably beautiful. 'Wanderers Nachtlied' ('Der du von den Himmel bist') may lack the simplicity of Schubert's heart-felt masterpiece, but it is an accomplished and sensitive song. Heard after the Schubert, it sounds old-fashioned but by no means absurd. Another of Loewe's early Goethe songs, 'Ich denke dein', also has to face competition from other more celebrated versions. Beethoven's approaches Goethe more closely, but there is no doubt that Loewe sees more in the poem, treats it more solemnly, and consequently brings to his setting an impressive weight of utterance. Also worthy of mention is 'Lynceus, der Türmer, auf Fausts Sternwarte singend' in which the poetic beauty of the words is enhanced by the composer's rapt response to them.

'Graf Eberstein' is among the more interesting of the other early ballads of Loewe. Its poem is by Ludwig Uhland (1787–1862), generally thought to be the finest German writer of ballads after Goethe and Herder, and it tells of a warning of danger uttered to the count by the king's daughter while they are dancing. Loewe's song is one long dance whose moods vary; this is one of his less literal settings. Another excellent Uhland setting is 'Der Wirtin Töchterlein'. Though he did not develop greatly throughout his long creative career, Loewe's style did noticeably alter over the years. The earliest ballads are in general the most dramatic. Three distinct creative periods can be distinguished, during the second of which Loewe wrote many of his finest songs, among them several from Goethe. 'Die wandelnde Glocke' is about the boy who would not go to church and who found himself being chased by the church bell. Humour is not Loewe's strong point, but this delightful song is an exception. Goethe's brilliant 'Hochzeitlied', like 'Die wandelnde Glocke' composed in 1832, is a splendid patter-song which Loewe himself used to perform to great acclaim. 'Der getreue Eckart' is Goethe's somewhat impenetrable rendering of an old Thuringian legend, from which Loewe has succeeded in fashioning a rather unusual song though not of sufficient melodic interest to captivate a non-German-speaking audience.

The sorcerer's apprentice of Goethe's 'Der Zauberlehrling' is best known musically through the programmatic orchestral piece, 'L'apprenti sorcier', by Dukas, which in turn reached its widest audience in Walt Disney's *Fantasia*. Loewe's setting of the poem, a vivid and amusing piece of narrative song, could surely become popular with English-speaking audiences in a singable translation. Another Goethe ballad graphically characterized in music by Loewe is 'Der Totentanz'.

A middle-period song which the composer himself used to perform is 'Heinrich der Vogler'. Heinrich is the king in Wagner's *Lohengrin* who, in the poem by Johann Nepomuk Vogl (1802–1866), happily greets a troop of horsemen who ride up to pay homage to him at 'the will of the German Empire'. The poem's patriotic sentiments appealed to Loewe whose music is frankly better than the words deserve. With a more interesting poet such as Rückert, the results are some particularly reward-ing songs: for instance, 'Süsses Begrabnis' and the brief 'Hinkende Jamben'.

In the later songs, one occasionally notices a greater elabora-tion in the piano parts, though not necessarily a greater ad-venturousness. 'Prinz Eugen, der edle Ritter', dating from 1844, is something of a *tour de force*, based on an old folk tune of which Loewe makes cunning and complex use. The poem is by Ferdinand Freiligrath (1810–1876). One of the most charming of Loewe's Goethe songs is 'Im Vorübergehen'. The poem is a dialogue between poet and flower, as in 'Das Veilchen', and the music needs only a little more southern lightness of touch to be called Schubertian. (Perhaps the most sheerly beautiful of Loewe's settings of Goethe is the little 'Canzonette' which is light and southern, in fact almost Bellinian in its *bel canto* sweetness.) On the other hand, many of Loewe's ballads, though superficially tuneful do little more than project the poem rhythmically over a thoughtless accompaniment. 'Odins Meeres-ritt' (poem by Schreiber) epitomizes this type of ballad. Two of the composer's most famous songs, which one still hears occasionally in recitals, are 'Archibald Douglas' and 'Tom der Reimer'. 'Archibald Douglas' (1857), though the poem by Theodor Fontane (1819–1898) is not a translation from English or Scottish, is about an incident which is supposed to have occurred during the feud between James V and the clan of Douglas, and which is also recounted by Sir Walter Scott. In the poem, the king pardons an old enemy. (According to history, he was wont to do nothing of the kind.) The poem is rambling and sentimental, but Loewe's scene painting and characterization are as masterly as ever, and musically the song is well organized, though the material can sound dangerously old-fashioned to modern ears, in a way that Schubert and Schumann avoid. Even quainter is 'Tom der Reimer' whose sweet sentimentality must have sounded considerably less cloying when it was written. The poem, by Theodor Fontane, is yet another account of a supernatural meeting in the forest. This encounter in Scotland, 'am Kieselbach bei Huntley Schloss' (by the pebbly brook near Huntley Castle), is between the rhymer Thomas and the queen of the elves, whom he at first mistakes for the Virgin Mary, but with whom eventually he rides off into the woods, her willing slave for seven years. Sentimental or not, the charm of Loewe's tunes and their accompaniment is still potent. Among the later works, the long and rambling ballad 'Die verfallene Mühle' has much to commend it. The cycle, Liederkranz für Bass (op. 145), consisting of five songs, to poems by Siebee, Scherenberg and von Redwitz, should be looked at by basses, for the songs are among Loewe's most typical, most dramatic and most tuneful especially no. 1 'Meeresleuchten', no. 3 'In Sturme', and no. 4 'Heimliehkat'.

Born thirteen years after Loewe, the Austrian Heinrich Proch (1809–1878), conductor, violinist and teacher of singing, as well as composer, was for thirty years chief conductor at the Vienna Opera. His songs, immensely popular in their day, are now seldom heard, though occasionally a soprano specializing in coloratura will essay his 'Variationen'.

Hardly less prolific than Loewe as a writer of Lieder was Wilhelm Taubert (1811–1891) who composed nearly 300 songs, many of which excited the admiration of Mendelssohn. With the exception of a display piece, 'Der Vogel im Walde' which enjoyed a popularity with lyric sopranos until the beginning of the 20th century, none of Taubert's songs survived him.

The songs of Felix Mendelssohn-Bartholdy (1809–1847) are closer in style and manner to Schubert than to Loewe. They might even be described as sub-Schubertian, for Mendelssohn had a charming sweetness of melody in common with Schubert, or with one aspect of Schubert, yet lacked the older composer's adventurousness and immense variety of mood and manner. Also, although he no doubt had a more assured literary taste than Schubert, Mendelssohn's feeling for words appears to have been considerably less intense, to judge by the manner in which he set them to music. This is perhaps only another way of saying that he was classical rather than romantic by temperament. It is certainly true that he was more adept at portraying quiet happiness, or contentment allied with a certain wistfulness, than with the larger emotions of anger, love and despair. He was an artist of exquisite sensibility, but had little feeling for, or response to, the tragic aspect of life.

Mendelssohn composed songs throughout the whole of his comparatively brief working career : he lived for only seven years more than Schubert. The twelve songs of his op. 8 include four which are by his sister Fanny (one of them, Goethe's 'Suleika und Hatem' is, in fact, a duet). Fanny's songs are very like those of her brother, and one of them, 'Einmal aus seinen Blicken', has character as well as charm, though it is somewhat too elaborate for its subject, a slight Spanish love poem. Mendelssohn's contributions to the group are, as was usual with him, settings of several poets. They include a 'Minnelied' of Hölty which Brahms was later to set more successfully, 'Italien' by Franz Grillparzer (1791–1872), a folk poem 'Erntelied' which, though somewhat archaic in manner, is interesting and individual, a lively 'Frühlingslied' by F. Robert, and, by far the most successful song of the entire group, 'Hexenlied', whose poem is by Hölty (1748–1776). This song is a lively and imaginative response to Hölty's picture of the fairy world, bringing to mind the Mendelssohn of the *Midsummer Night's Dream* music which was yet to come.

The songs of op. 9, still juvenilia, are a more varied collection than those of op. 8. This time, three of them are by Fanny : 'Sehnsucht', 'Verlust' and 'Die Nonne', to poems of Droysen, Heine and Uhland. They are unremarkable, and Mendelssohn's own songs are markedly superior. The music of 'Frage' (poem by J. H. Voss), a song of quiet charm, was later to be used again in the A minor String Quartet. 'Geständnis' begins with the same theme, but is much more passionate; 'Wartend' and 'Scheidend' anticipate the mature Mendelssohn, the latter especially in its quiet beauty and striking harmonies. Its poem is by Voss, while those of 'Geständnis' and 'Wartend' are by unknown poets. This group also contains 'Frühlingsglaube', Uhland's poem which Schubert had set so memorably. There is nothing in Mendelssohn's otherwise pleasant and lively song to equal Schubert's inspired simplicity.

Two individual songs, 'The Garland' to Thomas Moore's poem, composed in 1829, and a setting of Hoffmann von Fallersleben's 'Seemans Scheidelied' two years later, are of no especial interest, but the next group, the six songs of op. 19a, shows a considerable advance on the earlier ones. It consists of two Heine settings, two of Egon Ebert, one from Ulrich von Lichtenstein, and one from an unspecified Swedish poet. The Swedish song, 'Winterlied' is the least impressive of the six, though its final stanza is interesting. The two Heine songs are excellent. 'Neue Liebe' is an exhilarating and imaginative evocation of fairyland, gay and brilliant on the surface, but with a touch of strangeness, while 'Gruss', a strophic song in two stanzas, has something of the deceptive simplicity of Schubert and has attained quasi-folk song status in Germany. 'Frühlingslied' the Lichtenstein setting, is a squarely academic version of a banal poem. The two Ebert songs are more interesting: the warmly attractive 'Reiselied' and the more subtle 'Das erste Veilchen'. This latter is, for Mendelssohn, unconventional in its varying phrase lengths and the individuality and charm of its piano part.

Of the six songs of op. 34, 'Minnelied', its poem from the Old German, is perhaps no more than agreeably pleasant, and the same could be said of the two Klingemann songs, 'Frühlingslied'—there are a number of these in Mendelssohn—and 'Sonntagslied'; but the remaining three songs show the composer at his very best. 'Auf Flügeln des Gesanges' is well known in English as 'On Wings of Song'. The poem is by Heine. This is a song of great melodic charm, though Heine is said not to have cared for it. The other Heine song of the set, 'Reiselied', has an unusual power, and is also remarkable in its evocation of atmosphere. 'Suleika' is a touching and unusual response to

Goethe's poem. Two pairs of songs followed the op. 34 group. The first pair are undistinguished settings of Byron's 'There be none of beauty's daughters' and 'Sun of the Sleepless', though the piano part of the latter is rather free for Mendelssohn. The other two are from Eichendorff: 'Das Waldschloss' tells a typically Eichendorff tale of a knight enchanted by a nymph, set to simple but attractive music, and 'Pagenlied' is gay and charming.

The next group of six is op. 47, which contains some delightful and graceful songs, such as Tieck's lively 'Minnelied' and the two Klingemann settings: 'Der Blumenstrauss' and the particularly charming 'Bei der Wiege'. 'Volkslied' is simple and affecting, without, in this instance, sounding Schubertian, and the lively melody of Lenau's 'Frühlingslied', one of the best of Mendelssohn's spring songs, is particularly engaging. Op. 47 is completed by a simple unaffected setting of Heine's 'Morgengruss'. In the next group, the six songs of op. 57, we again find the composer in his best form. The songs, which include a 'Hirtenlied' by Uhland and another Suleika poem, 'Was bedeutet die Bewegung?', by Goethe, are never less than amiable, and one of them, 'Venetianisches Gondellied', a setting of a German translation of Thomas Moore's 'When through the Piazzetta', is a work of strangely sombre beauty. The folk poem setting, 'O Jugend' is interesting, if not perhaps compulsive listening.

Op. 71 consists of six songs written in the mid 1840s, all of them in Mendelssohn's mature manner, and some of them particularly interesting. 'Tröstung' (poem by Fallersleben) is fittingly sentimental, and the three Lenau settings are first-rate. The first, 'An die Entfernte', has delicacy and charm, the second, 'Schilflied', is a calmly flowing barcarolle, and the third, 'Auf der Wanderschaft', is a song of sombre beauty. The Eichendorff 'Nachtlied' is one of Mendelssohn's finest songs: strong, solemn and moving. The Klingemann 'Frühlingslied' is colourless.

Mendelssohn died in 1847, and, though a number of songs were published posthumously, they date from various periods in his life. Three songs written between 1831 and 1839 specifically for a low voice constitute op. 84. 'Da lieg' ich unter den Bäumen' is an unusual strophic song, which goes from major to minor in each of its six stanzas. The authorship of its poem is unknown. Klingemann's 'Herbstlied' arouses Mendelssohn to no greater heights than had his 'Frühlingslied', but the *Knaben Wunderhorn* 'Jagdlied' is an essay of delicate charm.

Op. 86 consists of Mendelssohn's usual number of six items. These include a number of interesting songs written at different times. 'Es lausche das Laub', from a Klingemann poem, is a product of the seventeen-year-old Mendelssohn; an unusual song which begins in a major key and ends in the minor. 'Morgenlied' displays the composer's fresh young charm, and Goethe's 'Die liebende schreibt' is a quite magnificent setting, freer and more imaginative in its response to the words than the composer was apt to be. The fourth is 'Allnächtlich im Traume', the poem from Heine's *Lyrisches Intermezzo* which was later to be set so perfectly by Schumann in his *Dichterliebe*. Mendelssohn's attempt, it must be admitted, is colourless by comparison, despite its agitated movement. 'Der Mond', poem by Geibel, is a rich and attractive song, while 'Altdeutsches Frühlingslied', whose poem is by Spee, is the last song Mendelssohn wrote. A somewhat perfunctory piece, alas.

Another posthumous group, op. 99, introduces one new poet, Count von Schlippenbach, and also contains settings of the familiar Mendelssohn poets, Goethe, Uhland, Geibel, Eichendorff, and the folk collection, *Des Knaben Wunderhorn*. *Des Knaben Wunderhorn* is a collection of German folk poems arranged and edited by Achim von Arnim (1781–1831) and Clemens Brentano (1778–1842). Published in 1806–8 it proved immensely popular, and became a profound influence on German poetry throughout the 19th century, as well as providing a number of texts for German and Austrian composers. Mendelssohn had set a 'Jagdlied' from the *Wunderhorn* in his op. 84, and op. 99 no. 3 is 'Lieblingsplätzchen', a tender and charming response to the poem. None of the other songs in this group is especially memorable, with the possible exceptions of the expressive 'Erster Verlust' (Goethe) and the plain yet not unappealing 'Wenn sich zwei Herzen scheiden' (poem by Geibel). 'Es weiss und rät es doch Keiner' begins as a pale adumbration of Schumann's setting of the same poem, 'Die Stille', in his op. 39 *Liederkreis*, and then becomes marginally more interesting as it proceeds. The poem is by Eichendorff. The second of two sacred songs, op. 112, was originally intended for inclusion in the oratorio *St Paul*. A final song without opus number, Schiller's 'Des Mädchens Klage' is first-rate, and is, for Mendelssohn, unusually passionate.

The songs of Mendelssohn, then, contain a great deal of pleasant and attractive music, though they cannot really be said in general to rise to the level of his instrumental and orchestral works. The songs of that many-sided, erratic genius, Franz Liszt (1811–1886) are less easy to classify. For one thing, the texts of his seventy-five or more songs range over five languages: German, French, Italian, Hungarian and English. Despite their composer's Hungarian birth, however, the majority of the songs are in German. Also, the songs are of various kinds, unlike, say, those of Mendelssohn, all of which conform to the requirements of the classical *Lied*. Understandably, the piano plays a prominent part in Liszt's songs which are, nevertheless, no mere appendage to the admittedly more important piano music, but an integral part of the composer's *œuvre*. They extend, too, over forty years of his creative life, and thus become increasingly adventurous as his style develops, loses some of its purely Hungarian quality and gains a cosmopolitan ease of manner. Liszt was primarily an instrumental composer, nevertheless his interest in German song appears to date from 1840, the year in which he first met Schumann, and in which Schumann wrote so many of his most miraculous songs. Prior to that year, Liszt had written only four songs, to Italian texts. These are 'Angiolin dal biondo crin' and *Three Petrarch Sonnets*. All four songs were later turned into piano pieces, the *Petrarch Sonnets* becoming movements in the Italian year of the *Années de pèlerinage*, and all four are more effective in their instrumental form, though a fine singer and pianist can make the *Petrarch Sonnets* sound convincing as songs. Liszt was a great, indeed a compulsive arranger of music, his own as well as other men's: most of his songs, we shall find, were to be transcribed for the voracious piano at some time or other. Another early song, this time to a French text by Delphine Gay, 'Il m'aimait tant', also in due course became a piano piece.

Liszt's first German songs, written shortly after his encounter with Schumann, are settings of Heine. 'Am Rhein' was followed by 'Die Lorelei' which subtly, perhaps over-subtly, matches verbal and musical phrases. There is no doubt, and this is true of almost all Liszt's songs, of the importance and independence of the piano part. Occasionally it is over-elaborate, giving an effect of studied unspontaneity, but only very rarely does it indulge in rhetorical display. The virtuoso pianist knew how to curb his virtuosity when writing song accompaniments. The sensitive response to words and the deep yearning of Liszt's 'Lorelei' are a far cry from the popular folk song setting of

Heine's poem by Friedrich Silcher. Indeed, it is positively Tristanesque in places. A most interesting song, though the pace occasionally seems, for all its brooding intensity, rather too slow for the events of the poem.

Hungarian was Liszt's first language. His German was never perfect, though it continued to improve throughout his life, and in many later versions of early songs, the composer corrects imperfect accentuation. This happens, for instance, in 'Mignons Lied', a setting of Goethe's 'Kennst du das Land?' which first appeared in 1843. The second version, published in 1856, is the finest setting of this text to have been composed before Wolf's great song. A third version, with orchestral accompaniment, was published in 1863. (Liszt orchestrated two more of his songs, 'Die Lorelei' and 'Die Vätergruft', as well as several by other composers including Schubert.) 'Comment, disaient-ils' (poem by Hugo) is a charming song, somewhat Spanish in rhythm and in its piano part which is marked 'quasi Chitarra'. Most of Liszt's French settings are of poems by Hugo. One of the best of them is 'Oh! quand je dors' with its langourous, romantic melody which, even without the words, sounds completely French in style and sentiment. The early 1840s also produced three fascinating Goethe songs, 'Es war ein König in Thule', 'Der du von dem Himmel bist' and 'Freudvoll und Leidvoll'. 'Es war ein König in Thule', Gretchen's song from *Faust*, is wonderfully effective although it lacks the artless, spontaneous quality which the poem displays in its dramatic context. If Liszt has one consistent fault as a composer of songs, it is that he sometimes tends to be over-emphatic, over-elaborate and unsubtle in his response to a poem. His setting of 'Der du von dem Himmel bist' is an example of this, though musically the song is first-rate. When Schubert set this beautiful Wanderer's Nightsong, he captured the mood of the poem beautifully and simply. So, too, did Liszt, but only after he had made three attempts, the first in 1843 and the last in 1860. In his 1843 setting, Liszt took Goethe's final line, 'Komm, ach, Komm in meine Brust' and repeated and elaborated it endlessly, as though hoping to improve or emphasize the feeling by repetition. Also, he insensitively altered the opening line from 'Der du *von dem* Himmel bist' to 'Der du *im* Himmel bist'. By 1860, Liszt had come to a clearer, saner appreciation of the poem. The repetition has gone, and Goethe's original opening line is restored. 'Freudvoll und Leidvoll' from Goethe's

Egmont also went through three versions, of which the most successful, certainly the most beautiful, is the last.

These revisions demonstrate Liszt's seriousness of purpose as a composer of *Lieder*, and it is almost invariably the case that they do improve the songs from version to version. When Hugo's 'Enfant, si j'étais roi', for instance, first published in 1844 (and arranged for piano shortly afterwards) was completely re-written in 1859, its more dramatic flourishes were simplified and its vocal line considerably modified. 'S'il est un charmant gazon', also by Hugo, similarly undergoes major changes between versions of 1844 and 1859. Among Liszt's Hugo settings of the mid 1840s, however, is one which he did not feel the need to revise later : a striking bolero of markedly Spanish character, 'Gastibelza'. His 'Du bist wie eine Blume', written at about the same time, is less successful. Heine's delicate poem had, in any case, been quite perfectly put to music by Schumann in 1840. Liszt misses the tremulous spontaneity of the poem. A miniature cycle of three songs from Schiller's *Wilhelm Tell*, composed in 1845, is undeserving of its present neglect, as is 'Jeanne d'Arc au bûcher' (poem by Hugo). Liszt himself in later years referred to this latter song as inadequate, perhaps because its climax is understated. But that strength of feeling does not have to be equated with vehemence of manner is proved by 'Ich möchte hingehn', the poem (by Herwegh) a typical piece of 19th-century *Weltschmerz*, but Liszt's music a fascinating anticipation of the Mahler of 'Ich bin der Welt abhanden gekommen'. 'Wer nie sein Brot mit Tränen ass' is hardly one of the most interesting settings of Goethe's much composed-upon poem, but 'O lieb, so lang du lieben kannst', whose poem is by Freiligrath, is deservedly popular. Liszt's yearning, romantic melody is appealing, particularly in this, its original form. He later transmuted and metamorphosed the song into the third of three 'Liebesträume' for the piano, from which form it has spread hackneyed wings and suffered countless transpositions and arrangements.

The voice of the authentic Hungarian Liszt is heard in 'Istenveled', a setting of a poem by the Hungarian Horvath, composed in 1846-7, and other, more cosmopolitan pieces from these years include settings of Béranger's 'Le Juif errant' and 'Le vieux vagabond', and Dinglestedt's 'Schwebe, schwebe, blaues Auge'. In 1848, Liszt came to Goethe's 'Über allen Gipfeln ist Ruh', the second of the 'Wanderers Nachtlieder'.

He had already set it for unaccompanied male chorus six years earlier, not very successfully, and it cannot be said that this solo song comes any closer to the mood of the poem. Much more successful is Uhland's 'Gestorben war ich', in which both vocal line and piano accompaniment are beautifully handled.

Of the songs of the 1850s—and there are barely a dozen of them, for Liszt's interests in these years were concentrated in other directions—the most sheerly beautiful in terms of melody is 'Es muss ein Wunderbares sein' (poem by Redwitz), whose mood and manner recall something of 'Oh, quand je dors' and 'O lieb, so lang du lieben kannst'. The short 'Nimm einen Strahl der Sonne' (Rellstab) is dramatically effective. In Liszt's Hungarian manner again, although this time to a German text, for the poem is by Lenau, is 'Die drei Zigeuner'. This is splendid gypsy music à la Liszt, instinct with drama and rhythmic excitement. The later songs of Liszt, and revised versions of earlier songs, those which follow after 'Die drei Zigeuner', tend to be less overtly dramatic. Some of them, 'La Perla' for instance, are frankly dull, but several are first-rate examples of the composer's most mature manner. One of the most impressive is 'J'ai perdu ma force et ma vie', a setting of de Musset's poem. 'Ihr Glocken von Marling' (poem by Emil Kuh), 'Sei still' (Henriette von Schorn) and 'Gebet' (Bodenstedt) are others almost equally good, though unfairly neglected today. 'Ihr Glocken von Marling' is especially interesting in its restraint and its feeling of strange serenity. In 1879, Liszt composed his Tennyson song, 'Go not, happy day', which would have been more interesting, perhaps, had he been less concerned to make the music sound as English as the words.

The songs of Liszt, then, constitute a by no means negligible part of his *œuvre*. From the extrovert drama of the earlier songs, to the unusual harmonies of the later ones, they cover a wide field, though it is true that they are, in the last resort, only the by-products of a great instrumental talent.

It would not be true to say this of the songs of Robert Schumann (1810–1856), Liszt's senior by one year. Schumann's genius was for the piano and the voice, and his stature as a composer of *Lieder* is due to this very fact. Although Schubert before him had brought increased interest to the piano part of his songs, had indeed made the piano an integral partner with the voice, it was Schumann who developed this even further, to the extent where some of his songs, in the *Dichterliebe* for instance, could be described as piano pieces with vocal obbligato. Schumann lacked Schubert's extraordinary range, but compensated for this by worrying away with great intensity at the vein he knew he could mine, a particularly German—as distinct from Austrian—romanticism, verging on the sentimental but, in Schumann's case, redeemed by his sensitivity to words. He is said, in addition, to have had very good literary taste, which is not the same thing and which, in the opinion of the present writer, is in any case not true. To Schumann, Jean Paul was as great an artist as Shakespeare, and he hailed as geniuses some very dubious cases indeed. But feeling for words he undoubtedly had; this is evident from the songs themselves.

Schumann's songs number more than 260, about half of which were composed during his *annus mirabilis* of song, 1840, when he was thirty. Only a dozen or so songs precede the vast outpouring of that year, and they are negligible. In his youth, as Schumann himself admitted, he used always to consider vocal music inferior to instrumental, and never thought of it seriously as art. The songs he had already written date from 1827 and 1828 when he was in his late teens. Two of them, 'Verwandlung' and 'Lied für XXX' remain unpublished, and a collection of eleven songs dedicated to Schumann's three sisters-in-law, settings of Goethe, Byron, Jacobi, Kerner and Ekert, contains little to suggest that he would later blossom into genius as a composer of the *Lied*. Schumann himself was dissatisfied with these songs, but made use of material from three of them in various piano works. A Kerner setting, 'Nicht im Thale', became the aria in his F sharp minor Piano Sonata (no. 1); Kerner's 'Im Herbste' was used as the andantino of the Second Sonata in G minor; and Ekert's 'Der Hirtenknabe' was used in the fourth of six intermezzi, op. 4.

Why did Schumann turn his attention to songs in 1840, the year of his marriage to Clara Wieck, to whom he had become engaged in 1837? As late as 1839 he was comparatively disinterested in vocal music, but on 19 February 1840, he wrote to a friend, 'At the present moment I am only writing songs, big and little . . . I can hardly tell you what a treat it is to write for the voice, compared with instrumental composition, and what a ferment I am in as I sit at work.'* The often advanced theory that Schumann took to writing songs as an expression of

* May Herbert (translator) *The Life of Robert Schumann told in his letters* (2 vols.) R. Bentley London 1890 (Edited by F. Gustav Jansen)

his great joy at marrying Clara is really hardly tenable. They were not married until the autumn, they had been engaged for three years, and Schumann had expressed his love in piano music dedicated to Clara. The answer is probably not to be found, though it may be that the composer wished to make his expressive meaning more explicit, and so resorted to words almost in the spirit of Beethoven in the last movement of the Ninth Symphony. Whatever the cause, he took to song in 1840 with a vengeance. Not only does half his song output date from that year, but also by far the better half of it. He was to write a number of superb songs later, but the majority of Schumann's finest *Lieder*, including all the great cycles, were composed in 1840.

The first fruits of 1840 were the nine settings of Heine which comprise the *Liederkreis* op. 24. Schumann was to compose more songs on Heine than on any other poet. The two were ideally suited, both in technique and spirit, for they had much in common : a spiritual affinity and a romanticism tempered with a somewhat bitter irony, as well as a gift for concision. Both were miniaturists, able to make their points swiftly, without preamble but with a telling directness. Schumann was to set forty-two of Heine's poems to music, all but five of them in 1840. In this, his first cycle, the composer had not yet completely come to terms with his poet. It is a true cycle, in the sense that there is a key sequence to be observed, and that the poems are not only all by the one poet but are also related in subject matter. Heine's subject in these poems is his familiar one of the pain of love. Schumann is more successful with some of these poems than with others, so that one cannot claim this early *Liederkreis* as one of the great cycles, though it contains some very lovely songs. It is a stepping stone on the way to, almost a rehearsal for the style and manner of, the *Dichterliebe*, although it does not begin to equal the neurotic intensity of feeling of the later work. Its style is in general that of the spare, terse Schumann rather than the romantic Schumann, conveying mood by various subtle means of phrasing in the voice part, and harmonies in the piano accompaniment. This *Liederkreis* lacks the charm and immediacy of appeal of much that Schumann wrote later in the year, but then it makes no attempt to display these particular virtues. Though its songs do not stand up well to performance outside the cycle, with one or two exceptions such as 'Schöne Wiege meiner Leiden', and its weakest songs are failures even within the cycle (e.g. 'Warte, wilde Schiffs-mann'), the work as a whole is effective in its hesitant, difficult way, and one of its songs, 'Ich wandelte unter den Bäumen', is Schumann at his most psychologically penetrating. It and its poem would not be out of place in the later *Dichterliebe*.

Myrthen op. 25 is not really a cycle, though it consists of twenty-six songs which begin with a 'Dedication' ('Widmung') and end with a 'Conclusion' ('Zum Schluss'). The poems appear to have been chosen at random, from such diverse poets as Rückert, Goethe, Heine, Burns and Thomas Moore (in transla-tion) and Julius Mosen, though the fact that Schumann intended the songs to be sung together is indicated by his having arranged them in key sequence. They are on a variety of subjects, rather than on Schumann's usual sole subject of ecstatic love. The Rückert 'Widmung' ('Du meine Seele, du mein Herz'), one of the most popular and frequently performed of *Lieder*, begins the collection in the composer's most ardent A major manner, dropping into a lower key for the more solemn middle section ('Du bist die Ruh, du bist die Frieden'). 'Widmung' is the most popular of the Rückert songs in op. 25, but the most beauti-ful, indeed one of Schumann's loveliest, is 'Aus der östlichen Rosen'. 'Freisinn' is the most successful, perhaps really the only successful, Goethe setting of the five to be found in *Myrthen*. The Goethe poems chosen are not particularly interesting, and in any case Schumann was never as much at ease with Goethe as with Heine. The three Heine songs, on the other hand, are all beautiful, typically Schumannesque love songs, pure confessions of his feelings for Clara. 'Die Lotosblume' and 'Du bist wie eine Blume', with their richly romantic harmonies and tender melodies, are among the most popular of Schumann's songs, but the more delicate 'Was will die einsame Träne' is, in its way, equally appealing.

Eight of Schumann's nine settings of Robert Burns, in German translations by Wilhelm Gerhard, are to be found in *Myrthen*. These, as befits Burns's style, tend to be more simply organized songs than, for instance, the Heine settings, and half of them are in fact strophic songs. The tunes are as good as the poems deserve, but Schumann's heart appears not to have been in the task, and it is not easy to understand why he should have tackled Burns at all. The other *Myrthen* songs call for no special comment. One of the two Thomas Moore translations is 'Wenn durch die Piazzetta' which Schumann makes into a curiously

Mendelssohnian song, though not one to compare with Mendelssohn's own setting.

Op. 27, the next group of songs to emerge in 1840, was published as Volume I of *Lieder und Gesänge*, and contains five songs to texts of five different poets. Only two are worth noting: the remaining Burns song, 'Dem roten Röslein gleicht mein Lieb', and Rückert's delicious 'Jasminenstrauch'. More interesting as a group are the *Drei Gedichte* of op. 30. The three poems by Emanuel von Geibel are character pieces, as the titles suggest: 'Der Knabe mit dem Wunderhorn', 'Der Page' and 'Der Hidalgo'. The liveliest of the songs is 'Der Hidalgo', a high-spirited bolero in which the piano suggests the Spanish gentleman's guitar. 'Der Knabe mit dem Wunderhorn' is equally gay and charming, but 'Der Page' has less musical character. The following opus number, 31, is a further group, *Drei Gesänge*. The distinction between *Gedichte* and *Gesänge* is not a consistent one, though Schumann tends to use *Gedichte* (poems) when the poems are all by one poet, and *Gesänge* (songs) when the poems come from varied sources, and when what unity there is is imposed by the music. That said, however, the *Three Songs* op. 31 are all from the same poet, Adalbert von Chamisso, though two of them are his translations of Béranger. Two of the songs, 'Die Löwenbraut' and 'Die rote Hanne', are ballads, and rather dull ones, but the third, another character-study, 'Die Kartenlegerin' ('The fortune-teller'), is both amusing and attractive; splendid material for a singing-actress, as a memorable recorded performance by Lotte Lehmann testifies.

The *Zwölf Gedichte* op. 35 are poems by Justinus Kerner (1786–1862) who studied medicine at Tübingen University and practised it for many years. He wrote books on hysteria and related subjects, and was one of a Swabian school of poets greatly detested in general by Heine who, however, made exceptions of Uhland and Kerner. Schumann, whose literary taste was, after all, catholic rather than selective, greatly admired Kerner's poetry. The *Zwölf Gedichte* do not really constitute a cycle. They are simply a collection of unrelated poems, and do not require to be performed together. Although Kerner was by no means the lyric genius that Heine was, many of his poems do possess a certain elegiac melancholy, and to these Schumann brought his own contemplative *Innigkeit*. The first song, 'Lust der Sturmnacht' is one of the relatively few dramatic songs in this collection, though even here the vocal line retains an almost

reflective quality, against a livelier piano accompaniment. 'Stirb,
Lieb' und Freud' ' is hymn-like in its plain harmonies, and
clearly influenced by Bach. The sentimental narrative tells of a
girl's renunciation of the world and of earthly love, to the
understandable distress of the youth who adores her. Schumann
captures the girl's religious fervour more easily than the frustrated
passion of the youth in the poem's closing lines : 'Sie weiss es
nicht/Mein Herz zerbricht,/Stirb, Lieb' und Licht'. ('She does
not know that my heart is breaking. Die, love and light.')
'Wanderlied' is a lively farewell to his comrades sung by a young
man as he sets out on his *Wanderjahre*. 'Erstes Grün' is imbued
with that bitter-sweet melancholy which came so easily to
Schumann, and this mood is sustained in the following song,
'Sehnsucht nach der Waldgegend', which is marked 'Innig,
phantastisch'. The poem is a typical piece of nature-worship of
its time, an expression of yearning for the mystery and romance
of the forest, but Schumann's sensitive melody and evocative
accompaniment make of it something more than that. 'Auf das
Trinkglas eines verstorbenen Freundes' is a solemn rather than
sad evocation of a dead friend, as the poet muses on the friend's
crystal goblet from which he is now drinking 'the golden juice
of German grapes'. Schumann makes an extraordinary song from
an awkward poem. 'Wanderung' is another lively wandering song,
hampered by a certain inelasticity of rhythm, and 'Stille Liebe' is
a delicate miniature in the manner of the *Dichterliebe*, as is also
the fragmentary 'Frage'. 'Stille Tränen' is the most immediately
attractive of these songs, in the manner of 'Die Lotosblume',
though its feeling of rapture is really not a proper musical equivalent to the bitterness of Kerner's poem. This quasi-cycle ends
with two short songs, 'Wer machte dich so krank?' and 'Alte
Laute', which share the same melody, quiet and reflective.

The *Sechs Gedichte* of Robert Reinick which comprise
Schumann's op. 36 consist of three rather engaging songs and
three quite dull ones. The first song, 'Sonntags am Rhein' fails
to transcend the picture-book tedium of the poem, but
'Ständchen' has a quiet charm and delicate romantic impulse,
and 'Nichts schöneres' an engaging innocence. The fourth song,
'An den Sonnenschein', is almost folk song-like in its artless
melodic freshness and gaiety. The poorest songs of the group are
the remaining two, 'Dichters Genesung' and 'Liebesbotschaft'.

Schumann selected twelve poems by Rückert for his op. 37,
Gedichte aus 'Liebesfrühling'. It is known that three of the

songs were in fact written by Clara—'Er ist gekommen', 'Liebst du um Schönheit' and 'Warum willst du andre fragen?' —and it is suspected that other songs may also have benefited from her collaboration. Clara's style was more akin to Mendelssohn's than to Schumann's, but since Schumann was at his least characteristic in this collection, it is not always easy to be certain who wrote what. 'Der Himmel hat eine Träne geweint" and 'O ihr Herren', though sentimental, are charming little songs, but there is not much to be said for the others. Rückert's pallid verses appear not to have excited either of the Schumanns to a high level of composition. Clara's 'Liebst du um Schönheit' would hardly appeal today even if Mahler had not later indelibly etched the poem into music of great beauty.

We come now to op. 39, the earliest of Schumann's three greatest cycles. This *Liederkreis*, settings of twelve poems by Eichendorff, has an assurance and inevitability that, for all their incidental beauties, one does not find in the songs of *Myrthen* or the Heine *Liederkreis*. In the spring of 1840, Schumann had written to Clara, 'I have been composing so much that it really seems uncanny at times. I cannot help it, and should like to sing myself to death like a nightingale. There are twelve songs of Eichendorff, but I have almost forgotten them now, and begun something else.'* (He had only just finished the Eichendorff *Liederkreis* and was about to begin his *Dichterliebe*!) This sense of effervescent creativity is evident throughout both these cycles, as well as in *Frauenliebe und Leben* which followed soon after. Each cycle has its own individuality, dictated of course to some extent by the poems. Eichendorff's romantic nature pieces have inspired Schumann in the op. 39 *Liederkreis* to an enchanted exploration of the world of nature, the mystery of the forest, and that mood of quiet ecstasy which is at the heart of German nature romanticism. Although it is perfectly possible to perform individual songs from this cycle out of context (which is not the case with *Dichterliebe*), it does have an organic unity, despite the fact that it is not an integrated cycle in that the poems do not combine around any one story or mood. Rather do they embrace a variety of moods, around a central theme of the heightened response of the romantic spirit to nature, myth and love.

'In der Fremde', the opening song, consists of a simple

* May Herbert (translator) *Early Letters of Robert Schumann* G. Bell London 1888 (Edited by Clara Schumann)

nostalgic minor-key melody over a harp-like accompaniment, setting the mood of quiet rapture which pervades the cycle. 'Intermezzo' is heartfelt, with a serene joy, its fine piano part anticipating the piano-writing in *Dichterliebe*. 'Waldesgespräch', a dramatic ballad in which a knight encounters the Lorelei in a forest near the Rhine, is one of the comparatively few extrovert songs in the cycle, in contrast to 'Die Stille', a song full of young, breathless rapture, intense and introverted. 'Mondnacht', frequently heard out of context, is one of Schumann's lyric masterpieces, instinct with the delicate ecstasy of a spring night, tinged with yearning, as, in the words of Eichendorff's poem, the poet's spirit 'flies over the quiet countryside as though heading towards home'. 'Mondnacht' has the beauty of genius and extreme simplicity. 'Schöne Fremde', equally beautiful, though less simple, is a miniature night-study, trembling with emotion. The apparent spontaneity of these songs, all of which sound as though they had been quickly poured out on to the page, is remarkable.

'Auf einer Burg', an atmospheric song portraying feeling under the guise of describing an old castle which has lain dormant for centuries, is followed by the second song in the cycle to be called 'In der Fremde'. 'In der Fremde II' conveys feelings of unease and anxiety through its use of forest imagery. Although the poet remembers past happiness, which Schumann has depicted in his independent piano part, the mood of the remembering voice is uncertain, hesitant. The neurosis comes to the surface in the next song, 'Wehmut' which is a deeply felt outpouring of sadness, a mood which develops into mistrust, cynicism and caution in 'Zwielicht', a song pervaded too by an air of mystery and foreboding. The poem is a curious one for Schumann to have chosen for this cycle, and, for that matter, to have chosen at all. 'Twilight spreads its wings', says the poet, 'and the clouds move past like bad dreams. What can this terror mean? If you have a friend, do not trust him at twilight. His eyes and his lips may smile, but he is thinking of war in false peace. What retires wearily from the world this night will be born anew tomorrow. But many things are lost in the night, so beware.' This is more like Heine than Eichendorff. Schumann's brooding, disturbing setting is followed by 'Im Walde' which appears to begin happily with its description of a passing wedding procession, only suddenly to change to a mood of despair. The manic-depressive, Florestan-Eusebius fluctuations are brilliantly conveyed. The cycle ends with 'Frühlingsnacht', a song whose surface suggests sheer rapture and ecstasy, though its exultant vocal climax is perhaps too feverish to convince us of the poet's happiness, and the piano postlude suggests that Schumann too had his doubts. This is a more subtle song than a superficial hearing of it would suggest, and its position as the closing song of the cycle emphasizes its ambiguity of mood.

The *Fünf Lieder* of op. 40 have been surprisingly neglected. The poems are by Chamisso, though four of them are his translations of Hans Andersen. The first, 'Märzveilchen', is a gentle warning of the transient nature of happiness. 'Muttertraum' and 'Der Soldat' are grimmer, larger songs of despair and betrayal. 'Der Spielmann' is a dramatic setting of Andersen's ironic text in which the musician finds himself condemned to play at the wedding of his beloved to another. The theme of this miniature cycle, then, is betrayal of one kind or another. The subject is treated comically, and brilliantly, in the final song, 'Verratene Liebe'. These five songs op. 40 deserve to be more widely known.

Schumann's next cycle is the *Frauenliebe und -Leben*, op. 42. Next in published opus number, that is, for it was composed later in 1840 than the *Dichterliebe* which is op. 48. Chamisso's cycle of nine poems, of which Schumann set the first eight, tells the story of a marriage from the woman's viewpoint. The young girl falls in love, speaks of the man effusively as 'Er, der Herrlichste von allen, wie so milde, wie so gut' ('He, the noblest of all, how kind, how good'), is proposed to, and marries. She announces her pregnancy, the child arrives, and the husband dies. The poems are sentimental but their language is not banal. The marriage relationship depicted is typical of the early, pre-industrial 19th century. Indeed, Chamisso's poems were no doubt prompted into existence by his marriage at the age of forty to an eighteen-year-old girl. Schumann lavished upon the poems his own feelings of domestic bliss, expressed in warm melody for the voice and the piano accompaniment. Both Chamisso's poems and Schumann's music for this cycle have been criticized—by people with little historic sense—for their old-world sentimentality and for the denigrating view of woman they propagate. But, although the poet's words are written to be spoken (and Schumann's music to be sung) by the woman, it is two men—Chamisso and Schumann—who are, in fact, expressing in these words, this music, their feelings of devotion towards the women they love.

The first song of the cycle, 'Seit ich ihn gesehen', is a simple, strophic melody in two stanzas, quiet and almost devotional in mood, in which the girl confesses her love; not a desperate, romantic love but the quiet certainty and assurance of affection offered and reciprocated, and enduring for ever. In 'Er, der Herrlichste von allen', the tempo is quicker, the maiden more excited as she catalogues the virtues of the man of her choice to Schumann's joyous and exultant voice part, with its urgent, though in this instance not particularly imaginative, accompaniment. 'Ich kann's nicht fassen, nicht glauben', 'I can't grasp it or believe it', she says in the third song, and the music has a jerky breathlessness which portrays and emphasizes her disbelief that such a paragon of virtue should actually have chosen her as his bride. The minor key of the music, and the ruminative postlude, add to the atmosphere of mingled doubt, modesty and hope. Serenity is attained in the major key of the following song, 'Du Ring an meinem Finger', as the bride contemplates her wedding ring. This is the only song which is occasionally heard out of context, perhaps because it does sound more self-contained than the others, also no doubt, because of its sweetly beguiling tunefulness. In 'Helft mir, ihr Schwestern', the actual day of the wedding has arrived, and the young bride addresses her sisters and bridesmaids, almost delirious with happiness and anxiety. The gaiety and charm of Schumann's music, flavoured with a wistful if momentary longing for lost innocence and youth at 'Aber euch, Schwestern, grüss ich mit Wehmut', make this one of the most attractive songs in the cycle. The weakest is the next song, 'Süsser Freund, du blickest mich verwundert an', in which the wife shyly announces she is going to have a baby. Schumann here retreats into a conventional sweetness of expression. Much fresher in its response to the situation is 'An meinem Herzen', in which the mother finds her greatest happiness in the arrival of her child, and the music gushes forth excitedly. But the family's bliss is tragically and abruptly shattered with the premature death of the husband. In the final song, 'Nun hast du mir den ersten Schmerz getan', which Schumann has set throughout as a kind of arioso, the widow apostrophizes the dead man. 'You sleep, you hard and pitiless man, the sleep of death', she accuses him. But her tone softens as she remembers past happiness, vowing to live within herself and her memories, and the music matches her remembrance of things past with a quotation from the first song.

Schumann published two volumes of *Romanzen und Balladen* ops. 45 and 49, each consisting of three songs. Of the op. 45 songs, two are settings of Eichendorff, and the third is from Heine. Op. 45 no. 1 is Eichendorff's 'Der Schatzgräber', a dramatic ballad about a seeker after buried treasure, whose greed is his undoing, and no. 2 is Eichendorff's 'Frühlingsfahrt'. The Heine song, 'Abends am Strand', is a curious, finally unsuccessful assault on a dull poem.

With the *Dichterliebe* op. 48, we come to Schumann's greatest achievement in song. Written during one week in May 1840, to sixteen poems from Heine's volume, *Lyrisches Intermezzo*, these miniature songs of love and despair are not only a perfect union of words and music but are also extraordinarily moving in their effect and in their implication. Both Heine and Schumann wrote from a dualism of sickness and health, gentleness and bitterness (the Florestan and Eusebius of Schumann's imagination), and it is in this cycle that we hear, perhaps for the first time in music, that modern *Angst* which continues through Wolf and Mahler. Schumann had already experienced the first attacks of that mental illness, probably inherited *dementia praecox*, which was later to overpower him completely, but he was temporarily recovered, and happy in his love for Clara. Although Heine's love poems are more often than not tinged with a bitter irony, many of them are gentle lyrics, and throughout the cycle Schumann has shown a sensitive and true affinity with the mood and intent of each poem, line by line. The poetry of Heine is not really translatable, for the romantic apparatus that he uses is very much of his time and place. His symbols reproduced in English seem robbed of their innocence. But although we may not be able fully to understand the transformation that nightingale, rose, dream and dreamer undergo in the language of Heine, we can be thankful that Schumann understood these poems so completely, and matched them with his own sympathy and lyric genius. The final songs of Schubert's *Winterreise* have in a way prepared us for the desperate loneliness of some of these songs, but not for the combination of calligraphic terseness and intense feeling of the cycle as a whole.

Dichterliebe is a beautifully integrated cycle, its key relationships from song to song carefully planned; the songs themselves, often very brief, need to be performed without tension-destroying breaks between them. The melodic interest is shared between voice and piano, and, although the tunes are usually

simple, their harmonic implications are not. There is not one
failure among these sixteen songs, and the climaxes are perfectly
placed. From the dream-like ecstasy of the first song, 'Im
wunderschönen Monat Mai', through the more tender desire of
'Aus meinen Tränen spriessen' and the happy, stammering,
breathless confession of 'Die Rose, die Lilie, die Taube, die
Sonne', one reaches the first shadow to fall across the poet's love
in 'Wenn ich in deine Augen seh', a poem which comes from
the very heart of Heine. The poet realizes that his beloved's 'Ich
liebe dich' is an empty lie, and weeps bitterly. Turning away
from his grief in the next song, 'Ich will meine Seele tauchen',
he dwells on the depth of his love and on its happier moments
in the past. 'Im Rhein, im heiligen Strome' begins broadly with
its picture of Cologne Cathedral and the Rhine, but mellows to
a tender melancholy, while, in the piano postlude, a heavy
fateful crescendo prepares for the violent emotion of 'Ich grolle
nicht', one of the finest songs composed by Schumann or any
other Lieder composer. 'I'll not complain, though my heart
breaks and my love flows away, though I feel the emptiness in
your heart.' The relentless vocal line, proud and bitter,
emphasized by heavy repeated chords in the piano, surges
forward to a great climax, taking the voice up to a high A which,
though optional and apparently an afterthought of Schumann's,
is really necessary to the shape and pattern of the vocal line,
and indeed called for by the emotional intensity of the song.

'Ich grolle nicht' is the biggest song in the cycle. It is followed
by briefer, more private expressions of despair : 'Und wüssten's
die Blumen', bitter and accusing, with a piano postlude which
underlines the angry grief of the words; 'Das ist ein Flöten und
Geigen', whose piano part is entirely independent of the vocal
line, a song aptly described by Lotte Lehmann as of 'a strange,
savage austerity'; 'Hör' ich das Liedchen klingen', a return to
the mood of longing for past happiness, in a song of quiet but
deep inner sadness. In 'Ein Jüngling liebt ein Mädchen', the
mood of psychopathic self-pity quivers beneath a mask of
objectivity until the end of the song, when it bursts forth with
the words 'Denn bricht das Herz entzwei' and the sudden
muddying of the harmony. 'Am leuchtenden Sommermorgen' is
surely the loveliest song in the cycle. The pathetic fallacy
intrudes perhaps too strongly for modern adult tastes, as the
flowers entreat the poet, 'Don't be angry with our sister, you
sad and lonely man'. But the blessed consolation of the piano

postlude, even more beautiful than the tune to which the words were sung, is beyond criticism. The pain returns in the tormented dream world of 'Ich hab' im Traum geweinet', a remarkable study of disillusion and total despair. 'Allnächtlich im Traume' is an even stranger, half-forgotten dream, and, in the penultimate song, 'Aus alten Märchen winkt es', the poet retreats into the world of fairy-tale, singing a gay marching song which fades away as he realizes that his imaginary world is dissolving before the morning sun. The final song, 'Die alten bösen Lieder', begins violently and ends in the familiar and strangely tender self-pity. The piano postlude places the entire cycle in position, containing the essence of the poems and a world of consolation. Time heals or numbs. The sighs grow fainter and retreat into silence.

Romanzen und Balladen Vol. II, op. 49, consists of three songs, two of them Heine settings. The first is the familiar version of 'Die beiden Grenadiere', the second a fierce ballad about brothers who are rivals in love, 'Die feindlichen Brüder'. The third is a rather sanctimonious setting of 'Die Nonne', a poem by Abraham Fröhlich which deserves no better.

The *Lieder und Gesänge* Vol. II, op. 51 contains Geibel's 'Sehnsucht' with its extraordinary piano cadenza; a 'Volkslied-chen' by Rückert which sounds like a heavily arranged folk tune; 'Ich wand're nicht' (Christern) and 'Auf dem Rhein' (Immermann), both rather dull, and a 'Liebeslied' by Goethe which is more sentimental than the verses require it to be. A third volume of *Romanzen und Balladen* op. 53 consists of two unsatisfactory ballads, 'Blondel's Lied' (poem by Seidl) and 'Loreley' (Lorenz), though the lyrical feeling in the latter song redeems it from failure. The miniature cycle *Der arme Peter* is a setting of three poems by Heine which tell the story of a young man who kills himself when his beloved marries someone else. The first song, of almost Mahlerian irony, is decidedly superior to the other two. A separate Heine ballad, 'Belsatzar', though uneven, is effective in performance, the piano part more imaginatively conceived than the vocal line.

The fourth volume of *Romanzen und Balladen* op. 64, consisting of songs written to texts of Mörike and Heine, is largely disappointing, though one of them, the composer's first setting of Mörike, 'Die Soldatenbraut', is pleasant. We have now moved beyond 1840, Schumann's great year of song. 'Die Soldatenbraut', for instance, was composed in 1847. From now on, the flame of Schumann's genius burns more fitfully.

Often, he appears to be copying his own manner of earlier and happier days, as his mental and physical condition enters its tragic decline. There were still, of course, some fine songs to come, though they must be searched for amongst much that is stolid and uninventive. *Lieder und Gesänge* Vol. III, op. 77, for instance, offers the gaily effervescent 'Aufträge' (poem by L'Egru) amongst five songs, the other four of which are mediocre. But there are several attractive songs to be found in *Liederalbum für die Jugend* op. 79, twenty-eight settings of various poets, composed in 1849. At least six of these songs for children could have come from the vintage year. 'Der Sandmann', a pleasant and simple song with a light, dancing accompaniment, is a setting of Kletke, a lyric poet who wrote mainly for children. 'Marienwürmchen' (from *Des Knaben Wunderhorn*) is a delightful nursery-rhyme, 'Des Sennen Abschied' (Schiller) a charming pastorale, and 'Er ist's' a happy spring song on a Mörike poem which Wolf was later to set more ebulliently. Rückert's 'Schneeglöckchen' is gently romantic, and 'Mignon', the last song of the twenty-eight, is Schumann's attempt upon Goethe's 'Kennst du das Land?' and a remarkably fine one. Lacking the fresh melodic charm of Schubert or the wild passion which Wolf was to bring to the poem, Schumann's attempt is nevertheless very close to Goethe in feeling, rich in harmony and impeccable in its actual word setting. 'Unter die Soldaten' a grim little narrative by Geibel, is given an inappropriately jolly strophic setting (perhaps in an attempt to make it sound suitable for children!) but, with another Geibel poem, 'Jeden Morgen', Schumann makes amends in a song of quiet but fervent romantic feeling.

Neither the three songs of op. 83, nor the isolated ballad, 'Der Handschuh' op. 87, need detain us. *Sechs Gesänge* op. 89 are settings of Wielfried von der Neun (a pseudonym for one Wilhelm Schöpff). The poems are sententious and mediocre, but in one of the songs, 'Röslein, Röslein', Schumann regains his earlier ease and lightness of touch, and in another, 'Ins Freie', there are some passages of real feeling. Considerably more successful as a collection are the *Sechs Gedichte* op. 90 of Nikolaus von Lenau. The songs are followed by an appendix, an additional song, 'Requiem' in memory of the poet, a melancholic who was to die in August 1850, after five years in an asylum, and some weeks after Schumann had composed his 'Requiem'. The Lenau songs are somewhat lowering, since the composer was only too well matched with his depressive poet, but one of them, 'Meine Rose', is, remarkably, of great lyrical beauty. Schumann had by now less than four years of increasingly difficult creativity left to him, and only six years of life. He had the previous year composed the *Drei Gesänge* op. 95, three settings of Byron's 'Hebrew Melodies' in German translation, whose musical interest is slight, except for the sensitive 'An den Mond' ('Sun of the sleepless, melancholy star'), and a fourth volume of *Lieder und Gesänge*, op. 96, five songs which included his only setting of Platen, 'Ihre Stimme', and the effective 'Gesungen', (von der Neun). *Lieder und Gesänge aus Wilhelm Meister* op. 98a are nine settings from Goethe's novel, beginning with the already published 'Mignon' op. 79 no. 28, now re-titled 'Kennst du das Land?'. Though these songs are musically uneven, they contain some remarkable things, flashes of the composer's former genius. The *Sieben Lieder* op. 104, settings of the mediocre Elisabeth Kulmann, are sadly uninventive, as are, for the most part, the *Sechs Gesänge* op. 107 to unrewarding texts by several poets, though the fifth, 'Im Wald' (poem by Wolfgang Müller) is not without merit. A curious little group of songs to have emerged from the peace-loving Schumann are the *Vier Husarenlieder* op. 117 (by Lenau), vigorous celebrations of violence.

From the remaining five collections of solo songs, very few individual ones remain to be singled out for attention. *Fünf Lieder und Gesänge* op. 127 includes the 'Schlusslied des Narren' which is the Fool's final song from Shakespeare's *Twelfth Night* ('When that I was and a little tiny boy'), composed several years earlier by Schumann, and quite dull, and two rejects from the *Dichterliebe* of 1840, one of which, 'Dein Angesicht', is a tender and beautiful song in Schumann's sweet, uncloying romantic style. Two other *Dichterliebe* rejects, 'Lehn' deine Wang'' and 'Mein Wagen rollet langsam', were published posthumously with two non-Heine items as *Vier Gesänge* op. 142. 'Mein Wagen rollet langsam' is a very fine song, though it would have been out of scale with the miniatures of the *Dichterliebe*; of the two non-Heine songs, Kener's 'Trost im Gesang' is the finer. The cycle of five songs by Mary Queen of Scots, *Gedichte der Königin Maria Stuart* op. 135, is sad but remote. All but one of the songs is in the key of E minor.

The essence of Schumann's creative genius is to be found in his short lyrical pieces, whether songs or works for the piano. Richard Wagner (1813–1883), on the contrary, revealed his genius in his large-scale music dramas, and cannot be said to have devoted much time or energy to the art of song. Nevertheless his few songs are interesting for the light they throw on the composer's larger concerns. Like every other 19th-century German, Wagner was unable to ignore *Faust*, and his first attempts to write songs are *Seven compositions from Goethe's Faust*, which he composed at the age of nineteen. Though these are student works, they are not without merit or individuality. The sixth song, Gretchen's 'Meine Ruh ist hin', though no rival to the masterpiece produced by the seventeen-year-old Schubert, is nevertheless an interesting and sensitive setting. The musical dramatist in Wagner emerges in the seventh of these compositions, which is not a song, but a piece of melodrama—spoken words against musical accompaniment—the words being Gretchen's prayer to the Virgin.

In 1838, during his period as conductor at the opera in Riga, Wagner set a poem, 'Der Tannenbaum', by Scheuerlein. This song shows a considerable advance upon the earlier work, not so much in the quality of its melody which is, in fact, negligible, but in its musical characterization. The brooding atmosphere of the poem, in which the fir tree and the boy confront each other and the tree reveals it is to be cut down to provide wood for the boy's coffin, is expertly caught, and the word-setting sounds easy and natural.

The remainder of Wagner's songs, with the exception of two occasional pieces, fall into two small groups : the songs he wrote in Paris in 1840 (Schumann's year of song, but a less golden year for Wagner in Paris), and the *Wesendonklieder* of 1857–8. The first of the Paris songs, a French translation of Heine's 'Die Beiden Grenadiere' suffers by comparison with Schumann's more famous setting. It lacks the movement and melodic interest of Schumann, though it curiously anticipates him in its use of the 'Marseillaise' at the end. The other Paris songs are generally dismissed as trivial, though they are all quite charming, if light, especially 'Mignonne' (poem by Ronsard) which is more graceful than the composer's German manner would lead one to expect, and 'Dors, mon enfant', a lullaby of individual character and distinction. 'Attente', a setting of Victor Hugo, is also not without charm, despite its dull accompaniment. Wagner's natural heaviness and slowness of gait are considerably lightened by his contact with the French language. It must be admitted that 'Les Adieux de Marie Stuart' is considerably less good than the other French songs, and that 'Tout n'est qu'images fugitives' (poem by Jean Reboul) wears its French manner less convincingly.

Wagner did not find time to compose songs again until after he had written *Die fliegende Holländer, Tannhäuser* and *Lohengrin*, and was three-quarters of the way through the *Ring*, from which he turned aside to work on *Tristan*. Mathilde Wesendonk, the wife of Wagner's current patron, was the inspiration behind *Tristan*, and it was during their love affair and the period of the composition of *Tristan* that Wagner set five of her poems, in Zurich during the winter of 1857–8. The songs were originally written with piano accompaniment, though the composer made an arrangement of one of them, 'Träume', to be played by eighteen musicians as a birthday serenade to his mistress, and the others were later orchestrated by the Austrian conductor, Felix Mottl, who was to conduct *Tristan* at Bayreuth after Wagner's death. The *Wesendonklieder* are really by-products of *Tristan*, and indeed were first published as *Sketches for Tristan und Isolde*. Fragments of theme and of mood from *Tristan* are to be found in all five of the songs. The first, 'Der Engel', contains echoes of Isolde's *Liebestod*. It and the second, 'Stehe still' are the least successful songs of the five, the remaining three perfectly catching the overheated romanticism of Mathilde Wesendonk's poems, 'Im Treibhaus' utilizing something of the mood and material of the Prelude to Act III of *Tristan*, and 'Träume' sharing the ecstasy of Act II. Lotte Lehmann, an admired interpreter of the *Wesendonklieder*, has written of 'Schmerzen': 'This whole song has something almost "military" in its pompous outbursts. I have never liked it— especially when I heard Toscanini describe it as musically rather weak.'*

With so sparse a song output, Wagner understandably exerted very little influence on younger German composers of *Lieder*, who found themselves developing in style from Schumann. Robert Franz (1815–1892), who concentrated on *Lieder*, attracted the admiration of Schumann with his first published set of twelve songs. Throughout his life he wrote more than 300 songs, the vast majority of them for the mezzo-soprano voice. Extremes of feeling or violence of emotion are avoided, and a placid charm pervades his work. If Franz had been less modest

* Lotte Lohmann *Eighteen Song Cycles* Cassell London 1971

—'My music does not pretend to be much in itself',* he wrote
to Liszt—and more adventurous musically, his *œuvre* might
have endured in the concert hall, for a great many of his songs
are impressive in their quiet way. He is scrupulous in his word-
setting, and it is unfortunate that he set so many poems which
other and greater composers had already treated more memorably. He was an excellent craftsman, but a minor, though
tasteful artist whose small-scale strophic songs tend to lack
imagination in their harmonies, and variety in their rhythms.
His melody is more individual, though again hardly memorable.
Among his settings of such poets as Chamisso, Eichendorff,
Geibel, Goethe, Heine, von Fallersleben, Lenau, Mörike, Rückert
and others (Heine being his favourite), Franz produced only a
few songs which are still occasionally to be heard. The best and
most typical of these include 'Aus meinem grossen Schmerzen'
op. 5 no. 1, 'Stille Sicherheit' op. 10 no. 2, 'Liebesfrühling' op.
14 no. 5 and 'Gute Nacht' op. 5 no. 7.

Peter Cornelius (1824–1874) was less prolific than Franz, but
more interesting as a musical personality. Several of his seventy-
five or more songs are written to his own texts, though he also
set Heine, Hölderlin, von Platen and others. Cornelius's verses
are at least the equal of those of a good many minor 19th-
century lyric poets (he published a volume of them, *Lyrische
Poesien*, in 1861), and his libretti for his own operas, certainly
those for *Der Barbier von Baghdad* and *Der Cid* are better
written than those of Wagner. The only songs by Cornelius that
one occasionally encounters today in recital programmes are
'Ein Ton', in which the voice part is confined to one single note,
the interest being sustained by means of rhythm and harmony,
and the six charming *Weihnachtslieder* of op. 8. (Incidentally,
'Ein Ton' is not, as is sometimes said, the only song to be
pitched on one note throughout, nor is it even the first. The
Bohemian composer and conductor, Joseph Drechsler (1782–
1852), whose working life was spent in Vienna, first as music
director of the Leopoldstadt Theatre and later as choirmaster at
St Stephen's Cathedral, introduced a song on one note, 'Alles
kleide ich in Häute', into the musical play *Jupiter in Wien*, in
1825.) Several of Cornelius's other songs are worthy of singers'
attention, for instance the rather Schumannesque cycle of four
songs, *An Bertha* op. 15 (poems by the composer), the six songs

* *Grove's Dictionary of Music and Musicians* (5th edition) Macmillan
London 1954

of op. 5 which include Hölty's 'Auftrag', and a magnificent setting of Heine's 'Warum sind denn die Rosen so blass?'

With Johannes Brahms (1833–1897) we are again considering one of the major composers of *Lieder*, a genius of the order of Schubert, Schumann and, later, Mahler, Wolf and Strauss. Brahms did not, of course, devote himself exclusively to the *Lied*, and his output of approximately 200 songs looms considerably less large in his *œuvre* than Schubert's 600 did in his; Brahms early in life came to see himself as the successor to Beethoven, and produced the large-scale symphonic works which he thought were expected of him. But this author's personal view, not one which is widely shared, is that Brahms's genius is more clearly revealed in his smaller-scale lyrical works, the songs and piano pieces, than in the larger and often stodgy symphonies and concertos. Brahms's highly individual melodic gift, smothered in the piano concertos under pages of passage work, flows un-trammelled through his songs with an almost Schubertian ease. Also Schubertian is his attitude to the words he set. Though he was not without literary taste, he was always willing to sacrifice correct verbal accentuation to the shape of the musical phrase. His range is wide, from an apparently artless folk style in some of the strophic songs (and there are also his arrangements of actual folk melodies) to the complex melodic and rhythmic patterns of those songs which are *durchkomponiert*. Brahms continued to write songs throughout his career, and it is possible to trace an orderly development from the songs he wrote at the age of twenty to the *Vier ernste Gesänge* which date from the last months of his life.

Brahms's first group of songs, published when he was twenty-one as op. 3, is by no means a mere apprentice work, though the six songs vary in quality, and are clearly the creation of a youth-ful talent. They are settings of various poets : the first song, 'Liebestreu' (poem by Robert Reinick), is a miniature dramatic scene which already anticipates the mature masterpiece 'Von ewiger Liebe', but is also completely effective in its own right. The second and third songs, 'Liebe und Frühling' nos. 1 and 2, are both pleasantly romantic settings of Hoffmann von Faller-sleben, somewhat in the manner of Schumann who was a strong early influence both musical and personal. Friedlaender, in his book on Brahms's *Lieder*,* draws attention to the fact that, in 'Liebe und Frühling I', Brahms sets the words 'Meine Tag- und

* Max Friedlaender *Brahms's Lieder* O.U.P., London 1928

Nachtgedanken' to the opening phrase of Zerlina's aria, 'Batti, batti, o bel Masetto' from Mozart's *Don Giovanni*. It does not seem at all likely that this was deliberate. The raw material of art being what it is, Brahms's phrase does not in context remind one of its earlier use by Mozart. (One thinks of Schubert's 'Sah' ein Knab ein Röslein steh'n' which one has heard before, sung by the three genii in *Die Zauberflöte*. But Schubert had no need to steal tunes, not even from Mozart.) The fourth song of Brahms's op. 3, 'Lied aus dem Gedicht "Ivan" ', his only setting of Bodenstedt, a volume of whose poems had appeared in 1852, is lively but unmemorable, while the remaining two songs, to poems of Eichendorff, are romantic mood pieces which contrive to sound authentically Brahmsian while at the same time echoing other composers. 'In der Fremde' recalls Schumann, which is not surprising since Schumann wrote so fine a song on the same poem in his *Liederkreis* op. 39, and 'Lied' is graceful enough to rival one of Schubert's nature songs.

The songs of the next two groups, ops. 6 and 7, also date from 1853 or earlier. Like virtually every such group of Brahms's *Lieder*, with the rare exceptions of the *Vier ernste Gesänge*, the *Magelonelieder* and the Daumer songs of op. 57, they are settings of more than one poet. Op. 6 opens with a 'Spanisches Lied' (poem by Paul Heyse) which is better known in Hugo Wolf's lovely setting as 'In dem Schatten meiner Locken'. 'Der Frühling' (poem by Johann Baptist Rousseau) is already mature Brahms in the confident shape of its melody, but the following two songs are less successful. The group ends well with Hoffmann von Fallersleben's 'Wie die Wolke nach der Sonne' and 'Nachtigallen schwingen'. The first song has an exultantly joyous air which is captivating, while the second has a voice part which is more subtle than it at first appears to be, and in the piano part a delicious imitation of the fluttering nightingales of its title.

The *Six Songs* op. 7 contain some of the best of the young Brahms. The first, 'Treue Liebe' (poem by Ferrand, the pseudonym of Eduard Schulz), is curiously neglected by recitalists who, in fact, tend to ignore all the songs which precede op. 32. It, again, is mature Brahms, a beautifully wrought lyric masterpiece. The two Eichendorff songs are also interesting. 'Parole' is the more individual of the two, but 'Anklänge' is perhaps even more attractive. 'Volkslied' is exactly what its title claims, a folk song. The words are from Georg Scherer's collection of *Deutsche Volkslieder*, and Brahms has treated them in a pastiche of folk style. 'Die Trauernde', whose poem is also traditional, is affectingly simple though less folkish. The final song of op. 7, 'Heimkehr', is a setting of a poem by Uhland which a number of minor composers also set, but which did not attract any other major composer. It is thought to be the earliest extant Brahms song, written in Hamburg when the composer was eighteen, a curious piece of recitative-plus-melody of a kind not found in the later Brahms.

Brahms in later years tended to avoid poems which he considered had already been successfully set to music. At the age of twenty-one, however, he was willing to challenge Schumann's beautiful 'Mondnacht' with his own sensitive and graceful setting, more a homage to Schumann, one feels, than an act of rivalry. It was published without opus number.

Six of the *Eight Songs and Romances* op. 14 make use of folk poems, the remaining two poems being translations by Herder from French and Scottish. The first two songs could almost be arrangements of folk melodies, though they are not. The third, 'Murrays Ermordung', is more ambitious, while the fourth and fifth songs, 'Ein Sonett' and the defiant 'Trennung' are by far the most successful in the set. The remaining three songs revert to the manner of the first two. A higher standard is maintained throughout the *Five Poems* op. 19. 'Der Kuss' is the first of Brahms's Hölty settings, a tender and reflective song with something of Schubert in it, though the piano part is clearly Brahmsian. 'Scheiden und Meiden', the first of three Uhland songs in this group, is less effective than its two fellows: 'In der Ferne' is quietly beautiful, and 'Der Schmied' somewhat more rumbustiously so, its pounded-out rhythm imitating the blacksmith's strokes on his anvil. The remaining song, Mörike's 'An eine Aeolsharfe', is quite different in style from the remainder of op. 19. Opening with a passage of recitative, it develops into a song of ethereal beauty, as fine in its way as Wolf's setting of thirty years later. The piano beautifully evokes the sound of the poet's 'Geheimmisvolle Saitenspiel'.

Five years separate the op. 19 songs from Brahms's next group for solo voice, the *Nine Songs* op. 32. The composer was now a mature thirty, and the fact is apparent from the wider range, deeper expressiveness and more assured style of the group as a whole. The poets are Platen (five songs) and Daumer (four). 'Wie rafft' ich mich auf in der Nacht' (Platen) is magnificent in the dark sombre quality of its melody, and the manner in

which the mood is maintained and emphasized in the piano part.
Incidentally, Friedlaender detects, in the order of the nine poems,
a story-line ('He tries to resist the spell of a beautiful and alluring
woman, but finally succumbs completely')* which, he claims,
parallels the interior life of the composer himself. This, to say the
least, is fanciful, if not downright misleading. Brahms's sexual
repression was so strong that he was unable to succumb completely to either woman or man, though there are indications
that his sensual thoughts were more usually directed towards
his own sex.

To return to op. 32 : the second song, 'Nicht mehr zu dir zu
gehen' is remarkably free in form, hovering between recitative
and melody, but never committing itself to either. Consequently
the declamation is truer, more potent than one expects to find
in Brahms. The passionate 'Ich schleich umher', on the other
hand, stakes all on its highly expressive melody. The fourth
song, 'Der Strom, der neben mir verrauschte', while highly
effective, is a superficial musicalization of Platen's poem about
memory, transience, change and decay. Brahms concentrates on
the present mood of anger at the disappearance of past pleasures
and past personality. The result, it must be admitted, is a
splendidly dramatic piece. The forward movement and momen-
tum of 'Wehe, so willst du mich, hemmende Fessel' are achieved
through its energetic accompaniment. This too is a highly
dramatic song, but this time also a perfect rendering of the
sense and mood of Platen's poem. 'Du sprichst, dass ich mich
täuschte' is a cry of grief and despair, and 'Bitteres zu sagen,
denkst du' a graceful expression of love, as, too, is the penultimate song of the group, 'So steh'n wir, ich und meine Weide'.
The last song 'Wie bist du, meine Königin', is one of the most
famous of *Lieder*, and understandably so, a tender love song
with a most appealing and graceful melody which, once heard,
is not likely to be forgotten.

Fifteen Romances from Magelone op. 33 is a cycle of songs
to poems by Ludwig Tieck. Tieck's *Wunderschöne Liebes-
geschichte der schönen Magelone und des Grafen Peter aus der
Provence*, published in 1797, describes the love of Count Peter
for the beautiful Magelone, daughter of the King of Naples.
It is in prose and verse, the poems occurring at various points
of the narrative. The strength of Brahms's cycle lies in the
cumulative effect of the fifteen songs. With the single exception

* op. cit.

of the lovely 'Ruhe, Süssliebchen', these are not songs to be extracted and sung out of context. Heard singly, they appear unsatisfactory, but together they form a whole of luxuriant richness of expression, now tender, now passionate. They are far removed from the Brahms of the simple strophic folk songs. It is not necessary to know the narrative from which the poems have been extracted in order to enjoy the songs. In fact, performances in which the songs have been separated by readings from Tieck's narrative have merely destroyed the unity of the cycle, while adding nothing of value. The lovers undergo exciting and unusual adventures when they leave Naples to travel in the Orient, but these are not relevant to the songs which, as a cycle, are completely self-contained.

The *Four Songs* op. 43 are all first-rate, though the first two are famous, and the other two virtually unknown. The poem 'Von ewige Liebe' formerly attributed to Joseph Wenzig, though now known to be by Hoffmann von Fallersleben, has inspired Brahms to one of his greatest songs. In the dark night, the lover is walking with his beloved. 'Do people reproach you because of our love?' he asks. 'Then let us part. I will not have you bear shame.' And the maiden answers: 'We shall never part. Our love is truer and stronger than iron and steel. They can be severed but our love shall never fail.' The music has the calmness and strength of true love, and the song is immensely affecting in performance. It is slightly disconcerting, however, to discover that the brave tune to which the words 'Eisen und Stahl, man schmiedet sie um,/Unsere Liebe, wer wandelt sie um?'* are sung, had been used by Brahms ten years earlier in a wedding chorus, for the words 'Das Haus benedei' ich und preis' es laut, Das empfangen hat eine liebliche Braut.'†

'Die Mainacht', gentle yet powerful, is a setting of Hölty. The melody of this sorrow-laden song is heavy with romantic yearning, and Friedlaender says of it, 'The poet and the composer met in complete harmony of feeling and of form, of outlook and of creative idea. Hölty and Brahms begin with veiled glamour, with romantic magic, dreamy and fanciful.'‡ What a satisfying yet terrifying song to sing, with those tender cadences and long climactic phrases, for instance at 'Und die einsame

---

* 'Iron and Steel can be forged into other forms, but who can alter love?'

† 'I bless and praise this house that has welcomed a beloved bride.'

‡ op. cit.

Träne rinnt'. No singer can fail to caress both words and tune at 'Wann, o lächelndes Bild, welches wie Morgenrot'. The song is an essay on the romantic attitude itself, portraying the tears that come to the lover's eyes as he wanders sadly through the forest, the quivering rapture, the intense yearning. It is presumably a coincidence that Levko's aria, 'How calm, how marvellous the night' from Rimsky-Korsakov's opera, *May Night*, composed about ten years later, should begin with the music of the opening phrase, 'Wann der silberne Mond', from Brahms's 'May Night'.

The two considerably lesser-known songs from op. 43 are 'Ich schell mein Horn ins Jammertal' and 'Das Lied vom Herrn von Falkenstein'. The folk poems have led Brahms to adopt a somewhat archaic style in these two songs, which reveal their quality less readily than the more accessible 'Mainacht' and 'Von ewige Liebe'. They are, nevertheless, both very fine songs. The *Four Songs* of op. 46, two from Daumer, two from Hölty, are less impressive, except for no. 4, Hölty's 'An die Nachtigall', which is imbued with Brahms's most richly romantic feeling. No. 3, 'Die Schale der Vergessenheit', was considered by the composer himself to be worthless, but his friend the famous singer Julius Stockhausen, to whom the *Magelonelieder* are dedicated, persuaded him to allow publication of it. Curiously, the very next opus number, op. 47, contains five songs of which four are absolute gems. The poem of 'Botschaft' is a Daumer rendering of Hafiz. The tender charm of the melody, and the rapturous manner of its expansion towards the end of the song, have made it a great favourite. 'Liebesglut', also by Daumer after Hafiz, is, by comparison, quite dull, but 'Sonntag', from a folk poem collected by Uhland, is a delight. 'O liebliche Wangen' (poem by Paul Flemming) is a passionate outpouring of love in three verses, the melody combining the sophistication of art with the freshness of the folk spirit. The poem is fatuous to the point of imbecility, which makes it all the more amazing that Brahms should have fashioned from it this wonderfully breathless, excited expression of a young lover's ardour. Op. 47 no. 5 is Goethe's 'Die Liebende schreibt', already set by both Schubert and Mendelssohn, the poem modestly but sensitively clothed in Brahms's charmingly self-effacing music.

The *Seven Songs* op. 48 are strophic, with the exception of 'Herbstgefühl' (Schack), and they vary considerably in character and worth. 'Der Gang zum Liebchen' could almost be a Slavonic dance, which is appropriate since its poem is a translation by

Wenzig of a Bohemian folk song. 'Der Überläufer' is disappointingly ineffective, but 'Liebesklage des Mädchens' is subtle and
original, and 'Gold überwiegt die Liebe' hardly less so. Goethe's
'Trost in Tränen' appears not to have engaged the composer
deeply, but the austerity of 'Vergangen ist mir Glück und Heil'
is unusual, and the gloomy 'Herbstgefühl' moved the musical
historian Spitta to write to Brahms : 'The song "Herbstgefühl"
is wonderful in its atmosphere of sadness . . . whoever has felt
the weird melancholy of dying nature in autumn must be deeply
moved by the faltering accompaniment which persists almost
throughout the song, by the undercurrent of sighs in the bass,
and the original harmonic construction.'* The song contains a
surely conscious quotation from Schubert's 'Der Doppelgänger',
at the words 'bald stirbt sie auch'. In the following opus number,
op. 49, Brahms collects five pleasant lyrics, none of them a
failure, though only one is heard frequently today. 'Am Sonntag
Morgen' is a vivid musical portrait, 'An ein Veilchen' a gentle
and melancholy setting of Hölty's poem, and both 'Sehnsucht'
and the restrained 'Abenddämmerung' are typically Brahmsian;
but it is 'Wiegenlied' which has become Brahms's best known
melody, known indeed to thousands who have hardly heard of
Brahms. It is a charming little cradle song, but it went through
so many editions and arrangements even during Brahms's lifetime, that at one moment the composer jokingly suggested to his
publisher a new arrangement in a minor key for naughty children. The song is dedicated 'to B.F. Vienna', B.F. being Frau
Bertha Faber, whom Brahms had once heard singing a Viennese
dialect song by Alexander Baumann. Brahms made use of this
Viennese waltz song, 'Du moanst wohl, du glabst wohl', for the
accompaniment, and later wrote to the dedicatee in Vienna,
'Has Hanslick perhaps noticed the Austrian element that has
been smuggled in?'

The *Eight Songs* op. 57 are all to poems by Daumer, but do
not make up an integrated cycle. Friedlaender speaks of the 'hot
passion and undisguised sensuality'† of many of these songs, but
the passion seems cooler today, the sensuality more disguised.
The first song, 'Von waldbekränzter Höhe', is certainly
passionate, the second, 'Wenn du nur zuweilen lächelst', more
tender, the third, 'Es träumte mir', calm, almost other-worldly.
'Ach, wende diesen Blick', though not an easy song to com-
prehend, repays study. 'In meiner Nächte Sehnen' and 'Strahlt

* Quoted in Friedlaender, op. cit.　　† op. cit.

zuweilen auch ein mildes Licht' are arguably the least interesting songs in the group, while 'Die Schnur, die Perl an Perle' is melodically expressive, and 'Unbewegte laue Luft' justifies Friedlaender's words about op. 57. It begins with a quiet restlessness, and moves through moods of increasing passion to a surging climax. A magnificent song.

The *Eight Songs* op. 58 do not include anything as fine as the best of op. 57, though several of them are light and charming. 'Blinde Kuh' is a delightful comic song, whose poem is by August Kopisch, the Silesian artist and poet who discovered the 'Blue Grotto' at Capri. There are two other settings of Kopisch in op. 58, 'Während des Regens' and 'Die Spröde'. Melchior Grohe is the poet of 'O komm, holde Sommernacht', one of the most popular of Brahms's gay songs of spring and summer. In 'Schwermut' Brahms's seriousness becomes too heavily solemn as he grapples with a rather poor poem by Candidus. The two Hebbel settings, 'In der Gasse' and 'Vorüber' are more success-ful, and Schack's 'Serenade' ('Leise, um dich nicht zu wecken') with its guitar-like accompaniment, is beautifully elegant.

In these songs of the 1870s, the rhapsodic Brahms begins to give way to a more reflective personality, though the old impulsiveness still returns on occasions. Op. 59 again contains eight songs, some of them as fine as anything the composer had written. 'Dämmrung senkte sich von oben' is a respectable attempt upon a very difficult poem by Goethe, a poem which contains within itself its own music. There are some fascinating things in Brahms's setting, though it can hardly be called a success. 'Auf dem See', however, is a complete success. Carl Simrock's poem about a beautiful Swiss lake has inspired a really delightful song. This is Brahms, the portrayer of nature, at his happiest. 'Regenlied', the first of Brahms's settings of his close friend, Klaus Groth, is a reticent song whose beauties do not yield themselves up too easily, though it is a song one can come to love. Its melody, echoed in the following song, 'Nachklang', also by Groth, was later used yet again in the finale to the A major Violin Sonata, op. 100. Both 'Agnes' (Mörike) and 'Eine gute, gute Nacht' (Daumer) are very simple, the latter a more engaging piece than the former. 'Mein wundes Herz verlangt nach milder Ruh' and 'Dein blaues Auge' are settings of Groth. 'Mein wundes Herz' is interesting rather than compelling, but 'Dein blaues Auge', using simpler means, is extremely moving in its avowal of love.

In addition to the two popular items found amongst the *Nine Songs* op. 63, there are several others which ought to be more frequently performed. The first four songs are from poems by Max von Schenkendorf, the next two (including 'Meine Liebe ist grün') from poems by Brahms's godson, Felix Schumann, the son of Robert and Clara, while the final three are settings of Groth. The first two Schenkendorf songs are first-rate, 'Frühlingstrost' warm and passionate, and 'Erinnerung' unpretentiously simple and endearing. The third Schenkendorf setting, 'An ein Bild' makes curiously little effect, but the fourth, 'An die Tauben', is graceful and pleasing. The Felix Schumann settings are both very successful. 'Junge Lieder I' ('Meine Liebe ist grün') has tended to over-shadow 'Junge Lieder II' ('Wenn um den Hollunder'); not surprisingly for the eighteen-year-old poet's exuberant outpouring of young love has been made into an exultant song which surges to a great climax. However, the quieter delights of 'Wenn um den Hollunder' are no less to be treasured. Brahms wrote this poetic, gentle song as a Christmas present for the young poet and his mother, Clara Schumann, eighteen years after the death of Robert Schumann. To the three Groth settings which conclude op. 63, Brahms gave the title *Heimweh I, II und III*. 'Heimweh I' is the charming 'Wie traulich war das Fleckchen', and 'Heimweh II' the lovely 'O wüsst ich doch den Weg zurück' with its nostalgic yearning for the distant joys and the vanished security of childhood. This is a song full of intense feeling, deepening into pessimism as it progresses. 'Heimweh III', 'Ich sah als Knabe Blumen Blühn' with its echoes of Schubert's 'Die Taubenpost' is pure delight.

The nine songs of op. 69, all of them written in March 1877, are intended to be sung by a female voice. Brahms instructed his publisher to describe the songs as *Mädchenlieder*, and, although the poems come from various sources, these songs do add up to form a portrait of a young girl in a variety of moods. Though the majority of them are strophic, and many of the poems derive from folk sources, the songs themselves are for the most part not at all folk-like in flavour. They are divided into two volumes, the first of which contains four settings of Joseph Wenzig's translations from Czech folk poetry, and one setting of Carl Candidus. The first three Wenzig songs are, in fact, decidedly more folkish in flavour than the remaining six songs. Both 'Klage I' and 'Klage II' could almost have derived from Slavonic folk song, while 'Abschied' seems no more than a simple folk melody. But 'Des Liebsten Schwur' breaks away from this idiom, and Candidus's 'Tambourliedchen' follows suit. The four songs of the second volume have poems by Eichendorff (from the Spanish), Carl Lemcke, Gottfried Keller and Siegfried Kapper (from the Serbian). Eichendorff's 'Vom Strande' is impressively expansive, Lemcke's 'Über die See' somewhat mundane, and Keller's 'Salome' graceful and high-spirited. 'Mädchenfluch' has something of that passionate sensuality which occasionally disconcerted Brahms's acquaintances, and is also the most elaborate song of the set.

Another Candidus song, 'Lerchengesang', is the most impressive of the *Four Songs* op. 70, its delicate accompaniment emphasizing the charm and imagination of the vocal line. The others are the sad 'Im Garten am Seegestade' (Lemcke), Goethe's 'Serenade' and Keller's 'Abendregen'. The Goethe poem comes from his opera libretto *Claudine von Villa Bella*, where it is sung by the hero who accompanies himself upon the zither. In Keller's 'Abendregen' Brahms returns to his earlier, somewhat Schumannesque vein.

After his thirtieth year, the North German Brahms resided in Vienna, where he remained until his death. Over the years, slowly but surely, a Viennese lightness of spirit began to invade his solemn Germanic soul, and although this may not have made itself apparent in his personality, it can certainly be heard in some of the later songs. The serious ones are no less serious, but the gayer ones are lighter, more waltz-imbued, responsive to a nature which is more beautiful in the country surrounding Vienna than in the flatter world of North Germany. Something of this is evident in the *Five Songs* op. 71, for instance; in 'Es liebt sich so lieblich im Lenze', a setting of a Heine poem called 'Frühling', or the voluptuous 'An den Mond' (poem by Simrock). The gentle 'Geheimnis', which a friend of Brahms likened to 'the most exquisite scent of lilies in the moonlight',[*] is a setting of Candidus, and the group is completed by 'Willst du, das ich geh?', a dramatic and passionate account of a poem by Lemcke, and Hölty's tender and melodious 'Minnelied', of which Theodor Billroth, the friend of Brahms quoted above, wrote: 'If anyone wishes to know what we call musically sweet without sugariness, full of feeling without sentimentality, he should hear this song.'[†]

---

[*] Quoted in Friedlaender, op. cit.
[†] Quoted in Friedlaender, op. cit.

Op. 72 is less overtly emotional. Again there are five songs, the first of which, 'Alte Liebe', to a poem by Candidus, is one of Brahms's finest, a work of deep feeling beautifully expressed. If it is not more popular than it is, this can only be because its melody makes no concessions to popularity, but goes its predestined way. The other Candidus song of op. 72, 'Sommerfäden', is beautifully lucid in texture, Clemens Brentano's 'O kühler Wald' is typically Brahmsian in its response to nature, and Lemcke's 'Verzagen' evokes the movement of a restless sea, with its accompaniment arpeggios encircling the sadder disquiet of the vocal line. Goethe's cheerful 'Unüberwindlich' concludes the set.

Romances and Songs for One or Two Voices op. 84 consists of five songs, the first four of which are dialogues and can be sung as duets, three of them between mother and daughter, and the fourth, the popular 'Vergebliches Ständchen', between a boy and a girl. 'Vergebliches Ständchen' uses a Lower Rhine folk poem refashioned by Zuccalmaglio, but the mother-daughter dialogues are poems by Hans Schmidt. The second of them, 'Der Kranz', has a sweeping urgency which comes across well in performance. None of these songs requires two singers, since any experienced singer of *Lieder* should be able to characterize the voices of mother and daughter, or even lover and beloved. The fifth song, 'Spannung', again a Lower Rhine folk text adapted by Zuccalmaglio, is pleasantly persuasive.

The first two songs of op. 85, settings of Heine, are thematically closely related. Brahms explained to a friend that the two poems, 'Sommerabend' and 'Mondenschein', were found together in Heine's cycle, *Heimkehr*. 'The moon is a central figure in both', he said, 'and it is very annoying for a musician to have to use four pretty lines only once, when he might repeat them with suitable and pleasing variations.'* The third song, 'Mädchenlied' is in deliberate imitation of Serbian folk song, the poem being one of Kapper's translations from Serbian; the fourth, another Kapper translation, this time from the Czech, is a somewhat characterless piece. Geibel's 'Frühlingslied' is by no means negligible, however, and the final song, 'In Waldeseinsamkeit' (Lemcke), is magnificent. Brahms's friends are his best commmentators : in a letter to the composer, Elisabeth von Herzogenberg wrote of this song, ' "Waldeseinsamkeit" is one of those pieces which the good Lord does not send every day even to you ... those rare pieces which make one involuntarily

* Quoted in Friedlaender, op. cit.

hold one's breath as one overhears them. A magnificent piece,
as full of radiant ecstasy and yet so humanly moving, born as it
is of the deepest inward experience.'*

The *Six Songs* op. 86, intended to be sung by a low voice,
contain two of Brahms's finest songs, 'Therese' and 'Feldeinsamkeit'. The simplicity of 'Therese' is deceptive, while in the serene
nature worship of 'Feldeinsamkeit' the lonely tranquillity of
Hermann Allmers' poem is beautifully captured. The remaining
four songs do not reach these heights, though all are excellent:
'Nachtwandler' with its restrained yet sensitive response to an
unpublished poem by Max Kalbeck, the composer's future
biographer; Brahms's only setting of Theodor Storm, 'Über die
Haide'; Felix Schumann's 'Versunken'; and the very fine
'Todessehnen' (poem by Schenkendorf).

The *Two Songs for contralto and piano, with viola obbligato*
op. 91 were probably composed in 1884, the year of their
publication. They are both very beautiful songs, their beauty
being of the resigned, autumnal hue that we associate with the
older Brahms. Both are quiet andantes, sharing the composer's
exquisite though low-toned feeling for colour. Classically reticent,
they are yet eloquent and touching. They were composed for
the wife of the violinist Joachim, and in both of them the vocal
line is so instrumentally expansive that they might almost have
been written for Joachim himself. The poem of the first song,
'Gestillte Sehnsucht' is by Rückert. The second song, 'Geistliches
Wiegenlied', makes use of the traditional German carol tune,
'Joseph lieber, Joseph mein', which is played by the viola. The
text is a version by Geibel, found in his *Spanisches Liederbuch*,
of a poem by Lope de Vega. The Virgin Mary sings the infant
Christ to sleep to a sweetly beguiling melody.

Op. 94 consists of five songs which, with the exception of the
best known of them, 'Sapphische Ode', are rather gloomy in
mood. Friedlaender tells us that when the famous *Lieder* singer
Julius Stockhausen 'first sang this moving song with Brahms's
accompaniment in Frankfurt, he was so overcome with emotion
that he broke down'.† The poem is by Rückert. 'Steig auf,
geliebter Schatten' (poem by Friedrich Halm) and 'Mein Herz
ist schwer' (Geibel) are sad in mood, without being especially
affecting, and Halm's 'Kein Haus, Keine Heimat' has the
distinction of being Brahms's shortest song. The lines come from

---

* Quoted in Friedlaender, op. cit.   † op. cit.

a long poem 'In der Sudsee', and are supposed to be sung by a negro immediately before his sacrificial death. One turns with relief to the calm and consoling beauty of 'Sapphische Ode', with its final cadence taken from Schubert's 'Am Meer'. The seven songs of op. 95 are generally lighter in mood. There are no masterpieces among them, but 'Das Mädchen' and 'Bei dir sind meine Gedanken' are quite charming, as is Halm's 'Der Jäger'. Op. 96, by way of contrast, consists of four more serious songs, three of them settings of Heine. The first and finest of the Heine songs, 'Der Tod, das ist die kühle Nacht', is one of Brahms's most beautiful and evocative melodies, terse, emotional yet beautifully controlled. 'Es schauen die Blumen' is more overtly agitated, and 'Meerfahrt' darkly impressive. The one non-Heine song of op. 96 is the tender, regretful 'Wir wandelten' with its gently wandering vocal line masking a deep intensity of feeling.

In the *Six Songs* op. 97 we find the lighter, Viennese-influenced Brahms predominant. 'Nachtigall' is the exception, a beautifully sensitive setting of Carl Reinhold's pleasant but not very remarkable poem. The bitter-sweet melody so perfectly fits the words, especially where the tune broadens warmly at 'Das ist von andern, Himmerschönen', that it comes as a shock to learn that Brahms originally wrote this song to a different Reinhold poem, 'Der Wanderer' (a poem he was to re-set as op. 106 no. 5). Of the lighter songs of op. 97, the most pleasing are 'Dort in den Weiden', an excellent imitation of folk song, and 'Komm bald' (poem by Groth) whose main tune turns up again in the Violin Sonata in A op. 100. A particularly remarkable set of songs is op. 105, five settings of poems by Groth, Hermann Lingg, Detlev von Liliencron, Lemcke and Zuccalmaglio. Groth's 'Wie Melodien zieht es' has brought forth one of Brahms's typically bitter-sweet melodies, meditative in character. At this stage of his life, Brahms was sparing of his best tunes, and the beginning of 'Wie Melodien zieht es' is used again in the first movement of the A major Violin Sonata. 'Immer leiser wird mein Schlummer', on Lingg's poem spoken by a dying girl, is one of the most beautiful *Lieder* imaginable, deeply poignant and moving. 'Klage' is in the composer's folk song manner, and excellent of its kind, while the melodramatic 'Verrat' is the least interesting of the five songs. 'Auf dem Kirchhofe' is a sombre and powerful piece which, in atmosphere, is not unlike the Biblical settings of 'Vier ernste Gesänge' which were to follow ten years later. Its style is more antique, based on 18th-century forms, and at the end there is a reminiscence of Bach's chorale 'O Haupt voll Blut und Wunden'.

The *Five Songs* op. 106 are predominantly lyrical. Franz Kugler's 'Ständchen' is made into one of Brahms's most immediately charming songs, and 'Auf dem See' (poem by Reinhold) is almost as attractive in its less sprightly, more tender vein. 'Meine Lieder' (poem by Adolf Frey), of which Elisabeth von Herzogenberg wrote, 'How can we resist such tenderness, such fine lines embroidered as with gold?',* is almost Schumann-esque in feeling, and the remaining two songs of the set, though less frequently sung, are just as fine: 'Es hing der Reif' is a sensitive setting of a poem by Groth, while 'Ein Wanderer' (Reinhold) is the poem for which the melody of 'Nachtigall', op. 97 no. 1, was originally composed. Brahms's song is a mechanical essay in *Weltschmerz*.

A similarly lyrical group is op. 107, again five songs and five poets. The best known is 'Das Mädchen spricht', Brahms's only setting of O. F. Gruppe, whose coy verses about the love life of the swallow hardly deserve so sweetly beguiling a tune. The other songs are almost equally successful, the best of them the touching little 'Mädchenlied'.

The last group of solo songs, written by Brahms in the final year of his life, is the magnificent cycle, *Vier ernste Gesänge*, composed on gloomy Biblical texts from *Ecclesiastes* and *Ecclesiasticus*. These four songs of doubt and despair are among the composer's greatest and most powerful utterances in song. 'Denn es gehet dem Menschen', 'Ich wandte ich' and 'O Tod, wie bitter bist du' are followed by the warmer tones of 'Wenn ich mit Menschen—und mit Engelzungen', but the over-riding impression left is one of black pessimism. Despite their use of words from the Bible, these are not religious songs. Brahms, in fact, feared that 'these altogether Godless songs, whose words, thank heaven, are in the Bible'† might offend against religious proprieties. In the *Vier ernste Gesänge* he faces his own secret fears about death, fears not to be banished by St Paul since the bitterness of the first three songs is by no means allayed by the hollow sentimentality of the 'faith, hope and love' tune in the fourth song. As Friedlaender says, 'It is a sort of personal confession, a struggle between the words of the Bible and his own life experience, that Brahms expresses in this music.'‡

---

* Quoted in Friedlaender, op. cit.   † Quoted in Friedlaender, op. cit.
‡ op. cit.

Brahms composed a number of songs for more than one voice. There are several volumes of duets and quartets, and one volume of the latter, the *Zigeunerlieder* op. 103, composed in 1887, was arranged two years later by the composer as a group of solo songs. It is as a solo group that these songs are now best known. Originally, there were eleven songs, all settings of Hungarian folk verse in German translations by H. Conrat. In arranging them for solo voice, Brahms decided to omit nos. 7, 8 and 9, so the solo *Zigeunerlieder* are eight in number. They represent Brahms's gypsy style at its most uninhibited, the melodies long-phrased, passionate and stirring, the accompaniments doing little more than marking the rhythm.

In addition to those songs composed to folk texts, which carry a strong flavour of folk song, Brahms also arranged a number of authentic folk melodies for solo voice with piano accompaniment : seventy-seven *Deutsche Volkslieder*, and a further fourteen *Volkskinderlieder*. These children's songs include the universally known 'Sandmännchen', while the adult songs range from noisy character sketches to the charming simplicities of 'Mein Mädel hat einen Rosenmund' the gentle sentiment of 'Da unten im Tale' and the pathos of 'Schwesterlein, Schwesterlein'. The dialect of the sly village maidens in songs like 'Och, Moder, ich well en Ding han' or 'We kumm ich dann de Pooz erenn' is an important ingredient. The Brahms folk songs are not pedantic arrangements, but in many cases imaginative reworkings of the original folk material.

The songs of Adolph Jensen (1837–1879) have not remained in favour, though a few of them are still known in German-speaking countries. The best of Jensen's fresh, spontaneous melodies recall the young Schumann, though he lacked that master's deeper poetic insights. The weakly sentimental 'Lehn' deine Wang' an meine Wang' (Heine) op. 1 no. 1 is occasionally heard in recitals, but many more attractive songs await rediscovery by an enterprising singer. Some of Jensen's *Spanisches Liederbuch* settings, though not seriously rivalling Hugo Wolf's settings of that same collection of verses, possess an undeniable charm. 'Murmelndes Lüftchen' is one of the most attractive of these.

Of all the major composers, Hugo Wolf (1860–1903) is the only one to have devoted himself almost exclusively to the composition of songs. He did, it is true, complete one opera and begin another, and his juvenilia include orchestral works.

chamber music and some pieces for piano. His mature output, however, consists almost entirely of solo songs, of which he composed some 250, and it is upon these songs that his reputation rests. Although Wolf recognizably derives from the earlier 19th-century composers of *Lieder*, especially from Schumann, he differs from them in one important respect: his greater emphasis upon the poem, indicative of his attitude to the setting of words in general. One does not find in Wolf the seemingly spontaneous melody of Schubert, nor should one seek it. Whether Wolf's melodic reticence is a consequence of his literary sensitivity or whether his subjugation of tune to text is due to the fact that he was no great melodist is not easy to determine, and in any case the question is both more complex than this, and, in a sense, pointless. There are, after all, some beautiful tunes to be found in the songs of Wolf. There is also a remarkable variety of mood and range. He is capable of writing lyrical pieces of great delicacy, as well as dramatic, quasi-Wagnerian character sketches, and songs of real humour, usually sardonic rather than boisterous.

Wolf's songs, understandably, are not as popular with non-German-speaking concert audiences as those of his predecessors, Schubert, Schumann and Brahms, or even those of his contemporaries, Richard Strauss and Mahler. Fully to appreciate a song by Wolf requires more than a superficial understanding of the words; for the composer's rhythmic subtleties, as well as the shape and the rise and fall of his vocal line, are conditioned by both the sound and the sense of those words. Wolf's comparatively brief life ended in madness. The majority of his songs were written at intense fever pitch during the three years 1888–91. In the mid 1890s he wrote his one opera and began a second, as well as a few more songs, but his last five years, from 1898 to 1903 were spent in an asylum.

The earliest surviving Wolf songs are those he composed in his mid-teens, none of which he chose to publish or acknowledge in his life-time, and only a few of which have been published posthumously. The earliest published songs are two volumes, each of six songs, which appeared in 1888, though they were written earlier. *Sechs Lieder für eine Frauenstimme* are to poems by Rückert, Hebbel, Reinick, and Mörike. Eduard Mörike (1804–1875) was a Swabian village clergyman who, at the age of forty, retired from the church to teach literature at a women's college in Stuttgart. If Mörike is still known today as a poet, it is almost certainly due to the fact that in 1888, Wolf set fifty-three of his poems to music. The Mörike song in *Sechs Lieder für eine Frauenstimme* was composed ten years earlier, when Wolf was seventeen, but it is one of the best-known and loved of his songs : 'Mausfallensprüchlein' or 'Mousetrap spell', in which a child is instructed how to charm a mouse into a trap. An appealing little song, if somewhat tougher than it is made to appear in the coy interpretations of most sopranos. Of the remaining songs in this volume, only Reinick's 'Wiegenlied im Sommer' and 'Wiegenlied im Winter' are worthy of the mature Wolf, tender and unusually individual and inventive little cradle songs.

The second volume published in 1888, *Sechs Gedichte von Scheffel, Mörike, Goethe und Kerner*, contains only one Mörike setting, 'Der König bei der Krönung', a rather Wagnerian portrait of a king at his coronation, dedicating himself to the service of his country. The Scheffel songs ('Biterolf' and 'Wächterlied auf der Wartburg') are disappointing, and Wolf's first encounters with Goethe, on whom he was to concentrate his attention in the winter of 1888–9, are also disconcertingly dull. This is all the more surprising when one considers that the poems are the marvellous 'Der, du von den Himmel bist', so memorably composed by Schubert, and 'Beherzigung', whose contrast of timidity with determination would seem to make it an ideal subject for music. The remaining song, Kerner's 'Zur Ruh, zur Ruh', the moving appeal of a tortured soul for rest and repose, is a remarkably strong and sensitive response to the poem, if somewhat Wagnerian in style.

It was Wolf's habit to work his way through a poet's *œuvre* until he had exhausted his interest in that poet. The fifty-three Mörike songs, for example, were composed between February and November 1888 (nine in February, twenty in March, eight in April, six in May, nine in October and one in November), during which period the composer also produced most of his Eichendorff settings and the first twelve of his Goethe songs. The published order of the songs in the Mörike volume (and this applies, in general, to Wolf's published volumes) is not that of composition. The first song, 'Der Genesene an die Hoffnung', in which someone convalescing from illness addresses himself to Hope, is followed by 'Der Knabe und das Immlein', a sweet little dialogue between a boy and a bee, whose melody, harmonies, and accompaniment figures completely reveal their

beauty and aptness only when the words are clearly understood. This is true of very many of Wolf's songs, though it
should also be pointed out that, as a group, the Mörike songs
are remarkable specifically for their musical virtues.

To emphasize Wolf's careful matching of musical to literary
form is not to imply that his songs do not stand on their own
feet; on the contrary, they represent a complex and highly
developed form of the *Lied*, in which words and music are in
every sense equal partners. This, at any rate, is the ideal to
which Wolf aspires, and his finest songs are those in which that
ideal is realized. In 'Der Tambour', for instance, a pleasant but
hardly first-rate poem about a drummer-boy who is on duty
in France but is dreaming of mother and home in Germany,
Wolf produces a highly enjoyable character-sketch in which the
skill with which the rhythms of speech are preserved and contained within the melodic framework appears not at all to in-
hibit that framework. The music is appropriate for the style of
the poem, and for its stature. The point can be made differently :
in Schubert, a poor poem can inspire a masterpiece of song, and
a great poem can sometimes result in an unsatisfactory song,
whereas in Wolf there are very few poor poems, though the
slighter poems result in slighter songs, and only the masterpieces beget masterpieces.

The delights of the Mörike songs are many and varied. Spring
races through the pages of 'Er ist's' as though bursting into
bloom; loneliness and loss are achingly evoked in the sparse A
minor harmonies and bleak melodic style of 'Das verlassene
Mägdlein'; the strange sweetness of the poem 'An eine Aeolsharfe' in which a girl, mourning the loss of a brother, addresses
the Aeolian harp gently stirred into life by the breeze as her
feelings are stirred by thoughts of the past, is turned into
memorably heightened recitative, the arpeggios of the harp
sustaining and varying at the caprice of the wind. 'Verborgen-
heit' is a song which became popular during Wolf's lifetime,
to such an extent that he angrily exclaimed he wished he had
never written it. With its uncomplicated ABA form, its sentimental and easily remembered melody, it is hardly typical Wolf,
though it remains a pleasant, accessible and unpretentious song.

Equally melodious, but of a higher order altogether, is 'Im
Frühling' in which Wolf can be heard responding not simply
to the overall mood of the poem, but phrase by phrase, and
image by image. Magically he gathers all the strands together

into a seamless masterpiece, which is not simply a song about lying on a hillside in spring and experiencing vague yearnings, but a musical expression of a complex of moods, feelings, fleeting images, and half-remembered memories of 'Alte unnennbare Tage', these last three words of the song themselves hardly translatable into another tongue. (The literal meaning of the adjective is 'unnameable': the phrase means something like 'past days that can no longer be grasped or even conceived of'.) By way of strong contrast with 'Im Frühling', 'Elfenlied' is all dazzling melodic recitative, brilliantly clothing the kind of elf poem which, though it sounds perfectly acceptable in German, does not come across happily to the English language or imagination.

The Mörike volume, like all the other Wolf volumes of 1888–91—the Eichendorff, Goethe and Keller poems, and those of the *Spanish* and *Italian Song Books*—is full of magnificent miniatures. Among the finest and most enchanting of the Mörike songs are the fairy-tale-like 'Der Gärtner', the charming and melodic 'Zitronenfalter im April', and the poignant 'Auf ein altes Bild' in which the Christ-child is pictured playing on his mother's lap, while the trees, one of which will become his cross, grow to maturity in the sunny forest. Wolf responds with a devout sympathy to Mörike's religious poems, especially in 'Schlafendes Jesuskind' and 'Karwoche' ('Holy Week'). This latter song, perhaps somewhat undervalued, is a richly sensuous setting of an unusual poem of love both earthly and spiritual.

Wolf's volume of twenty songs to poems of Joseph von Eichendorff was published in 1889. The majority of the songs were composed in 1888 at the same time that the composer was concentrating on Mörike and Goethe, though five of them were written in 1887, and two songs, 'Erwartung' and 'Die Nacht' are much earlier, dating from 1880. We have already encountered Eichendorff in our survey of Schumann's songs, but whereas Schumann chose to present the Eichendorff of magic forests, elves and ruined castles, Wolf attempted to complement the earlier composer's settings by depicting the rougher, more humorous aspect of Eichendorff's art. This he did in a delightful collection of songs which, while not attempting to compete in variety or depth with the Spanish and Italian volumes which were to come, nevertheless show Wolf at his most captivating. These twenty songs may be generally lighter in mood than much else in Wolf, but almost every one of them is highly attractive, and one or two are absolutely magnificent. The volume opens with 'Der Freund' which is the least interesting of the songs; one suspects it may be an earlier work, added to or improved in 1888. The poet contrasts two types of man : he who accepts life with calm passivity, and he who takes it by the throat. That Wolf's sympathies are not one-sided is revealed by the tenderness of the first ten bars; but for the greater part of the song, the piano ranges up and down the keyboard behind a stern vocal line, and the effect, though enjoyable in itself, suggests a somewhat superficial reading of the poem. 'Der Musikant', which follows, is a real gem, a gay little character-study of the wandering minstrel who makes light of adversity. Simple but delightful, this is Wolf at his finest and most immediately appealing. 'Verschwiegene Liebe', a beautiful, quietly rhapsodic mood-picture, is one of the composer's most attractive miniatures, and the fourth song, 'Das Ständchen', is also regarded as one of his finest. An old man, hearing a youth serenading his beloved, is reminded of his own sweetheart of many years ago, long since dead. 'Sing on for ever', he advises the youth. The atmosphere of the scene is beautifully realized in the piano part, and the vocal line, though restrained, conveys the essence of the romantic attitude.

There are two songs in the Eichendorff volume with the title of 'Der Soldat', both of them inventive, with bouncy accompaniments making it clear that the soldier is a cavalryman. To the jaunty tune of the first song, whose accompaniment depicts his horse's brisk trot, the soldier sings of riding to the house where a maiden waits to welcome him. If she begins to talk of marriage, he can quickly mount and ride off again. In the second song, more serious in intent, more violent in manner, the horseman gallops through the night, pursued by fears of death. Tersely effective in performance, the song is marred only by a certain theatricality of gesture. 'Die Zigeunerin' is blatantly and unashamedly theatrical, but this time appropriately so, with much bravura and gypsy flourish. The poem of 'Nachtzauber' may be more conventional Eichendorff, though none the less pleasing for that, but there is nothing conventional about the song, whose fervent romanticism completely captures the mood of the poem, conjuring up by its quietly beautiful melody and richly varied harmonies a magical evocation of woodland lakes and mountains as evening draws on. 'Der Schreckenberger' is a strange, wild poem in which the dreaded fearless rider is called into action by Fortune herself, to fight his way to immortal glory. The poem obviously appealed to Wolf's imagination, for he has emphasized and underlined its mood with a most bombastic postlude on the piano, directed to be played *fff*. Though it is difficult to take 'Der Schreckenberger' seriously, the song is immensely effective and exhilarating in performance. The swagger of 'Der Glücksritter' is equally likeable, and the poem even more removed from modern taste. A knight claims to tame the shrewish Dame Fortune, to drink with her and make her pay, and then to lead her forth, acknowledged by all as her master. 'Lieber alles' is a slight but pleasing little sketch of a young man who wonders whether to be a soldier, a student or a poet, and finally decides he'd rather be a horseman, winning fame as he rides lustily through life.

'Heimweh', in the company of such fine songs, is relatively unimpressive, 'Der Scholar' is a cheerful character-sketch, and 'Der verzweifelte Liebhaber' an amusing trifle in which a jilted young lover lashes out in what seems to him to be tragic despair. In 'Unfall', the narrator indignantly relates how one night he was waylaid by a young ruffian with a rifle. In the scuffle, the narrator falls on his nose. The piano part describes the fight, in racing triplets, and his fall. All is allegory: the ruffian's name is Cupid. Eichendorff's confident love poem, 'Liebesglück', its images drawn from the grandeur of nature, becomes even more confident, indeed exultant, in Wolf's setting, and the lively 'Seemans Abschied' is a brilliantly and humorously graphic sea-picture. The following two songs are the much earlier pieces which Wolf inserted into the volume: 'Erwartung', though it sounds curiously Brahmsian in these surroundings, is a most attractive song of young love, and 'Die Nacht', which likens night to a calm sea, could easily be mistaken for mature Wolf. Joy, sorrow and the torments of love seem far away, like voices heard distantly across the water. The volume ends with 'Waldmädchen', one of Eichendorff's less impressive 'woodland sprite' poems, which Wolf treats to a bravura setting. Should the Eichendorff volume be performed complete and in sequence, 'Waldmädchen' would make a rousing conclusion.

With Germany's greatest poet, Goethe, Wolf was suitably matched: not as Austria's greatest composer, which he was not, but as the composer of song with qualities closest to those of the poet. Wolf has left us fifty-one Goethe songs, all but one of them composed between late October 1888 and early February

1889. Though some of the poet's exquisite small lyric poems are included, the over-riding tone of the volume is earnest, and its greatest achievements are large-scale songs. It has been mentioned earlier that Wolf deliberately avoided well-known poems whenever he considered that they had already been successfully put to music. In this volume, then, he consciously challenges Schubert, whom apparently he considered had not fully understood Goethe in the *Wilhelm Meister* songs and elsewhere. Ten songs written to poems from *The Apprenticeship of Wilhelm Meister* are placed at the beginning of Wolf's Goethe volume, eight of which had already been set by Schubert (and nine by Schumann). First are the Harper's songs, 'Harferspieler I, II und III'. No. 1 is 'Wer sich der Einsamkeit ergibt', a nobly restrained setting of the Harper's sorrowful meditation. In 'An die Türen will ich schleichen' the expression is rather more overt, though never uncomfortably dramatized. These, and the third of the Harper's songs, 'Wer nie sein Brot mit Tränen ass' are among the finest of Wolf's *Wilhelm Meister* settings. The satirical 'Spottlied' is less successful, perhaps because the poem itself makes little effect away from the context of the novel. Three of Mignon's four songs follow (the fourth, the famous 'Kennst du das Land?' is simply titled 'Mignon', without identifying number). 'Mignon I' is the poem which begins 'Heiss mich nicht reden', a cryptic utterance not made any clearer by Wolf; 'Nur wer die Sehnsucht kennt' had been set by numerous composers, most memorably by Schubert and Tchaikovsky. Wolf lacks their lyrical spontaneity, but substitutes a greater psychological penetration which, in this instance, is highly effective. The third Mignon song, 'So lasst mich scheinen', too, benefits from Wolf's intellectual approach to the problem of wordsetting. In this gravely memorable song he has somehow succeeded in composing the context of the poem as much as the words themselves. These three Mignon songs and 'Kennst du das Land?' are separated by 'Philine'. Philine is the soubrette of the theatrical company in the novel, and at a certain point in the action she sings 'a very graceful and pleasing melody'* to these lines. The song Wolf has given her perfectly fits the occasion and the words.

We come now to 'Mignon', or 'Kennst du das Land?' one of the greatest poems in the German language, and, in Wolf's setting, certainly one of the most magnificent *Lieder* ever com-

* So described in Goethe's novel

posed. Wolf's song is sometimes criticized for being too elaborate for Mignon's pathetic, childlike dream, but such criticism is surely invalid and unimaginative, for Goethe's poem rises above its immediate context to make a statement about *Sehnsucht*, about the mystery of the past, and the fever of dreams. The poem is, of course, also susceptible to a simpler musical treatment than Wolf gave it, but so instinctively to have grasped its poetic resonance and significance as Wolf did is itself an act of genius. The greater the music, the more difficult it is to attempt a verbal description of it. To describe Wolf's 'Kennst du das Land?' is virtually impossible, one can but point to its magnificence, and listen to it. It is a song of such imaginative richness and power that to hear it sung by a Lehmann, or a Schwarzkopf, is to experience one of the most intense of musical pleasures.

The last of the *Wilhelm Meister* songs in Wolf's Goethe volume is, anti-climactically, 'Der Sänger', another of the Harper's songs. The poem itself is poor, and Wolf makes little more of it than did Schubert and Schumann who also chose to grapple with it.

The next twenty Goethe songs are taken from miscellaneous lyric poems, among them some of Goethe's most famous. 'Der Rattenfänger' is his version of the Pied Piper, boasting of his powers as rat- child- or woman-catcher, and Wolf has made an irresistible song of it. For the children of some friends, he composed 'Epiphanias', to be sung and acted at Christmas, a charming miniature scene for the three wise kings in search of the newly-born Christ. The tender and delicate 'Blumengrüss', which looks forward to the manner of the *Italienisches Liederbuch* is utterly enchanting, as is the song which follows it, 'Gleich und Gleich'. A rare masterpiece is 'Anakreon's Grab', Goethe's beautiful and reverent poem clothed in music of wistful tranquillity and human warmth.

From the *Westöstlicher Divan*, Goethe's late collection of poems based on texts of the Persian poet Hafiz, Wolf chose sixteen lyrics in praise of wine or women. 'Ob der Koran von Ewigkeit sei?' begins by asking solemnly whether the Koran has always existed, but soon turns to the more interesting subject of wine. A difficult poem to set to music, one would have thought, but Wolf brings it off superbly, and makes an even greater effect with 'Trunken mussen wir alle sein!', the drinking song to end all drinking songs. 'Erschaffen und Beleben' at first hearing sounds rather disjointed, but closer acquaintance reveals it to be an appropriate musical vehicle for Goethe's amusing poem. 'Als ich auf dem Euphrat schiffte' and 'Dies zu deuten bin erbötig', both delightful and approachable songs, are linked verbally and musically, the second being an answer to the question posed by the first. They are followed in the sequence by a third song related thematically to the second: 'Hätt' ich irgend wohl bedenken'. These three songs ought really to be performed together. Most of these *Westöstlicher Divan* miniatures tend to be neglected by singers. but they are all worth investigating, especially perhaps the love songs such as 'Komm, Liebchen, komm'.

The Goethe volume ends with three of Goethe's greatest poems about the relationship of man to the Gods: 'Prometheus', 'Ganymed' and 'Grenzen der Menschheit'; three poems, it may be remembered, which Schubert had already turned into masterpieces of song. Though Wolf here directly challenges Schubert, we are fortunate in not having to make a choice between his versions and those of the earlier composer. Their approaches to the poems differ so widely that it is idle to ponder, for instance, whose 'Prometheus' is the better song, or whose is closer to the spirit of Goethe. It would be interesting to hear all six songs sung as a group of Goethe interpretations: first Schubert's 'Prometheus', then Wolf's, then Wolf's 'Ganymed' followed by Schubert's. Apart from questions of temperament and method, there is the fact that Wolf is writing more than fifty years later than Schubert. The melodic tradition they share is fifty years less fresh, but knowledge of Goethe has fifty years' more experience. If one prefers the tremulous lyricism of Schubert's 'Ganymed' to the purer intellectual experience of Wolf's setting of the same text, one is guided by one's temperament. Another might think Schubert's 'Grenzen der Menschheit' superficial alongside Wolf's extraordinary vision.

The forty-four songs of Wolf's *Spanish Song Book*, composed during six months of 1888–9, are settings of poems taken from the *Spanisches Liederbuch*, a collection of 16th- and 17th-century Spanish poems,* translated into German by Emanuel Geibel (1815–1884) and Paul Heyse (1830–1914), and published in 1852. Geibel and Heyse divided their collection into sacred and secular songs and, in making his selection, Wolf did likewise. The first ten are sacred songs, the remaining thirty-four

* Some of the poems are by such famous names as Lope de Vega, Cervantes and Camões, but many are folk poems

secular. The sacred songs contain some of Wolf's most intensely felt dramatic portraits, of souls in anguish, of sinners repentant and of religious ecstasy. 'Nun bin ich dein', a prayer to the Virgin Mary, is beautiful in its single-minded concentration and its feeling of contrite dedication, and these qualities are found even more strongly in the second song, 'Die du Gott gebarst', a similar prayer uttered not with the solemn devotion of the northern European, but with the completely consuming religious passion of the Spanish Catholic. 'Nun wandre, Maria' is sung by Joseph to Mary on the way to Bethlehem. 'Journey on', he says, 'we shall soon reach Bethlehem, where we are sure to find lodging, and you can rest and sleep.' The quiet, steady walking rhythm of the song and the tenderness of the solicitous and anxious husband's words combine in a gentle, devout way to present a touching musical portrait. 'Die ihr schwebet um diese Palmen' is the Lope da Vega poem which Brahms had set for contralto and piano with viola obbligato. Wolf's version of the song sung by the Virgin over the cradle of her child is less abstractly poetic, more graphic than that of Brahms. His piano part gives us the angels hovering overhead and the waving of the palm trees in the wind, while in the voice-part we hear the devoted mother-love of the Virgin. In 'Führ mich, Kind', another gravely beautiful song, a penitent implores the holy child to lead him to Bethlehem, and 'Ach, des Knaben Augen' is a sweet outpouring of devotion to the Christ-child, with melody of tender simplicity, and an articulate and expressive piano part.

One of the most admired of the sacred songs is 'Mühwoll komm' ich und beladen', to a poem by Don Manuel del Rio in which a penitent sinner petitions Christ. The poem has something of the psychological sickness of the religious masochist who revels in his abasement, something of the self-flagellant about it, and this is emphasized, perhaps exaggerated in Wolf's anguished setting. Not a likeable song by any means, but a memorable one. 'Ach, wie lang die Seele schlummert', an anonymous mystical poem, is sensitively set by Wolf, though the final effect is somewhat remote and uninvolved. The next song, 'Herr, was trägt der Boden hier', is anything but uninvolved. Cast in the form of a dialogue between Christ and a sinner, the poem is a fine parable of the ambivalence of experience. The anguish of the questioner, the calm fore-knowledge of Christ, these are beautifully conveyed by the composer, both in his setting of the words and in the rhythms and harmonies of the piano part. The dialogue continues in the last of the sacred songs, 'Wunden trägst du, mein Geliebter', whose poem is by Jose de Valdivivielse. The words, this time, are less affecting because more affected, but Wolf's response is to the spirit, not the matter of the text, and his music vividly portrays both the spiritual anguish of the sinner and the consolation offered by his Saviour.

The contrast between 'Wunden trägst du, mein Geliebter' and the song which follows it in the *Spanisches Liederbuch* is enormous. 'Klinge, klinge, mein Pandero', the first of the secular songs, returns us to the world of the flesh with a vengeance. Pain is still present, but it is the relievable pain of love, not the ecstatic torment of religious fanaticism. The singer sings of his torment, but the rhythm of his tambourine persists throughout. The next song is 'In dem Schatten meiner Locken', the epitome of the brief, musically slight, yet endearing character sketch of which Wolf, here and in the *Italian Song Book*, proved himself a past master. The singer is a woman whose lover has gone to sleep in her arms. Three times she wonders if she should awaken him, and answers herself with a tender falling phrase, 'Ach, nein'. With the lightest, most delicate touch, Wolf is able to bring a character and a situation before us, as clearly as though we were seeing them on the operatic stage. The singer of this kind of Wolf song must be able to act with the voice, and to refrain from acting with the body. Expressive performance of the text brings these delicious miniatures alive, even the not completely successful ones, such as 'Seltsam ist Juanas Weise' or 'Treibe nur mit Lieben Spott' in which the musical material is less strongly individual. 'Auf dem grünen Balkon' is superb : music perfectly matched to the shape and sense of the five stanzas of the poem.

In these secular songs Wolf frequently resorts to a suggestion of Spanish colouring in the rhythms, whereas he refrains from this in the sacred songs. Not all of the secular songs thrust their Spanish provenance at one, however. 'Wenn du zu den Blumen gehst' could be an original German poem, and Wolf's delightful setting of its message of love has something of the melodic fluency and even the inflections of Schumann. This is a song of great charm, though not one strongly characteristic of Wolf. Even more charming is 'Wer sein holdes Lieb verloren', a tender and plaintive love song, which is followed by a song more plaintive still, 'Ich führ über Meer', sung by an unsuccessful seeker after happiness. Three songs further on, we encounter 'Herz, verzage

nicht geshwind' which always promises more on the page than
it delivers in performance. Obviously it is not an easy piece to
interpret: its harsh words about women are not to be taken too
seriously, but the exact tone of the song is not easy to catch.
No such difficulties are presented by 'Sagt, seid Ihr es, feiner
Herr?', addressed to a young man by a mocking young woman.
This is one of the composer's most delightful little character
pieces, but very dependent upon clearly enunciated and impeccably acted performance.

Some of these Spanish poems, it must be admitted, are
distinctly less good than others. It is not easy to understand, for
instance, why Wolf should have chosen to set such texts as 'Bitt'
ihn, o Mutter' or 'Liebe mir im Busen zündet'. Yet the composer
is able to make something even of such unpromising material. The
former song, in which a girl tells her mother she must beg Cupid
to stop aiming his arrows at her, can be made to go with a swing
by a soprano of strong personality, and the latter is at least short
enough not to outstay its welcome. 'Schmerzliche Wonnen', a
relative failure, is followed by six songs which are works of sheer
genius. 'Trau' nicht der Liebe' is not a particularly interesting
poem, but the music is so spontaneous that it sounds as though
it had written itself, and the lilting rhythm of the accompaniment propels the song along winningly. 'Ach, in Maien war's' is
curious in that the words tell of languishing in a dungeon, while
the music sounds quite blithe! Perhaps the dungeon, the guard,
and the killed bird are symbols of some odd kind of delight?
The next song, 'Alle gingen, Herz, zur Ruh' is a song of real
and deep sorrow, and a very beautiful one. 'Dereinst, dereinst,
Gedanke mein' develops a similar theme, a longing for release
from torment, heart-achingly portrayed in Wolf's weary vocal
line. Equally grief-laden, yet quite different in expression, are
'Tief im Herzen trag' ich Pein' (poem by Camões), and
'Komm, o Tod', a startlingly fine evocation in musical terms of
the death wish. Of the remaining songs in the *Spanish Song Book*,
the most noteworthy are 'Bedeckt mich mit Blumen', the underrated 'Wer tat deinem Füsslein weh', and the final song, the
marvellous 'Geh, Geliebter, geh' jetzt', in which a girl begs her
lover to leave, for it is almost dawn and the village will soon
be stirring. The operatic sweep and passion of Wolf's urgent
setting are remarkable.

These Spanish songs reflect in a definite though subtle way
the world from which the poems sprang. The almost sensual

ecstasy of the religious songs, the urgent passion of some of the secular ones, these qualities are far removed from the more introspective fervour of, for instance, many of Wolf's Mörike settings. But what has not altered is the composer's gift for characterization in music, whether he is portraying religious devotion, romantic love, or comic frustration. Rhythm, melody, verbal accentuation and dramatic characterization, all are combined in these superb sound-portraits.

In the early summer of 1890, between concluding the *Spanish Song Book* and embarking upon the *Italian*, Wolf wrote a group of six songs to poems of Gottfried Keller (1819–1890), under the collective title of *Alte Weisen*. The poems include 'Du milchjunger Knabe' which had already inspired Brahms's beautiful 'Therese'; unfortunately none of Wolf's six settings represents the composer at his best. Perhaps his creative faculties were biding their time, awaiting the *Italian Song Book*, for the later collection of forty-six miniatures, composed between September 1890 and April 1891, is surely Wolf's finest achievement in song.

The translations of the Italian poems are the work of Paul Heyse alone, whose *Italienisches Liederbuch* was published in 1860. Most of the poems are anonymous, quite brief, and popular in style, though some are by such poets as Leopardi, Giusti and Carducci. They are portraits of Italian life, which Wolf has translated into his own individual musical shorthand. Though small, these songs are precious, and the opening one virtually says as much. 'Even small things can bring delight', it begins. 'Auch Kleine Dinge' is exquisite, delicate and memorable.

'Gesegnet sei, durch den die Welt entstund' is one of the few religious poems of the *Italian Song Book*, and the song Wolf has fashioned from it is a masterpiece of deceptive simplicity, yet overwhelming effect, with a particularly beautiful setting of the poem's last line, 'Er schuf die Schöinheit und dein Angesicht'. Among the highlights of the volume are the comic sketches, such as 'Wer rief dich denn?' 'Who asked you to come here?' cries the jealous maiden. 'Why not go to your other sweetheart?' The piano part offers stage directions and details of mood, and the vocal part finds the real meaning beneath the apparent anger of the girl's utterance. 'Der Mond hat eine schwere Klag' is a long and imaginative song, and in 'Nun lass uns Frieden schliessen' a lover makes peace with his beloved after a quarrel, to music of ineffable tenderness and love. Another of Wolf's angry or sarcastic girls is met with in 'Du denkst mit einem Fädchen mich zu fangen', which can be brilliantly effective in performance, though it requires the interpretative powers and personality of a Lehmann, a Seefried or a Schwarzkopf fully to bring it off, for the musical material itself is thin.

'Wie lange schon' is one of the best of the humorous songs. The girl has long yearned for a lover who is also a musician, and now the good Lord has sent her one, 'with a delicate air, his head bowed, and playing the violin'. After the last words of the poem, the piano takes over, giving its impression of the shy young violinist who ends his careful little solo with a slow and effortful trill. The following two songs are equally delightful examples of Wolf's comic vein. In 'Nein, junger Herr' the maiden chides her young man who, she says, pays attention to her on working days but is on the lookout for something better at holiday time. The gay rhythms and light-hearted melody are perfectly judged, as they are, too, in 'Hoffärtig seid Ihr' in which, this time, a young man addresses the girl of his choice, accusing her of haughtiness. 'You are no princess', he warns her. His words are hurt and angry, but Wolf does not ignore the underlying tenderness which is also present. The song that follows is a brilliant character-sketch in which a young man suggests to his friend that they should dress themselves as monks, knock on people's doors begging for alms, and offer to visit sick girls to hear their confessions behind locked doors. The musical portrait of the bogus friar is built up mainly by splendid touches in the piano part, and the deliciously sanctimonious voice part is a gift to a singer with a talent for dramatic characterization. 'Mein Liebster ist so klein' survives its amusing but absurd little poem about the lover who is so small that he is frightened by a snail in the garden. We are not meant to take the words literally: the speaker is another of those snide girls who are forever complaining, but she is quite obviously fond of her sweetheart who comes from Maremma, where the men are said to be small. A song of exasperated affection.

Delightful though these Italian miniatures are, to hear a number of them in succession can lead to a certain tedium. The practice of performing the *Italian Song Book* as a complete cycle is not to be recommended: far better to pick out a group of songs for performance together with other Wolf songs. Singly, however, or in small groups, Wolf's little character pieces are brilliantly effective. In 'Ihr jungen Leute', the bossy maiden this time addresses her sweetheart's regiment, telling them to look after him, as this is his first battle, and his chest is weak, so he must not be made to sleep in the open. This is a little masterpiece of wit and affection. It is followed by a serious love song, and one of the most beautiful in Wolf's entire *œuvre*, 'Und willst du deinen Liebsten sterben sehen', in which the rapt adoration of the words is set to music of immense tenderness. Even tenderer and more affecting is 'Wir haben beide lange Zeit geschwiegen', words spoken in peace and love after a quarrel, and clothed in music of rare sensitivity and feeling. These love songs, some light, some grave, are even finer, musically, than the character-sketches. Of the lighter ones, 'Ein Ständchen euch zu bringen' is perhaps the most charming, and of the more deeply serious expressions of love, 'Was für ein Lied?' is one of the most beautiful. The lover wonders where to find a song worthy to be sung to his beloved, and hopes to find something never before heard. Wolf obliges with one of his most original and beautiful settings.

Both original and impressive is 'Schon streckt' ich aus im Bett', a song whose beauties may not reveal themselves at a first casual hearing, but which grows to haunt one. The same can perhaps be said of 'Wohl kenn' ich Euren Stand', another song of helpless and hopeless adoration. A more immediately accessible masterpiece is 'Sterb' ich, so hüllt in Blumen'. It is number thirty-three of the forty-six songs of the *Italian Song Book*, and the remaining thirteen songs, with the possible exception of the penultimate one, 'Verschling' der Abgrund', are all minor masterpieces. The melodically generous 'Und steht Ihr früh am Morgen auf' is radiant with love and devotion, and contains some of Wolf's most imaginative harmonic effects. 'Benedeit die sel'ge Mutter' is one of the most popular songs in the collection, unusual for Wolf in being in strict ABA form, its passionate middle section contrasting most effectively with the serene melody of the opening and closing sections. 'Wenn du mein Liebster' is perhaps somewhat too extrovert in manner for the delicacy of the sentiments expressed, but for all that it is a splendid song. 'Wie viele Zeit verlor ich' is a tender and moving love song of simple beauty, and the equally disarming simplicity of 'Wenn du mich mit den Augen streifst' is enormously appealing. 'Gesegnet sei das Grün' is thought by some not to represent Wolf at his best, but to this writer the suggestion of sadness beneath its surface freshness and spring-like charm is attractive and unusual. 'O wär dein Haus durchsichtig' is less immediately appealing, though it is an excellently constructed song, in some ways curiously Debussian. The brief, eighteen-bar-long 'Heut Nacht erhob ich mich' is one of Wolf's finest, achievements despite its miniature size, a poignant song of great melodic inventiveness. The serenade, 'Nicht länger kann ich singen', and its unkind response, 'Schweig einmal still', are both delightful, and 'O wüsstest du' is a passionate lament of the kind that Wolf seemed able to produce so easily. 'Verschling' der Abgrund' is disappointingly empty, though full of sound and fury, and the gay bravura of 'Ich hab' in Penna', which concludes the entire collection, is irresistible.

We have almost come to the end of Hugo Wolf's voluminous output. All that remain are four collections, each consisting of three or four songs. The three settings of poems by Robert Reinick were published in 1897, though two of them had been composed some years earlier. The poems are not particularly engaging, but Wolf makes something of 'Gesellenlied' and 'Morgenstimmung'. The three songs from Ibsen's *The Feast at Solhaug*, composed in 1891 but not published until 1897, are uninteresting, and the four settings of Heine, Shakespeare and Byron published in the same years are somewhat uneven. Heine's 'Wo wird einst' elicits a lifeless response from the composer; Bottom's transformation song from a *A Midsummer Night's Dream* is rather heavy, and not helped by Wolf's interpolated braying noises at the end of each stanza, while the two transla-tions (by Otto Gildemeister) from Byron—'Sun of the sleepless! melancholy star' and 'There be none of Beauty's daughters'— though somewhat better, are far from being first-rate Wolf. They were composed in the last week of the year 1896. Three months later, unexpectedly, came Wolf's last three songs, master-pieces of pessimism and despair, settings of poems by Michel-angelo translated by Walter Robert-Tornow. It had been the composer's intention to set several more of these translations, but his final breakdown came after he had completed the first three : 'Wohl denk' ich oft', 'Alles endet, was entstehet' and 'Fühlt meine Seele'. Not easy songs to know, these dark and brooding last utterances of Wolf are dignified, noble, and inhumanly impressive. 'Wohl denk, ich oft', in which the poet remembers the past before he was burdened with the responsi-bilities of fame and love, is solemn and dignified, its expressive vocal line strongly supported by a piano part which, though not one of Wolf's most imaginative, is nevertheless completely in keeping with the restless mood of the poem. The second song, 'Alles endet, was entstehet', is the finest of the three, and one of the great glories of German *Lieder*. The mood is one of Ecclesiastican pessimism and gloom : 'Everything that is created comes to an end, thought, speech, sorrow and joy. . . . Once we too were men like you, joyful and sad, but now we are dead, we have turned to dust.' The music, like the poem, seems to speak as from the dead, quickening into a remembrance of life, then returning to death, disillusion and decay. This extraordinary song does not reveal itself fully at first hearing; it takes some knowing. Eric Sams, in *The Songs of Hugo Wolf*,* rightly says that 'it is not a song one can live with or love'. True, but it is a song one comes in time to be haunted by. The last of the Michelangelo *Lieder*, 'Fühlt meine Seele', is Hugo Wolf's last completed song. It is, in a way, the most difficult of the three, a complex love song which seems to question the very concept of love, a searching and profound piece of music, and a worthy end to the career of a genius who devoted his life to the art of song.

Gustav Mahler (1860–1911), born in the same year as Hugo Wolf, is undoubtedly a composer of much greater stature than his contemporary. If he occupies less of our attention in this survey, it is not only because he composed considerably fewer songs than Wolf but also because the majority of these songs were for voice and orchestra. Song is a highly important aspect of Mahler's art; it infiltrates into several of his symphonies, and could even be said to form the basis of his symphonic thinking. But, except at the beginning of his career, he tended not to produce many separate songs for voice and piano. The majority of the texts he did set were taken from the *Knaben Wunderhorn* collection already mentioned in connection with Brahms.

The earliest songs of Mahler to have survived are two fragments and five completed pieces, mentioned by Donald Mitchell in his *Gustav Mahler: The Early Years*.† One of the two fragments is approximately twenty-three bars of unidentified text, and the other is eighteen bars of a setting of Heine's 'Im wunderschönen Monat Mai'. According to Mitchell, the D minor fragment is a faint adumbration of the style of the *Wunderhorn* songs of ten years later, while the Heine fragment is in a style of 'Tristan-esque yearning'. Mahler composed these

* Metheun, London 1961
† Rockliff, London 1958

pieces in his mid teens. At the age of twenty, he completed three more songs, the words of which he also wrote: 'Im Lenz', 'Winterlied' and 'Maitanz im Grünen'. This last song, under a new title, 'Hans und Grete', was included in his first published volume in 1885. This volume, *Lieder und Gesänge*, Book 1, contains four other songs, whose texts are either original poems or translations by Richard Leander. 'Hans und Grete' is a pleasant little *Ländler*, an Austrian country waltz, in which, for all the obvious immaturity of the music, the individual voice of Mahler can already be heard. 'Frühlingsmorgen' (poem by Leander) is less individual, in fact somewhat reminiscent of Schumann, but 'Erinnerung' (Leander) has a curious blend of resignation and yearning in its vocal line, bitter-sweet in quality, which proclaim it to be *echt*-Mahler. The other two songs of this early volume are settings of Leander's translations from Tirso de Molina's *Don Juan*. 'Serenade' is somewhat colourless, indeed stodgy: a curiously middle-aged Don Juan for so young a composer. 'Phantaisie' is more successful in its restrained, remote manner.

Before Books 2 and 3 of *Lieder und Gesänge* appeared, Mahler wrote his first orchestral song-cycle, *Lieder eines fahrenden Gesellen*, four songs composed on his own texts, in which his individual voice is heard most distinctly. Possessed of a more spontaneous melodic gift than his friend Wolf, he composed instinctively from the apparently endless stream of music he felt welling up within himself. As a result, he required less in the way of inspiration from his texts than Wolf did. In Mahler's songs, the feeling is conveyed entirely by the music. The words may tell a story or serve as a prop for the mood of a song, but they are seldom anywhere near as important as they are in Wolf.

The poems in Books 2 and 3 of the *Lieder und Gesänge*, published in 1892, are all drawn from *Des Knaben Wunderhorn*. The four songs of Book 2 are: 'Um schlimme Kinder artig zu machen', a pert little tale intended to make bad children good; 'Ich ging mit Lust', a sensitive improvement on an unpromising text; 'Aus! Aus!', a pleasant marching song; and 'Starke Einbild-ungskraft', whose delicacy is rather characterless. Book 3 contains five songs. 'Zu Strassburg auf der Schanz' is an oddly compelling ballad, to the rhythm of a funeral march, recounted by a deserter on the eve of his execution. In 'Ablösung im Sommer', the mock pathos of the death of the cuckoo, and his replacement as a singer by the nightingale, is treated with gentle detachment by Mahler. 'Scheiden und Meiden' fails to make much effect, but 'Nicht Wiedersehen' has a numbed, grief-laden quality which lifts it out of the ordinary. 'Selbstgefühl' suffers from Mahler's inability to take the poem at its face value. In none of these songs is the piano part particularly interesting, or at all independent. Mahler was essentially an orchestral composer, to whom the piano was merely an accompanying instrument.

The remainder of Mahler's songs were all composed for voice and orchestra. Since, however, with the exception of the two cycles *Lieder eines fahrenden Gesellen* and *Kindertotenlieder,* they are frequently encountered in recital programmes performed with piano accompaniment, some mention of them will not be out of place in this volume. The collection of ten songs known as *Songs from 'Des Knaben Wunderhorn'* was published in two volumes in 1905, in which year two separate songs for voice and orchestra, also with *Wunderhorn* texts, appeared. All twelve are frequently performed, sometimes together, though they do not in any sense constitute a cycle. Some of the poems are in the form of dialogue between two characters, and this has led to duet performances by two singers, though strictly speaking the songs are solos. 'Der Schildwache Nachtlied' is a grim night-piece in which a sentry, dreaming of his beloved, meets his death. In lighter vein, 'Verlor'ne Müh' utilizes the rhythm of the *Ländler* to tell its story of the foolish village maiden clumsily attempting to woo a disinterested village boy. 'Trost im Unglück' is a gay song of parting, and 'Wer hat dies Liedel erdacht?' is an entrancing nonsense song. 'Das irdische Leben', by contrast, offers a grim picture of a child starving to death. In 'Des Antonius von Padua Fischpredigt', St Anthony preaches an amiably ineffective sermon to the fish, while in 'Rheinlegendchen' Mahler has composed one of his most captivating songs, with a lilting, insinuating tune of immense charm. 'Lied des Verfolgten im Turm' is an affecting dialogue piece in which a prisoner in a tower dreams of peace and freedom with his beloved in the summer meadows. Equally affecting is 'Wo die schönen Trompeten blasen' in which a girl dreams she is visited by the spirit of her dead lover, a soldier who has fallen in battle. 'Lob des hohen Verstandes' is a light piece of nonsense, and both 'Revelge' and 'Der Tamboursg'sell' are sombre songs of military life.

In his five songs to poems of Rückert for voice and orchestra, composed between 1901 and 1904, Mahler has produced music of rich, autumnal beauty. These songs must be heard with their orchestral accompaniment to be fully understood and appreciated, though they do quite often appear in recital programmes with piano. 'Ich atmet' einen linden Duft' is music of a shimmering delicacy, 'Liebst du um Schönheit' a touching love song addressed by Mahler to his wife Alma, and 'Blicke mir nicht in die Lieder' the least interesting of the five. 'Ich bin der Welt abhanden gekommen' is certainly the most moving and beautiful, the quintessential Mahler *Lied* of farewell and withdrawal from the world. 'Um Mitternacht' is a huge song, less personal in manner than the other Rückert settings, but impressive as a cry of exaltation.

Four years younger than Mahler, Richard Strauss (1864–1949) lived nearly forty years longer. He was as devoted to the human voice as Wolf was, and, although he was primarily an opera composer, he continued to write songs from his teens to the last months of his life, songs noted for the late romantic appeal of their melody and, later, for their subtlety and charm. Strauss thought of himself as being in the tradition of Schumann and Brahms as a composer of *Lieder*, and his earliest songs have something of the rhapsodic quality of much of Brahms. But he developed in several directions during the course of his long career, and there is a world of difference between the popular 'Zueignung' of 1882 and the *Four Last Songs* of 1948, though their musical language remains essentially the same. Unlike Wolf, Strauss was not methodical in his choice of poets or in the manner in which he set to work on them. In a letter to a friend, he once described his method, or lack of it :

For some time I will have no impulse to compose at all. Then one evening I will be turning the leaves of a volume of poetry; a poem will strike my eye. I read it through; it agrees with the mood I am in; and at once the appropriate music is instinctively fitted to it. I am in a musical frame of mind, and all I want is the right poetic vessel into which to pour my ideas. If good luck throws this in my way, a satisfactory song results.*

'Instinctive' is the key word here. Strauss's feeling for words

* *Grove's Dictionary of Music and Musicians* (5th edition) Macmillan London 1954

was instinctive and untutored. Sometimes it led him to excellent poems, sometimes not; it hardly mattered. Where his sympathies were engaged, he was able to compose with spontaneous warmth. Where they were not, he could sound laboured and heavy.

Strauss's earliest published *Lieder* (except for juvenilia) are the *Eight Songs* op. 10 (1882–3) written for tenor voice, the poems from *Letzte Blätter* by Hermann von Gilm. The group begins with the best known of all Strauss *Lieder*, 'Zueignung', a rhapsodic expression of love which is a splendid romantic gesture of the kind that came easily to the composer. Not all of the eight songs are on this level; in fact, some of them—'Nichts', for instance, or 'Geduld'—make very little impression. But the general level of this first group is remarkably high. 'Die Nacht' is Strauss in his vein of quiet ecstasy; rich, even over-ripe in style, it is still hard to resist. 'Die Georgine', Gilm's poem to the dahlia, is a rather pleasant song, and unfairly neglected, but the real beauty of op. 10 is the final song, the popular "Allerseelen' in which the spirit set free by All Souls' Day addresses his still-living beloved. The poem is preposterous and touching, the music serious and full-blooded in feeling.

Of the *Five Songs* op. 15, the first is a setting of Michelangelo, while the other poems are by A. F. von Schack. The Michelangelo 'Madrigal' is solemn and impressive, but the first of the Schack songs, 'Winternacht' is disappointingly pedestrian. The other three all have something to commend them. 'Lob des Leidens' has that ardent fervour which redeems even the most turgid of Strauss's songs of love or contemplation of nature. The same could be said of 'Aus den Liedern der Trauer' though its musical material is less distinguished. The piano part is considerably more interesting than the voice line. 'Heimkehr' is the finest of these songs, a quiet and tender expression of relief at returning home to the beloved. In both these groups, op. 10 and op. 15, one is conscious that one is listening to a young and ardent voice. With the next group, op. 17, a certain maturity becomes evident. The development is a subtle one, for there is no loss of ardour or diminution of the sweeping romantic style where this is appropriate. Perhaps it is simply that Strauss is already beginning to think somewhat more carefully about the piano parts, and that, from op. 17 onwards, these are, if not necessarily more independent, at least more thoughtfully planned, and not mere duplications of what is being expressed vocally. The *Six Songs* op. 17 are all settings of von Schack.

It is easy to see why these largely mediocre verses appealed to Strauss, who was not particularly concerned with the problem of setting great poetry to music, as we have seen. All he required of a poem was that it should appeal to his temperament. The flowery romanticism and somewhat faded language of Schack were ideal for his purpose, and in op. 17 they have drawn from him four hits and only two misses. The first song, 'Seitdem dein Aug', which sounds like Strauss idly improvising, is one of the misses, but it is followed by the delightful 'Ständchen' in which the composer magically brings alive a romantic night, an assignation and a feeling of trembling ecstasy. The decorative piano accompaniment adds immeasurably to the effect of this splendid serenade. 'Das Geheimnis' is subtler, but no less full of feeling, and 'Aus den Liedern der Trauer' is much finer than the song of the same title in op. 15. For that matter, the poem is better too, simpler and more direct in expression. Two lovers are parted by death, and the living one concentrates his gaze on the twilit distance where he imagines his beloved calling him. 'I have gone on before you', she says. 'Why do you delay?' Of the two remaining songs, 'Nur Mut!' is grandiose but dull, and 'Barkarole' utterly charming in its evocation of a lover's feelings as he rows through the rippling water to his beloved's house.

The op. 19 songs are settings from Schack's volume, *Lotosblätter*, and are for the most part very much in the style of the previous group. 'Wozu noch, Mädchen' is the most successful, and 'Breit über mein Haupt' can also be effective in performance; the others, all competently constructed, seem rather lifeless, as though their composition had been a mere exercise, as perhaps it was. After op. 19, Strauss forsook Schack, and the five songs of op. 21, titled as a group *Schlichte Weisen*, are by Felix Dahn. 'All mein Gedanken' is fanciful but slight, and 'Du meines Herzens Krönelein' an attractive love song, but 'Ach, Lieb, ich muss nun scheiden' is unconvincing. In op. 21 generally, as in op. 19 and, for that matter, the following group of songs, op. 22, Strauss appears not only to be marking time but also to have lost his previously sure touch. Op. 21 no. 4, 'Ach, weh mir unglückhaftem Mann' though an effective character piece of its kind, owes much to Hugo Wolf, and in the final song of op. 21, 'Die Frauen sind oft fromm und still', Strauss hardly does justice to Dahn's touching little tribute to woman's spiritual qualities. *Mädchenblumen* op. 22 is a rather pleasant miniature cycle of four songs to Dahn's poems which compare girls to different types of flowers, the cornflower, the poppy, the ivy and the water-lily, but one has the feeling that the composer is embarrassed by the naïve sentimentality of the poems, and that he is pulling his romantic punches somewhat. The two songs of op. 26, to poems by Nikolaus Lenau, mark a return to a more confident manner. 'Frühlingsgedränge' is a rapturous welcome to spring, and the text of 'O wärst du mein' is a morbidly passionate outpouring of grief to which the composer's sombre music brings a certain nobility. Still in his twenties, Strauss produced, in the four songs of op. 27, four of his most popular songs. There is a tendency to denigrate the more popular Strauss songs, to refer to them as superior drawing-room music. In a sense, the whole of Schubert is superior drawing-room music, so the insult, if it is one, fails to strike home; but it is wrong to attempt to divide the *œuvre* of Strauss into difficult, worthy works, and popular, unworthy ones. Generally speaking, singers and audiences have had the taste to prefer the songs which are also the more successful in aesthetic terms. Of course, there are exceptions, cases of unaccountable neglect. But the four songs of op. 27 fully deserve their popularity. 'Ruhe, meine Seele' almost Wagnerian in the shape of its vocal line, and its feeling of size, is an impressively quiet description of fortitude and courage. Shortly before his eighty-fourth birthday Strauss was to return to this song, and orchestrate it. 'Cäcilie' is in the composer's finest vein of romantic ardour, and so is 'Heimliche Aufforderung' with its superb musical contrast of drunken chatterers and secret assignations. 'Morgen!' is simply a very beautiful song, its voice part stealing in, in melodic recitative, over the piano melody. The voice subsides, but the poem's mood of blissful anticipation is still carried on in the piano part.

It is interesting to note how Strauss avoided not only those poems already set by earlier composers of the *Lied* but also almost the whole of classical German poetry. Instead of continuing to set Goethe, Schiller, Heine, and Eichendorff to music, he made use of contemporary poets, three of them in the *Four Songs* op. 27. 'Ruhe, meine Seele' is by Karl Henckell (1864–1929), a young socialist and innovator in German poetry, born in the same year as Strauss. 'Cäcilie' is by Julius Hart, and the poems of 'Heimliche Aufforderung' and 'Morgen!' are by John Henry Mackay (1864–1933) who, like Henckell, was one of the leaders of the Naturalist revolt in German literature. Mackay was a Scotsman who was brought up in Germany and who wrote a number of novels in German, as well as poetry. Another contemporary poet, Otto Julius Bierbaum, provided the poems for the *Three Songs* op. 29. Bierbaum (1865–1910), poet and novelist, is remembered today mainly as the virtual founder of the intellectual and political cabarets of Germany. His poems are very much the German equivalent of the English aesthetic school of the nineties, a kind of verbal 'Jugendstil'. From the over-scented style of 'Traum durch die Dämmerung' Strauss has fashioned one of his most gently erotic love songs. 'Schlagende Herzen' is a rather tiresome poem, and its coyness has under-standably infiltrated into Strauss's music for it. In mood and style 'Nachtgang' is not unlike 'Morgen!'; 19th-century romanticism at its finest.

Two more modern poets are introduced in the four songs of op. 31, written in 1895–6 : Carl Busse and Richard Dehmel. The more important of the two, Dehmel (1863–1920), was one of the 'Jugendstil' poets whose twin themes were social protest and love. The rich harmonies of Strauss's setting of 'Blauer Sommer' (Busse) make this the most attractive song of the four. The other two Busse settings are less successful. 'Wenn' sounds artificial and self-consciously archaic, as though Strauss were consciously imitating Brahms, and 'Weisser Jasmin' is oddly characterless. Dehmel's 'Stiller Gang', an interesting, impression-istic little lyric, becomes a little too explicit, over-stated in Strauss's otherwise clever setting, with viola obbligato. The five songs of op. 32 include three settings of Karl Henckell, one of Detlev von Liliencron (1844–1909), and one from Brentano and von Arnim's *Des Knaben Wunderhorn*. 'Ich trage meine Minne' (Henckell) is one of Strauss's finest love songs, but the other op. 32 songs have not worn well. The *Knaben Wunderhorn* setting, 'Himmelsboten zu Liebchens Himmelbett' is the most enjoyable of them. 'Liebeshymnus' is hefty rather than rhapsodic, 'Sehnsucht' uneven, though with a fine conclusion, and 'O süsser Mai' disappointingly conventional in expression, though not unpleasing. Op. 36 consists of four songs, the first of which is an exception to Strauss's unwritten rule to avoid poems already successfully set. It is Klopstock's 'Das Rosenband', and no rival to Schubert's enchanting song, though quite attractive in its heavier, late romantic manner. It is followed by two charming *Wunderhorn* settings, 'Für fünfzehn Pfennige' and 'Hat gesagt —bleibt's nicht dabei', both sounding rather too like a melodic-ally more generous Wolf, and a setting of Rückert's 'Anbetung' which is really more contrived than inspired. The six songs of op. 37 are perhaps not first-rate Strauss, but most of them are immensely enjoyable. 'Glückes genug' (poem by von Liliencron) makes up in tenderness what it may lack in originality; the poem of 'Ich liebe dich', also by von Liliencron, is a violently aggressive expression of love, and Strauss has set it accordingly, with a great deal of swagger and romantic gesture; 'Meinem Kinde' (Gustav Falke) is a touching cradle song of great beauty, 'Mein Auge' (Dehmel) sensitive and appealing, 'Herr Lenz' (Emanual von Bodmann) an ebullient outburst in praise of spring, and the Viennese poet Anton Lindner's 'Hochzeitlich Lied' gets no better a setting than it deserves.

Four of the five songs of op. 39 are settings of Richard Dehmel. 'Lieses Lied', one of the unfairly neglected songs, is a lyrical gem, and 'Der Arbeitsmann', one of Dehmel's poems of protest in which the worker complains of his lack of leisure time, is given dramatic though perhaps somewhat superficial treatment by Strauss. This is, in its way, a remarkable song, but one can imagine what Mahler would have made of Dehmel's poem. 'Befreit' is addressed by a husband to his dying wife. Dehmel's poem avoids being mawkish, and Strauss has given it music of great tenderness and beauty. This is one of a handful of Strauss *Lieder* worthy to rank with Schubert, Schumann or Brahms. 'Lied an meinen Sohn' is a dramatic ballad of much sound and fury, and the non-Dehmel setting, Bierbaum's 'Junghexenlied' is negligible, though no doubt as exhilarating for its pianist as is 'Lied an meinen Sohn'. There are two Dehmel songs among the five of op. 41; the charming and melodious 'Wiegenlied' and the beautiful though static 'Am Ufer'. The setting of Mackay's 'In der Campagna' is loud and inflated, and both poem (von Liliencron) and music of 'Bruder Liederlich' are boring and boorish. The last of the group, 'Leise Lieder' (poem by Christian Morgenstern), is in Strauss's yearning vein, but somewhat sub-standard. 'Muttertändelei' (Bürger) is the best of the three songs of op. 43. The others are 'An Sie', a dull setting of Klopstock, and Ludwig Uhland's 'Die Ulme zu Hirsau' which is Strauss at his most pedestrian.

Poems by Rückert were used for the *Five Songs* op. 46, which are pleasant though hardly important; the *Five Songs* op. 47, to Uhland poems, however, contain more interesting things. The second, 'Des Dichters Abendgang', explores that vein of rich romantic ecstasy which Strauss was to remain so adept at mining right up until the time of the *Vier Letzte Lieder* of 1948. Op. 47 dates from the beginning of the century, but Strauss's musical language altered very little across the years. The 'stiller Rührung' of Uhland's poem continued to come easily to him. If he is uneasy with the sickly imagery of Uhland's 'Rückleben' op. 47 no. 3, and falls back on his more conventional manner, this speaks well for his taste. 'Einkehr' is attractive, and so is 'Von den sieben Zechbrüdern', though this moral tale of the seven drunkards who hated the sight of water almost outstays its welcome. Of the five excellent songs of op. 48, the first is a setting of Bierbaum, and the others of Karl Henckell. The Bierbaum is the famous 'Freundliche Vision', a masterpiece of romantic song, and the Henckell songs are hardly less magnificent, though less often performed: the delicate 'Ich schwebe', the exultant 'Kling!' spoilt only by a somewhat over-emphatic conclusion, the gently touching 'Winterweihe', and the rapturous 'Winterliebe'.

The eight songs of op. 49, by various poets, include 'Waldseligkeit', a serenely beautiful setting of Dehmel that bears comparison with Brahms's 'Feldeinmaskeit', the politically conscious 'Lied des Steinklepfers' of Karl Henckell, and the charming 'Sie wissen's nicht' (poem by Oscar Panizza). Then, after almost twenty years, each of which had produced its crop of songs, Strauss, no doubt preoccupied with the 'Symphonia domestica' and other large-scale projects, wrote no songs for three or four years. When he returned to the genre in 1904 and the immediately following years, it was with settings of Goethe, Heine and Conrad Ferdinand Meyer as well as of his own contemporary Henckell. The *Six Songs* op. 56 begin with Goethe's 'Gefunden' in a rather colourless setting, and continue with Henckell's 'Blindenklage', a blind man's lament, turned by Strauss into extremely dull music. But the third song, 'Im Spätboot', is absolutely magnificent, and its neglect by singers is difficult to understand. The poem by Conrad Ferdinand Meyer (1825–1898) is a strange, original piece, and Strauss's music an industrial-age equivalent of Schubert's 'Meeresstille'. His setting of Heine's 'Mit deinen blauen Auge' has both sweetness and strength, and the remaining two Heine poems also make interesting songs—'Frühlingsfeier' and 'Die heiligen drei Könige'.

A gap of several years separates op. 56 from Strauss's next group of songs, the cycle *Krämerspiegel* op. 66, composed in 1918. These twelve pieces are almost valueless as songs, having been composed by Strauss in a state of fury with his publishers after a copyright dispute. The clumsily punning poems were written for the composer by the Berlin music critic Alfred Kerr, with copious references to Strauss's publishers Bote und Bock ('Bote'—'messenger' and 'Bock'—'goat') and most other German publishers as well. 'Einst kam der Bock als Bote/Zum Rosen-kavalier an's Haus' ('The goat once came as a messenger to the house of the Rose Cavalier') is the opening line of the second song, which wittily continues 'O Botenbock, zieh mit gesenktem Sterz hinterwärts'. ('O goat messenger, back out with your tail lowered'.) There is a beautifully lyrical piano interlude which has little connection with the surrounding mood, but which turns up again in the finale of the opera *Capriccio* in 1942. In fact, the piano music throughout the cycle is considerably more interesting than the word-setting.

Op. 67 consists of three settings of Ophelia's songs from Shakespeare's *Hamlet*, which are neither particularly interesting as music nor suitable for Ophelia, and three of Goethe's difficult *Westöstlicher Divan* poems, in which Strauss is certainly interesting if not very spontaneous. Op. 68 reveals a welcome return to the romantic style, with six songs to poems by Clemens Brentano (one of the *Des Knaben Wunderhorn* editors). Though these magnificent songs are not a cycle, they make a splendid effect when sung together, preferably by a lyric coloratura. They were dedicated to Elisabeth Schumann. The first song, 'An die Nacht,' sets the mood of romantic *Sehnsucht* beautifully, both with its soaring arioso line, somewhat in the style of Strauss's *Frau ohne Schatten* music, and with the suavity of its gesture. 'Ich wollt' ein Sträusslein binden' makes demands on the soprano's flexibility, and sometimes rather arbitrary-sounding demands. It is the least successful song of the group. The melodic rambling of 'Säusle, liebe Myrte', now forging ahead, now sinuous, is highly engaging throughout, but the emotional and musical climax of these songs when performed as a group is no. 4, 'Als mir dein Lied erklang', a magnificent, ecstatic out-burst of romantic longing, with an elaborate accompaniment. 'Amor' is light, gay and written as though for a Zerbinetta, while 'Lied der Frauen', the final song and the longest, makes an inspired and exciting conclusion, its poem a tribute to women whose men risk their lives in battle.

The *Fünf kleine Lieder* op. 69, settings of Brentano's co-editor Achim von Arnim and Heine, are pleasant, if nothing more.

Only one of them, 'Schlechtes Wetter', has retained a place in the recital repertoire, though the charming 'Einerlei' is occasionally heard. 'Waldesfahrt' is Heine's 'Mein Wagen rollet langsam' in a rather fussy setting.

Ten years passed before Strauss composed his next songs, in 1929. These are the five *Gesänge des Orients*, translations by Hans Bethge from Chinese and Persian, in which Strauss's language sounds tired, almost played out.

The four songs posthumously published as op. 87 date from 1922 (no. 2) and the early 1930s. No. 2 is Goethe's 'Erschaffen und Beleben'; the other three are Rückert settings, the finest of which, no. 4, 'Im Sonnenschein', is vintage Strauss. The three songs of op. 88 consist of 'Das Bächlein', composed in 1933 and dedicated to Dr Goebbels, and two settings of the Austrian poet Josef Weinheber, written for Weinheber's fiftieth birthday in 1942.

Strauss made orchestral versions of a number of his song accompaniments, and also wrote several songs for voice and orchestra, the best-known among them being 'Hymnus' from near the beginning of his career, and the *Four Last Songs*, poems by Eichendorff and Hesse, which ended it with a magnificent and elegiac nostalgia.

Of Strauss's younger contemporaries who made important contributions to the *Lied*, the names of five stand out : Pfitzner, Reger, Marx, Wellesz and Hindemith. Hans Pfitzner (1869–1949) composed more than 100 songs, romantic in style, to texts largely drawn from the 19th-century German poets. Though several of the songs are enjoyable to perform or to hear, their language is insufficiently personal to Pfitzner for them to make any real impact. Max Reger (1873–1916) composed well over 250 songs to texts of the usual German poets. The majority of these, distinctly Brahmsian in style, exhibit a fluent yet hardly memorable melodic gift, and on the occasions when he tackled poems which had already been set by his predecessor, Strauss, he invariably came off second best, for instance in 'Traum durch die Dämmerung', and 'Morgen!'. The best known of Reger's songs is the simple, tuneful 'Mariä Wiegenlied'. The songs of the Austrian, Joseph Marx (1882–1964) owe little to Brahms, but a great deal to Hugo Wolf. While around him the new Viennese school of Schoenberg, Berg and Webern were extending the language of music, Marx, like Strauss, remained firmly within traditional tonality. Few of his songs, which number more than a hundred, are heard nowadays outside Austria. The songs of the Viennese, Egon Wellesz (b. 1885) are fewer. Since the Austrian Anschluss he has lived in England, so it is not surprising that his more recent songs are to English texts. Paul Hindemith (1895–1963) in his songs also ranged beyond the confines of German poetry to produce settings in their original languages of Shelley, Blake, Keats, Rimbaud and Baudelaire. His cycle *Das Marienleben* (poems by Rilke), composed in 1924, is enjoyable music to listen to, though it lacks the imprint of a strong personality. Boris Blacher (b. 1903), one of the most original talents of his generation, has written very few songs. His *Fünf Sinnsprüche aus dem Persischen* op. 3 are effective, and lie well for the medium voice. The main stream of German song in the first half of the 20th century was the atonal stream, and this survey of the German *Lied* will most appropriately end with a glance at the songs of the three leading composers of the second Viennese school, Schoenberg, Berg and Webern.

Arnold Schoenberg (1874–1951), it should be remembered, composed a great deal of music in the traditional manner before his break with tonality and his experiments with the twelve-note system. Though his earliest songs pre-date his atonal period by several years, they are nevertheless the products of a fully developed musical personality. His earliest published works are the songs of ops. 1, 2 and 3. Op. 1 consists of two songs for baritone voice, to poems by Karl von Levetzov. The voice parts of these two songs, 'Dank' and 'Abschied', are not unlike Wolf, but Schoenberg's individuality reveals itself in the piano accompaniments which are of a remarkable polyphonic richness, almost orchestral in effect. These, and the songs of op. 2 and op. 3 were written by Schoenberg in his mid-twenties. Between op. 1 and op. 2, however, there is already evidence of further musical development, for the accompaniments to op. 2 are more pianistic in style, and there is no trace of rhetoric either here or in the voice parts. The first of the four songs of op. 2 is 'Erwartung' (poem by Richard Dehmel), still somewhat reminiscent of Wolf, but put together with a concision and deliberation which anticipate the later Schoenberg. The second song, 'Schenk' mir deinen goldenen Kamm', the text again by Dehmel, is tender in feeling, its voice part natural, simple and affecting. The remaining two songs, 'Erhebung' (Dehmel) and 'Waldsonne' (poem by Johannes Schlaf), are melodically and harmonically simpler, though no less attractive.

Op. 3 consists of six songs, with texts from various sources. The first, 'Wie Georg von Frundsberg von sich selber sang', based on one of the *Knaben Wunderhorn* poems, is immensely powerful in expression, and the second, a setting of Gottfried Keller's 'Die Aufgeregten', is a pleasant little nature-piece. 'Warnung', written to a poem by Dehmel, is a dramatic song of great energy and passion, 'Hochzeitslied' (poem by Jens Peter Jacobsen) and 'Freihold' (Hermann Lingg) are the least interesting of the group, and Gottfried Keller's 'Geübtes Herz' the most sheerly beautiful.

It was five years later when Schoenberg's next group of solo songs appeared, five years which saw the composition of such major works as the String Sextet, *Verklärte Nacht*, inspired by a poem by Dehmel, and the huge *Gurrelieder* for solo voices, chorus and orchestra. The *Eight Songs for voice and piano* op. 6 were, in fact, preceded by *Six Orchestral Songs* op. 8. Apart from the orchestral colour, there are no essential differences between these warm and romantic songs and those with piano accompaniment. The most interesting, harmonically and melodically, of the op. 6 songs is 'Traumleben' (poem by Julius Hart) but, indeed, all the songs in this set are remarkable for the close accord between voice and piano, and for the imaginative and poetic manner in which the piano is used to convey the mood and intention of the poems. The finest of the songs are the delicate 'Alles' (Dehmel), the mysterious 'Lockung' (Kurt Aram) and the final song, whose poem is 'Der Wanderer' by Friedrich Nietzsche. As Egon Wellesz wrote, fifty years ago:

> [These] songs are among the most compact and the most unified that were produced on the lines of development from Schumann through Wolf. Written with the means at a composer's disposal in the first decade of the twentieth century, they surpass everything that has been created on these lines, through their logically developed musical ideas and through the personality that is behind every note.*

When these songs were first performed in Vienna, audience reaction was predominantly hostile, and there were violent demonstrations both for and against the composer, who himself later observed: "Since then, the scandal has never ceased.' It is with the three pianoforte pieces of op. 11, in 1908, that Schoenberg

* Egon Wellesz *Arnold Schoenberg* J. M. Dent London 1925

made his break with tonality, thus banishing the concept
of dissonance from the western musical world. Immediately prior
to this, he had pushed the harmonic implications of tonality as
far as they could be extended, in the two ballads of op. 12,
'Jane Grey' (poem by Heinrich Ammann) and 'Der verlorene
Haufen' (Victor Klemperer). A bridge between these and the
first songs in Schoenberg's new atonal manner are the two songs
of op. 14, 'Ich darf nicht dankend' (poem by Stefan George)
and 'In diesen Wintertagen' (Georg Henckell). The first atonal
songs are the fifteen which make up the cycle of poems from
Stefan George's *Das Buch der hängenden Gärten*. In these songs,
the piano is no longer an accompanying instrument as in the
19th-century songs of Schubert, Brahms and Wolf, or even as
in the earlier songs of Schoenberg himself, but pursues an entirely
independent course. In an essay which appeared in the periodical
Der Blaue Reiter in 1912, the composer attempted to describe
how he arrived at the method by which he set George's poems
to music. He had found that, inspired by the opening words of
a poem, he would embark upon a setting without giving any
further thought to the sense of the words of the rest of the poem.
'Then', he wrote,

> to my greatest astonishment I discovered that I was never
> more faithful to the poet than when, led as it were by the
> first contact with the opening sounds, I felt instinctively that
> all must necessarily follow from these initial sounds. Then it
> became clear to me that it is with a work of art as with every
> perfect organism. It is so homogeneous in its constitution that it
> discloses in detail its truest and inmost being. Thus I came to
> a full understanding of the Schubert songs, together with the
> poetry, from the music alone; and of Stefan George's poems
> from their sounds alone; and this with a perfection that could
> hardly be attained by analysis and synthesis, and which in
> any case could not be surpassed.*

Whether or not one is prepared to accept Schoenberg's conten-
tion, one has to admit the beauty and aptness of the songs from
Das Buch der hängenden Gärten. Of them, the composer himself
said, 'With the op. 15 songs, I have succeeded for the first time
in approaching an ideal of form and expression which has
hovered before me for years. ... I am conscious of having

* *Der Blaue Reiter* Munich 1912

removed all the traces of a past aesthetic.'* It was a quarter of a century before he was to return to composition for solo voice and piano, with three songs (op. 48) to poems by Jakob Haringer. Schoenberg no doubt considered he had said the last word about song in the George settings.

Alban Berg (1885–1935), Schoenberg's pupil, is one of the strongest creative musical personalities of the first half of this century. To offer the encapsulated opinion that he was a greater composer than his teacher is hardly useful in this context. Certainly it is true that his music is easier to assimilate than Schoenberg's. His masterpieces are the operas *Wozzeck* and *Lulu*, the Violin Concerto and the Lyric Suite for String Quartet. He was not a prolific writer of songs, and his most highly regarded songs are the *Altenberg Lieder*, five songs with orchestral accompaniment, to picture-postcard texts by the Viennese prose-poet Peter Altenberg (1862–1919). Berg's works for solo voice and piano begin and end with settings of 'Schliesse mir die Augen beide' by Theodor Storm. Berg's first setting of this poem was composed in 1907. Actually, before this time, Berg had already written ninety songs, thirty-five of them between 1901 and 1904, the year in which he became Schoenberg's pupil, and the remainder between 1904 and 1908 during the period he was studying with Schoenberg. He chose neithei to publish nor acknowledge them, naming the Piano Sonata composed during the years 1906 to 1908 as his op. 1. Of the songs written under Schoenberg's tutelage, Berg selected seven which he grouped together later as *Seven Early Songs*, and whose piano accompaniments he orchestrated in 1928. These settings of seven poets reveal that in those years under Schoenberg, Berg's musical style had not severed its close connections with the world of Schumann and Brahms. More modern in feeling and technique, though still direct in their emotional impact, are the *Four Songs* op. 2, to texts of Friedrich Hebbel and Alfred Mombert (1872–1942). In 1925, Berg again set Storm's 'Schliessen mir die Augen beide', and thereafter turned his back on the *Lied*.

The least accessible of the three geniuses of the second Viennese school is Anton von Webern (1883–1945). The angular shape and extremely difficult intervals of his vocal line combined with the general concision and economy of his style have militated against his songs finding favour with the general musical public.

* H. H. Stuckenschmidt *Arnold Schoenberg* John Calder London 1959

It takes a Webern expert to discern and identify melody in the isolated notes of his songs, though he is respected as a musical innovator of a high order. He composed several groups of songs for solo voice and small instrumental ensemble, and four sets of songs for voice and piano. The first of these is the op. 3 set of five songs from Stefan George's *Der siebente Ring*, written in 1909; it is also the first of Webern's atonal compositions. In the same year he completed the five songs of op. 4, again to texts by George; their similarity to the style of Schoenberg's George settings, *Das Buch der hängenden Gärten*, is clearly noticeable. In the years 1915 to 1917, Webern produced his third group for voice and piano, *Four Songs* op. 12, to texts from Bethge's translations of Li-Tai-Po, from Strindberg's *Ghost Sonata*, and the Goethe lyric 'Gleich und gleich' of which Wolf had made an exquisite setting. These op. 12 songs are closer to traditional melody than the earlier groups, with greater development of the vocal line than one normally associates with Webern. It is of these songs that his colleague Alban Berg wrote to Webern : 'A song of yours is a bringer of joy to me, a bringer of joy which irradiates my whole being. As when on dull days the sun suddenly breaks through and one doesn't know why one is suddenly happy.'*

Webern's last two groups of songs, *Three Songs from 'Viae Inviae'* op. 23 and *Three Songs* op. 25, are settings of poems by the Viennese poet and painter, Hildegard Jone, a life-long friend of Webern. Composed in the middle 1930s, they are among the more intractable of his vocal compositions. If this is to take too unsympathetic a view of a difficult artist, the words of the 20th-century's greatest composer should perhaps be placed here as a corrective : in 1955, ten years after Webern's death, Stravinsky wrote of him : 'We must hail not only this great composer but a real hero. Doomed to a total failure in a deaf world of indifference and ignorance, he inexorably kept on cutting out his diamonds, his dazzling diamonds, of whose mines he had such a perfect knowledge.'†

* Willi Reich *Alban Berg* Herbert Reichner Verlag Vienna 1937
† Igor Stravinsky and Robert Craft *Conversations with Igor Stravinsky* Faber & Faber London 1959

II

FRANCE

SOLO SONG WAS slow to develop in France during the
18th century. The hundred or so romances of Jean-Jacques
Rousseau (1712–1778), so popular in their day, are now completely unknown; and, although one or two celebrated French
recitalists of our own time, most notably the baritone Gérard
souzay, have included French airs of the 18th century and earlier
in their programmes, there is no individual composer whose
music can be said to be familiar to modern audiences, with the
exception of the German, Schwartzendorf (1741–1816), who
changed his name to Giovanni Martini, made his career in
France, and is remembered today for one charming and plaintive
song, 'Plaisir d'amour'. In the 19th century, the earliest composers of merit are Louis Niedermeyer (1802–1861) and
Hippolyte Monpou (1804–1841). Niedermeyer's reputation rests
almost entirely upon one song, 'Le Lac', his setting of a poem
by Lamartine, although he wrote a number of other songs which
are equally attractive, among them 'L'Automne', 'La Voix
humaine' and 'Le Cinq Mai'. Saint-Saëns was later to write of
him: 'Niedermeyer was above all a precursor. He was the first
to break the mould of the antiquated and insipid French
romance; taking his inspiration from the beautiful poems of
Lamartine and Victor Hugo, he created a new type of song of
a superior artistry, analagous to the German *Lied*. The resound-
ing success of "Le Lac" paved the way for Gounod and all those
who followed this path.'*

Like Niedermeyer, Monpou was equally attracted by texts
from the romantic poets, in particular Victor Hugo and Alfred
de Musset. His setting of de Musset's 'L'Andalouse' in 1830
brought him immediate success, and many of his other songs

* In Preface to *Vie d'un compositeur moderne* by Baron Lovig Alfred
Niedermeyer (Paris, 1893)

also exploit the exotic colouring of the Iberian peninsula. Monpou's chief asset was his melodic gift, for in other aspects of his art his technique verged on the primitive.

Although they are completely neglected today, it is worth remembering that the songs of the German-born composer of opera, Giacomo Meyerbeer (1791–1864), who virtually invented Parisian 19th-century grand opera, were greatly admired in the Paris of the 1830s. The majority of Meyerbeer's songs were written before the première, in 1836, of his opera *Les Huguenots*. They include lyrical romances, religious songs, lighter salon pieces, quasi folk songs, and understandably hybrid French language equivalents of the German *Lied*. Meyerbeer also composed songs to German and Italian texts; indeed the vocal style of most of his French songs is Italianate, as was much of his juvenilia. This musical dramatist was not really in his element in the lyrical world of song, though it is probably true to say that his public success encouraged and influenced certain later French composers.

The important period of French song begins with Hector Berlioz (1803–1869). Though his primary interest was in larger-scale work, Berlioz composed songs at the beginning of his career, and continued to do so until 1850. The earliest song of his that is known to us is 'Le Dépit de la bergère', written around 1825 and published by the composer at his own expense. Neither in it, nor in 'Toi qui l'aimais, verse des pleurs' and 'Le Maure jaloux' which followed shortly afterwards, can one discern any trace of the individuality which Berlioz was soon to develop. A mere four years later, however, he produced *Irlande*, a collection of five songs, settings of French translations of Thomas Moore : 'La Belle Voyageuse' a simple but charming little melody, 'Le Coucher du soleil' rather more interesting, 'L'Origine de la harpe' typically Berlioz at least in its eccentricity, 'Adieu, Bessy' a fascinating song which the composer re-wrote twenty years later, and the curious 'Elégie'. 'Elégie', which Berlioz prefaced with an account of the execution of Robert Emmet in 1803, an event which inspired Moore to write the poem, is a song which obviously meant a great deal to the composer, who wrote it in a state of intense emotion. Viewed objectively, the song appears overwrought and pretentious. Yet, in his *Memoirs*, Berlioz speaks of it with pride and affection. He has been describing his habit of wandering aimlessly about Paris, and continues :

It was on my return from one of these wanderings (during which I looked like a man searching for his soul) that I came upon my copy of Moore's *Irish Melodies* lying open on the table at the poem which begins 'When he who adores thee' and, taking up my pen, wrote the music to that heartrending farewell straight off.... This is the sole occasion on which I was able to express a feeling of the sort directly in music while still under its active influence. But I think I have rarely found a melody of such truth and poignancy, steeped in such a surge of sombre harmony.*

He points out that the French translation is so close to Moore's English that he was later able to fit the English words to his tune, and prophesies that the English and Germans will respond sympathetically to it, though the French will find it incomprehensible and the Italians nonsensical.

Two early songs, 'Le Pêcheur' and 'Chant du bonheur' were later revised and used in *Lélio*, the sequel to the 'Symphonie fantastique', and several of the *Irlande* songs were in due course provided with orchestral accompaniments. One of Berlioz's defects as a song-writer, indeed, was that he had virtually no feeling for the piano, for which he therefore tended to write dully. In the early 1830s, he composed several more songs, some of which are among his best. 'Le Jeune Pâtre breton' is a pleasant little melody with a horn obbligato part, and 'La Captive' (poem by Victor Hugo), which went through several versions and revisions, emerged as a remarkably fine song, its melody highly expressive, its accompaniment livelier and more meaningful than any that Berlioz had previously composed. Two other songs of this period, 'Les Champs' (poem by Béranger) and 'Je crois en vous', are charming, innocuous pieces, but much more important is the cycle or collection of six songs to poems of Théophile Gautier, *Nuits d'été*. 'Absence' is perhaps the most perfectly beautiful and unspoiled piece of music ever written by Berlioz, a song of poised melancholy whose graceful lines have a marvellous simplicity and spontaneity rare in this composer. 'Villanelle', too, is an exquisite song with a flowing melody of great delicacy and charm. The other four songs of the *Nuits d'été* are almost equally impressive, 'Sur les lagunes' a remarkable expression of despair, 'Au cimitière' elegant and melancholy, and 'Le Spectre

* David Cairns (ed.) *The Memoirs of Hector Berlioz* Victor Gollancz London 1969

de la rose' and 'L'Ile inconnue' both poetic and accomplished,
the former a remarkable transformation of Gautier's highly
mannered poem.

The remaining few Berlioz songs are of lesser interest. 'La
Belle Isabeau', written in 1844, is extremely dull, and 'Le
Chasseur danois' and 'Zaïde' of 1845 are hardly less so. 'La
Mort d'Ophélie', after Shakespeare, was later turned into a
chorus for female voices and orchestra, in which form it is even
less effective than it was as a solo song. 'Le Matin' and 'Petit
Oiseau' are pleasant if unmemorable.

The modestly talented Henri Reber (1807–1880), not even a
name today, enjoyed a certain vogue in his own lifetime with
his urbane, elegant *mélodies*, literate, classically balanced, though
lacking any strongly defined character. His contemporary, the
critic Ernest Legouvé, wrote of him : 'Reber is not of this age . . .
his music has the strangeness of works from another period; he
is the contemporary of Haydn, the Boccherini of our day.'* The
sixty songs of Reber's contemporary Félicien David (1810–1876)
sound today like pallid imitations of Schubert's weaker pages,
though they were admired in their time.

French song, or *mélodie*, which is the word generally used as
the French equivalent of the German *Lied*, developed during
the 19th-century, not along lines laid down by Berlioz, who was
too original a genius to found a school or to influence followers,
but in the direction pointed to by the songs of Charles Gounod
(1818–1893). Although Gounod is remembered today only for
his operas, and then only for two—*Faust* and *Roméo et Juliette*
—of the twelve that were produced during his lifetime, he was
also a prolific composer of church music, oratorios and songs.
Comparatively few of his 150 or more songs are performed today,
but the lyrical charm of the best of them is still fresh, and can
be heard echoed in the songs of such later 19th-century French
composers as Bizet and Chabrier. Gounod was an admirer of
Schumann's music, and it was through him that the influence
of Schumann's gentle and lyrical songs spread to the younger
French composers. Gounod's first songs, settings of Lamartine's
'Le Vallon' and 'Le Soir', were written when he was twenty-two,
after which time he produced no more songs for at last fifteen
years. His religious songs, of which there are many, strike us today
as being both over-sentimental and sanctimonious, though the
popular 'Ave Maria' of 1892, a meditation on the second prelude

* *La France Musicale* Paris 26 March 1843

of Bach, has certainly proved durable. An earlier 'Ave Maria' (1877) is musically more attractive. But his secular lyrical songs represent Gounod at his best. Their qualities of purity, expressive charm and melodic sweetness are emphasized by the sober yet penetrating harmonies of the accompaniments. Such songs as 'Sérénade' (1855: poem by Victor Hugo), 'Au printemps' (1865: Jules Barbier), 'Medjé' (1865: Jules Barbier) and 'Ce que je suis sans toi' (1882: de Peyre) have retained their appeal today. Gounod's few Italian and many English songs have fared less well, though some of his settings of English poets are splendidly authentic Victorian songs, and ripe for revival. The most successful of them are 'Goodnight' (1871: Shelley), 'The Worker' (1873: Frederick Weatherly), and a boating song, 'Gliding down the river', composed in 1888 to words by H. B. Farnie.

By comparison with Gounod, the songs of César Franck (1822–1890) are extremely sparse in number: there are only sixteen of them. The earliest ones, such as 'Souvenance' (Chateaubriand), 'L'Emir de Bengadar' (Joseph Méry) and 'L'Ange et l'enfant' (Jean Reboul), are negligible, and a patriotic song, 'Les trois exilés', whose poem is by Colonel Bernard Delfosse, though popular when it was published in 1848, is banal in the extreme. After this, the remaining few songs of Franck are better, though nowhere near as good as the sensitive and poetic works which his pupils Chausson and Duparc were to produce. 'Le Mariage des roses' (poem by Eugène David) and two Hugo settings, 'Passez toujours' and 'Roses et papillons', are particularly attractive, and 'Nocturne' (poem by Louis de Fourcaud) is quite beautiful, with its broad melody and imaginative accompaniment. 'La Procession', Franck's most famous song, written in 1888, is a piece of religious pomp for voice and orchestra.

Camille Saint-Saëns deserves mention here as an important composer who produced a number of songs, in fact more than 100, though there is little among these settings of Hugo, Lemaire and other French poets that is at all memorable. 'Danse macabre', in its original form a song with words by Henri Cazalis, was turned into a symphonic poem by its composer, though it is by no means ineffective as a song. 'La Sérénité (Marie Barbier), 'Rêverie' (Hugo) and 'Uncle flûte invisible' (Hugo) have a certain faded charm. The unseen flute of the last named song is not unheard: it alternates with the voice part.

The songs of Georges Bizet (1838–1875) have much in common with those of Gounod, but they have, in addition, a greater range and passion, as well as personality of their own. Most of them were composed before Bizet reached the age of thirty. The earliest two date from the composer's mid teens. They are 'Petite Marguerite' and 'La Rose et l'Abeille', both hardly distinguishable from the sweet melodic style of Gounod, but undeniably pretty. The poems by Olivier Rolland which Bizet originally set are mediocre, and when the songs were re-published in 1888 they were given new words by Armand Silvestre. 'Vieille Chanson', words by Millevoye, and 'Après l'hiver' (Hugo) are both delightful, but the finest of the songs composed in 1866 is undoubtedly 'Adieux de l'hôtesse arabe' sung by an Arab girl whose lover has deserted her. This exotic, harmonically adventurous and passionate setting of a poem by Hugo is as fine as anything in *Carmen*. 'Chanson d'avril' is gay and attractive, and the songs of this year are completed by a set of six *Feuilles d'album*, settings of six poets, among them Alfred de Musset and Pierre de Ronsard as well as the ubiquitous Victor Hugo. All six are excellent songs, their melodies fresh and appealing, though not always sensitively fitted to the words; their accompaniments are perhaps less happily contrived. 'A une fleur' is an exquisite setting of de Musset, and the other de Musset song, 'Adieux à Suzon', is even better, the ambiguous mood of the poem perfectly caught. Ronsard's 'Sonnet' is first-rate, 'Guitar' is in the bolero rhythm to which Bizet always responded happily, and 'Rose d'amour' (Millevoye) and 'Le Grillon' (Lamartine), though hardly of strong character, are both delightful, undemanding songs. In 1867 Bizet appears to have written no original songs, but merely to have provided unexceptionable accompaniments for six folk songs, *Chants des Pyrénées*. The following year, he produced his last songs. Although they include nothing as fine as 'Adieux de l'hôtesse arabe' there are several notably successful pieces among them, including 'Pastorale' (Regnard), 'Ma vie a son secret' (Félix Arvers) and 'Absence' (Théophile Gautier). 'Berceuse' (words by Marceline Desbordes-Valmore) is interesting in that its accompaniment is based on a folk tune which was later to be used both by Fauré in his *Dolly Suite* and by Debussy in *Jardins sous la pluie*. It is also a very pleasant song. 'Vous ne priez pas' (Casimir Delavigne) has an unexpected passion, and 'Aubade' a unique charm. One is left with the impression that Bizet could have contributed more significantly to the song repertoire had he worked at it. But, to him, songs were a mere by-product of opera.

Another composer who, under different circumstances, might have become a major figure in the world of French *mélodie* is Emmanuel Chabrier (1841–1894), whose gifts for characterization and caricature were employed in a mere handful of songs. Apart from two early unpublished settings of Baudelaire ('L'Invitation au voyage') and Hugo ('Sommation irrespectueuse'), and three undistinguished songs published in the 1880s—'Tes yeux bleus' (Maurice Rollinat), 'Credo d'amour' (Armand Silvestre) and 'Chanson pour Jeanne' (Catulle Mendès)—his entire output is virtually contained in *Six Mélodies* (1890), in which he set to music the farmyard sketches of Edmund Rostand and Rosemonde Gérard, and produced songs in which the chirping of cicadas, the quacking of ducks, the snorting of pigs and the throaty gurglings of turkeys are translated into amusing musical terms; 'Villanelle des petits canards', 'Ballade des gros dindons', 'Pastorale des cochons roses' and 'Les cigales' are, however, also not without lyrical charm. The set of six songs was completed by the graceful 'Ile heureuse' (poem by Ephraim Mikhaël) and 'Toutes les fleurs' (Rostand), less quirkily individual songs, the latter of which Chabrier himself referred to, not unfairly, as 'd'un baveux de salon irrésistible'.* The farmyard pieces in *Six Mélodies*, however, are superb comical sketches, compounded of humour, irony, and acute observation. The 'Ballade des gros dindons' mysteriously quotes from 'Deh! vieni alla finestra' in Mozart's *Don Giovanni*. Ravel surely had these songs of Chabrier in mind when he composed his own *Histoires naturelles* sixteen years later.

Jules Massenet (1842–1912) composed a number of songs some of which are quite charming but of no great individuality. A minor contemporary of Massenet, Emile Paladilhe (1844–1926) also composed pleasant, graceful songs. In his lifetime, 'La mandolinata', from his one-act opera, *Le Passant*, attained great popularity, but he is barely remembered today, and that only because of Maggie Teyte's championing of the charming love song, 'Psyché'. ('Je suis jaloux, Psyché, de toute la nature.')

In the person of Gabriel Fauré (1845–1924), France's long-delayed answer to Schubert arrived upon the musical scene. Fauré's art is intimate; his voice is not loud or assertive. Even

* G. Servières *Emmanuel Chabrier* Paris 1912

in his comparatively large-scale works such as the *Requiem*,
scored for two soloists, chorus, organ and orchestra, he never
strives for effects of massive sound. The mood of the *Requiem*,
his major masterpiece, a gentle resignation transformed into
serenity, is one that pervades many of his smaller compositions
as well. The prevailing qualities of his songs are tenderness,
grace, *douceur*. Unlike most of his predecessors in the field of
French song, Fauré very rarely wrote strophic songs, and the
few that he did compose in this form are early works. In his
attitude to the poems he set, in his scrupulous respect for the
value of words and the care with which he clothed them in
music, he closely resembles Hugo Wolf (who was his junior by
fifteen years), though he lacked Wolf's occasional extrovert
panache. Fauré's gift of close identification with his poets led
him to evolve a completely homogeneous, *durchkomponiert*
form for his songs, which gives the best of them a uniqueness
and inevitability that stamp them as the products of genius. His
first songs were composed when he was about twenty, and he
continued to produce them until within two years of his death
at the age of seventy-nine.

Fauré's op. 1 consists of two songs, written to poems of Victor
Hugo. 'Le Papillon et la fleur' and, to a slightly lesser degree,
'Mai', are pleasant, not unlike Gounod, but giving no hint of
the manner in which their composer was, within months, to
develop. In op. 2, the second of the two songs, 'Les Matelots',
is similarly immature, but the first, 'Dans les ruines d'une abbaye'
(poem by Hugo) is unmistakably the work of Fauré. Op. 3,
again consisting of two songs, offers 'Seule/' (Théophile Gautier)
which is less individual, and 'Sérénade toscane', a graceful
serenade (to words translated by Romain Bussine) which
exquisitely conjures up, in its graceful vocal line and its flowing
accompaniment, the warm beauty of a Tuscan night. The two
songs of op. 4 are absolute gems. 'Chanson du pêcheur', a gentle
yet deeply felt, melodically generous setting of Théophile
Gautier's poem about a fisherman lamenting his dead love, is
a masterpiece, and 'Lydia' (Leconte de Lisle) has an enduring,
typically Fauré-like charm and grace.

These first four opus numbers have each consisted of two
songs. The next four, ops. 4 to 8, still creations of Fauré's youth
(c. 1865), offer three songs each. Those of op. 5 are Charles
Baudelaire's 'Chant d'automne', the best of the three, "Rêve
d'amour', a setting of Hugo's 'S'il est un charmant gazon' which

is disappointingly slight, and 'L'Absent', also by Hugo, a poet to whom Fauré did not return after this song. The three songs of op. 6 are vintage Fauré; 'Aubade' (Louis Pommey) is ingratiating, while 'Tristesse' (Théophile Gautier) is deservedly popular, and does not commit the aesthetic error of taking the poet's 'tristesse affreuse' too seriously. It is both a dramatically restrained and highly attractive song. No. 3 is 'Sylvie', which rises triumphantly above its puerile text by Paul de Choudens. Op. 7 opens with the famous 'Après un rêve' (another of Romain Bussine's Tuscan translations), a gently rhapsodic and compelling setting of a fine romantic lyric. Baudelaire's 'Hymne' makes considerably less effect, but Marc Monnier's 'Barcarolle' is another absolute gem. The last of these youthful songs are to be found in op. 8 : 'Au bord de l'eau' (Armand Sully-Prudhomme) with its lulling barcarolle motion and quiet confidence, Baudelaire's 'La Rançon' which is disappointing, and 'Ici-bas' (poem by Sully-Prudhomme), charming but pale.

A gap of about fifteen years separates these youthful yet mature songs of Fauré from the rest, after which each year usually sees the composition of a group of songs. The three songs of op. 18 are all splendid. 'Nell' (poem by Leconte de Lisle) is ardent, graceful and altogether enchanting, 'Le Voyageur' (Armand Silvestre) unusually dramatic for Fauré, and 'Automne' (also Silvestre) a beautifully constructed song. Op. 21 is a miniature cycle of three poems by Charles Grandmougin, *Poème d'un jour*. In the first song, 'Rencontre', the poet meets his beloved, in the second, 'Toujours', he swears eternal fidelity, and in the third, 'Adieu', he leaves her. The passions are never over-stated, either in Grandmougin's poems or Fauré's charming but forceful setting. In the three songs of op. 23, the composer returns to Sully-Prudhomme and Silvestre. The former's 'Les Berceaux' is magnificent in its restraint, its perfect evocation of mood, its confident motion. The two Silvestre songs are also fine. 'Notre amour' enhances its rather banal poem, while 'Le Secret', a much better poem, is given a fine, restrained and sensitive vocal line, supported by a simple, perfectly apt accompaniment.

Most of the Fauré songs we have been discussing, though they may not possess the popular appeal of German *Lieder*, do turn up in the recital programmes of French singers. But the two Silvestre settings of op. 27 are rarely encountered. This is a pity, for both 'Chanson d'amour' and 'La Fée aux chansons' are worth listening to, particularly the latter which is a lively and graceful little song. More popular are the four songs of op. 39, three of them to poems by Silvestre, whose underrated lyrics obviously attracted Fauré. 'Aurore' is suffused with a delicate melancholy which perfectly reflects the underlying unease of the poem, 'Fleur jetée' matches its poem's desperation, and 'Le Pays des rêves' is subtly attractive. The fourth song, a setting of de Lisle's 'Les Roses d'Ispahan', is one of Fauré's loveliest creations. Leconte de Lisle's languorous oriental exoticism is beautifully caught in the composer's dreamily evocative melodic line. The two songs of op. 43 are unaccountably neglected. 'Noël' (poem by Victor Wilder) is excellent, and 'Nocturne' (Villiers de l'Isle-Adam) mysterious and intriguing. No. 1 of op. 46 is another Villiers de l'Isle-Adam poem, 'Les Présents', elegant, sensitive, and also hardly known. Op. 46 no. 2, on the contrary, is famous: Verlaine's 'Clair de lune'. This exquisite song is Fauré's first encounter with the poetry of Paul Verlaine (1844–1896), and, as we shall discover, his settings of Verlaine are unquestionably among his finest achievements in song. He seemed to have a special affinity with Verlaine's delicate, occasionally melancholic lyric gift, and sometimes actually enhances the beauty of the words, revealing even more clearly, but with an infinite tact, the poet's meaning and his mood. This sympathetic collaboration of poet and composer recalls famous earlier ones such as those of Schumann and Heine, Wolf and Mörike.

The four songs of op. 51 represent Fauré at his best. 'Larmes' is unusual in its vigour and violence, and hardly known at all. 'Au cimitière' is also untypical, also neglected. Verlaine's 'Spleen' is surely the perfect musical equivalent of the famous poem, 'Il pleure dans mon coeur', and 'La Rose' (poem by Leconte de Lisle) a vivid and appropriate setting of its poem. The next two opus numbers are both collections of Verlaine, and among the most valuable of Fauré's songs. *Cinq Mélodies* op. 58 opens with the elegant 'Mandoline', and contains also the inspired, melancholy 'En sourdine', the charming 'Green', 'A Clymène' and the exquisite 'C'est l'extase'. Op. 61 is the cycle, *La Bonne Chanson*.

From Verlaine's collection of twenty-one poems, *La Bonne Chanson*, Fauré chose nine for his cycle which was composed during 1891–2 and dedicated to its first interpreter, Madame Sigismond Bardac, who was later to become the wife of Debussy.

The cycle was not published immediately, since a publisher, Enoch, had rejected it in 1895 as being both dissonant and incomprehensible. But, after repeated performances, it began to achieve popularity and acclaim. It is a cycle which reveals itself most readily to those ears which are attuned to its language. It is by no means a 'difficult' work, but it does ask to be listened to with sympathy and care. Verlaine's words and Fauré's music are of equal importance here, blending to become a perfect example of lyric art which is in turn rhapsodic, intense, vital, joyous, tender, fragrant, of an extreme variety and an incomparable and indefinable unity.

'Une Sainte en son auréole' opens the cycle in a mood of quiet reverence as the poet speaks of his beloved's grace and purity. The emotional temperature is deliberately kept low in this, the lover's shy admission of his feelings. In 'Puisque l'aube grandit', the lover's ardour mounts as his joy wells up within him, and Fauré's beautiful and rhapsodic setting is perfectly indicative of the poet's amorous intensity. The third song, 'La lune blanche luit dans les bois', comes as a sharp contrast. The poem is a mood picture in which the lover equates the deep stillness of the moonlit night with his own feeling of inner peace and fulfilment. The song flows along with a sweet tenderness, the vocal line, though wandering, seeming to possess a kind of inevitability, almost a certain trustfulness.

'J'allais par des chemins perfides' begins in uncertainty and anguish. The lover walks along an unknown path, his only guide the voice of his beloved. But his love dispels this unease, and the song ends in one of those superb bursts of rapture towards which so many of Fauré's loveliest songs move. In 'J'ai presque peur, en verité', the lover's fever becomes more breathless and agitated, and he trembles to think of the almost deranged intensity of his feeling, which he can no longer control. Finally his passion bursts through, and he makes another avowal of love. The composer adds a formality and control to the poet's lines without lessening the tension in any way.

'Avant que tu ne t'en ailles' begins softly, but rises to a final mood of triumphant ecstasy in the poet's vision of happiness and content. Verlaine's intoxicated joy and Fauré's warmth and clarity are perfectly matched. A mood of expansive, affirmative joy and serenity is expressed with great power in 'Donc, ce sera par un clair jour d'été', a mood which Fauré was often to revert to in his later works, several of which derive in some way from

La Bonne Chanson. Here the poet anticipates the day of complete union with his beloved. Verlaine's poem 'N'est-ce pas?' has a youthful charm and confidence, and Fauré adds his own maturity to this utterance of careless young love. The final song is 'L'hiver a cessé'. The winter passed, the poet's heart is filled with spring. This joyous melody, which makes so perfect an end to the affectionate, lyrical cycle, was later to be transformed by the composer into the finale of his second Violin Sonata. In the song, it quotes thematically from earlier in the cycle, thus completing it as it climbs towards its radiant and passionate conclusion.

The two songs of op. 76, which did not appear until five years after *La Bonne Chanson*, admirably complement each other. 'Le parfum impérissable' is a veritable masterpiece. The very quintessence of Fauré is to be found in this song, in which the almost Proustian images of Leconte de Lisle's poem have inspired the composer to a setting ineffably tender, mysterious and sad beyond words, even beyond de Lisle's words. 'Arpège' is almost superficial by contrast, but it does not aim at the emotional profundity of 'Le parfum impérissable'. Albert Samain's poem has a Watteau-like formal grace, and Fauré has exquisitely translated this into musical terms in a song of imaginative elegance and charm. For the two songs of op. 83, Fauré drew on Verlaine and Samain. Verlaine's 'Prison' makes an admirable song, the composer's restraint providing a perfect balance to the poet's anguish, but 'Soir' is of an altogether higher order of romantic beauty, compassion and melancholy, expressed in one of Fauré's most gloriously flowing melodies. The three songs of op. 85 do not reach this level, though all are very attractive. 'Dans la forêt de septembre' is touching, and 'La fleur qui va sur l'eau' lively. Both are settings of Catulle Mendès. The third song, Albert Samain's 'Accompagnement' is a sweetly appealing barcarolle. For op. 87, Fauré returned to the poems of Armand Silvestre, a poet he had neglected since his op. 39, and composed settings of 'Le plus doux chemin' and 'Le ramier', though without equalling the success of his earlier Silvestre songs.

Before the important cycle, *La chanson d'Eve*, written between 1907 and 1910, there are three separate songs to be considered. 'Le don silencieux' op. 92, a setting of a poem by Jean Dominique, is a particularly fine example of the later Fauré, the melody more reticent than in earlier years, but no less sensitive to verbal nuance than formerly, and the structure more compact. The op. 94 setting of Henri de Régnier's 'Chanson', though less memorable, is quite charming, and a wordless vocalize without opus number, which began its life as a piece for oboe, was published in a volume of vocalizes by various composers.

The songs that Fauré wrote in his sixties and seventies may seem at first hearing to lack the immediate appeal of much of the work of his earlier maturity. The texture, for instance, is thinner, the harmonies generally lacking in richness, the melodic impulse noticeably less ardent. But the beauties of these later songs are no less real for being reflective in nature. *La Chanson d'Eve* op. 95, a cycle of ten songs to poems of Charles van Lerberghe, is less frequently heard than *La Bonne Chanson*, but is, in its less passionate manner, a work of equal or perhaps even greater beauty, dealing with the freshness of creation and the serenity of age in verbal and musical images both sensitive and profound. It was followed some years later by another cycle, *Le jardin clos* op. 106, composed during the First World War, also to poems by Van Lerberghe, and consisting of eight songs again in the manner of the *Chanson d'Eve* settings, and *Mirages*, op. 113, composed in 1919, four rather pale settings of not very interesting poems by the Baronne de Brimont. 'C'est la paix' op. 114, an isolated song (poem by Georgette Debladis) was followed in 1922 by Fauré's last composition for the voice, the miniature cycle, *L'Horizon chimérique*, whose poems are by a young poet, Jean de la Ville de Mirmont, who was killed during the 1914–18 war. These four songs of departure and of fulfilment are quietly moving, contemplative, and an apt conclusion to Fauré's subtle art as expressed in song.

Rarely can any composer have left his mark on the world of music with a slighter, smaller *œuvre* than that of Henri Duparc (1848–1933) who produced only fourteen songs and a handful of other pieces. His reputation rests on the songs alone, for the other works, including an orchestral nocturne, *Aux étoiles*, a symphonic poem, *Lénore*, and a three-part motet, *Benedicat vobis Domine*, are now totally forgotten. Not, in any case, a prolific composer, Duparc was unable to continue to write music after his thirty-seventh year, when he suffered a nervous collapse which left him incapable of work for the remainder of his long life. He was one of the earliest pupils of César Franck, though his songs are not in any way Franckian. Grove's Dictionary quotes Georges Servières* who asserts that Duparc's songs 'are absolutely original, rich and abundant in strength, with a depth of sentiment rarely found in French music'. Much in this statement is hyperbolic—though it is true that one must look beyond French music for influences on Duparc, the strongest of which was undoubtedly the erotic chromaticism of late Wagner. And the songs of Fauré certainly do not lack depth of sentiment. Nevertheless, it is probably true that Fauré and Duparc are by far the finest composers of French *mélodie*. Duparc's fourteen extant songs were composed between 1868 and 1884, a period of sixteen years, yet it is not easy to discern stylistic differences over the years. The style, it appears, came to maturity early, and, though some songs are superior to others, one cannot talk of a maturing process in Duparc.

Eleven of the fourteen songs were composed for high voice, a fact which is nowadays obscured due to the songs having in recent years become widely known mainly through gramophone records by French baritones (Charles Panzéra, Gérard Souzay). It is, however, an important fact : these are songs of passion, and they soar. Although two of them, 'La vague et la cloche' and 'La vie antérieure' were originally written for voice and orchestra, and the composer later wrote orchestral accompaniments for another five ('L'Invitation au voyage', 'Phidylé', 'Testament', 'Chanson triste' and 'Au pays où se fait la guerre'), the versions for voice and piano are to be preferred, for Duparc's orchestration was not particularly skilful. It is also true that his piano writing lacks the audacity and originality of Fauré's, but it is invariably sensitive, and perfectly supports his distinctive and affecting vocal line.

The earliest song, 'Chanson triste', is one of the greatest of *mélodies*. The poem is by Jean Lahor (1840–1909) to whose verses Fauré also frequently turned. His poems inspired three of Duparc's songs, which makes him that composer's most often used poet. The faded romantic gestures of Lahor's verse have lost whatever charm they might once have possessed, but his phrases still sound magical when uttered on Duparc's melodies. The weak, self-pitying verses of his 'Chanson triste', for instance, are made vibrant with ecstasy in the song, with its wide-ranging voice part, the flourish of its accompanying arpeggios and its mood of tender nostalgia. The climaxes in Duparc are always beautifully judged and placed, the movement always assured.

* *Guide musical* Paris 1895

Duparc contrives, too, never to distort the normal spoken stresses of declamation, though he is no slave to them in the way that Debussy can sometimes appear to be. In 'Chanson triste' the vocal tessitura is raised, from stanza to stanza, as the singer's passion mounts, to subside somewhat in the fourth and final stanza, at the possibility of cure by satiety.

> Et dans tes yeux pleins de tristesses
> Dans tes yeux alors je boirai
> Tant de baisers et de tendresses
> Que peut-être je guérirai.

'Soupir', like 'Chanson triste', dates from 1868, when Duparc was twenty, and is an equally impassioned love song. But Sully-Prudhomme's poem is one of hopeless, unrealized love, a poem about the romantic attitude rather than an outpouring of love for any one person, and Duparc's setting eerily catches the mood of tender masochistic devotion to an unattainable ideal, which it expresses with a poised restraint in striking contrast to the ardour of the earlier song. The original key is D minor, which is considerably more effective than the downward transposition by a whole tone which is necessary to bring the song within the range of the medium voice. The controlled passion of the vocal line is by no means easy to convey in performance; but, when rendered by a singer whose intelligence and feeling are not at war with each other, 'Soupir' can sound like the masterpiece it is.

Another song of 1868, 'Le Galop', was one of three subsequently suppressed by Duparc who was fiercely self-critical. However, in 1948, the centenary of the composer's birth, it was reissued, though it is still not included in the 'complete edition' of Duparc's songs which contains the other thirteen extant songs. Sully-Prudhomme's ecstatic verses are set to an excited, expansive melody which can sound immensely effective in performance, even though the song is not one of Duparc's more characteristic pieces. 'Au pays où se fait la guerre' (1869) is the only one of the songs manifestly unsuitable for the male voice. In Théophile Gautier's poem, a woman longingly awaits the return of her lover who has gone 'to the country which is at war', and Duparc has given the words a setting which begins simply but develops to a pitch of great intensity. A song of less immediate appeal than some of the others, this is a miniature dramatic scene which responds well to interpretative boldness in the singer.

How different in temperament, and, for that matter, working habits, Duparc was from Schubert. When we consider how many masterpieces the Viennese composer was likely to produce in any one year, it may seem almost absurd that Duparc was capable sometimes of composing no more than one song in a period of twelve months. The year 1870 yields up only one, but it is one of the finest not only in 19th-century France, but in the entire song literature. This is 'L'Invitation au Voyage', Duparc's setting of Baudelaire's great poem from the volume *Les Fleurs du Mal* of 1875, or, to be exact, his setting of the first and last of Baudelaire's three stanzas. The shimmering ecstasy of the poet's nostalgic vision is transmuted into the texture and shape of the piano accompaniment; the voice part, magically natural, poised, sensual and elegant, captures to perfection the languid yearnings, stirring almost but not quite to excitement, of the poem. The sense of a shining goal glimpsed intermittently through mists of wilful inactivity pervades this remarkably beautiful and poetic song.

'La Vague et la Cloche' (1871), to a poem by François Coppée is one of the two songs originally written for voice and orchestra. The poem, a portentous and obscure allegory, has not inspired Duparc to one of his more successful creations, though the vocal writing is accomplished and the orchestration interesting. This is perhaps the least valuable of Duparc's songs. With 'Elégie', composed in 1874, we return to the heights. The words are a translation in prose of Thomas Moore's 'Lament on the death of Robert Emmet' (the Irish youth who was executed in 1803 for having led an uprising against the British). The poem, whose opening lines are

> Oh, breathe not his name, let it sleep in the shade
> Where cold and unhonoured his relics are laid

is perhaps even more moving in the French prose translation, which is probably by Duparc himself, than in Moore's rhymed verse; and the music, while thoroughly in accord with the sombre restraint of the words, has a more complex and subtle life of its own, expressed in its harmonies, the texture of its piano part, and the sensitive accentuation of its vocal line.

Trembling on the verge of preciosity perhaps, yet exquisitely beautiful in its delicacy of feeling and expression, is 'Extase' (1878), a setting of a poem by Jean Lahor: 'Sur un lys pâle mon cœur dort/D'un sommeil doux comme la mort.' Duparc wrote this song in the style of *Tristan und Isolde* as his creative response to the anti-Wagnerism of French criticism, but it is by no means merely an act of homage to, or imitation of, the German composer. Quietly, and without passion, with an air of infinite regret, it draws into sound an expression of the death-wish which is far removed from Wagner's erotic death-longing.

'Le Manoir de Rosemonde', composed in 1879, is dedicated to Robert de Bonnières, who wrote the poem. Like 'La Vague et la Cloche', it is a vivid and dramatic setting of a fairly worthless poem, but it is an infinitely more successful song than the earlier one. Its movement has more vitality, its melody is firmer in outline, and, though on paper it hardly suggests it, 'Le Manoir de Rosemonde' can sound not only dramatic but strange and intense in a good performance. There could be no greater contrast to it than Duparc's next song, the graceful little 'Sérénade florentine' of 1880 whose poem is by Jean Lahor. With his two earlier settings of Lahor, 'Chanson triste' and 'Extase', Duparc had created two of his most beautiful songs. The Florentine Serenade is perhaps not on that level of achievement, but it is a most exquisite and delicate song, more a lullaby than a serenade.

'Phidylé', written in 1882 and dedicated to Ernest Chausson, is a setting of parts of a very fine poem by Leconte de Lisle, and is a superbly passionate song whose vocal line swells with feeling. It has, too, an exciting accompaniment and an almost operatic stature. It is arguably Duparc's greatest achievement, beginning in classical calm to develop into romantic exultation. The following year produced two songs, 'Lamento' and 'Testament'. 'Lamento', dedicated to Fauré, is a setting of Théophile Gautier, and actually a rather Fauré-like setting, though it manages at the same time to sound unmistakably like Duparc. 'Testament' (poem by Armand Silvestre) turns a feeble poem into a remarkably fine song, powerful and expressive.

Duparc's last song is also one of his greatest. 'La vie antérieure', composed in 1884 on Baudelaire's poem, goes to the heart of the poet's uneasy nostalgia, and combines with it the composer's own deep sadness. The song is by no means mawkish, but almost serenely beautiful in its despair, a despair which Duparc was to endure stoically for almost another fifty years.

The songs of Ernest Chausson (1855–1899) tend to be too

easily dismissed, perhaps because those of his teacher, César Franck, are not generally admired. But Chausson is more than simply a reflection of his master, especially in his songs. His untimely death at the age of forty-four caused by a bicycle accident, and the fact that he always worked slowly, are together responsible for the relative sparseness of his output; nevertheless, of his thirty or more songs, a large number are works of individuality and considerable interest. Although he composed three operas, only one of which was performed in his lifetime, Chausson was essentially a lyrical miniaturist, and it is arguable that the essence of his musical character is to be found in his songs, all written during the last sixteen years of his life. What distinguishes these songs from, for instance, those of Franck, is Chausson's ability to project an air of delicacy and refinement without any suggestion of preciosity. Like most other French composers of his period, he is rarely, if ever, inelegant, but to this negative virtue he adds a positive and personal charm of manner which gives his songs a distinct character of their own, a character compounded of tenderness and melancholy, but with a directness and sincerity which prevent any suggestion of mawkishness. While never obtruding his personality upon the texts of the poems he sets, but rather responding to the mood and imagery of his poets, Chausson nevertheless contrives to compose melody which is always characteristic of himself; not assertive, yet by no means pallid or wan. From the earliest songs of 1882 to the last ones of 1898, his voice remains constant, and, within that constancy, varied.

The earliest published songs by Chausson are the seven of op. 2, dating from 1882, settings of such popular poets as Leconte de Lisle, Armand Silvestre, Théophile Gautier and Paul Bourget. These are, in the main, simple but pleasant songs. 'La dernière feuille' has an artless charm, 'Les Papillons' and the graceful 'Sérénade italienne' are equally attractive and de Lisle's 'Le Colibri' even more so; but there are greater riches to come. The four songs of op. 8 are written on poems by Chausson's friend, Maurice Bouchor, a lesser artist than many other poets set by the composer, but one close enough to him in temperament and sympathy to have been able to provide him with exactly the right kind of material. These op. 8 songs are distinctly superior to the earlier set, more interesting rhythmically (as in 'Nocturne' and 'Nos Souvenirs') and with more characterful piano parts (as in 'Amour d'antan' and the beautiful 'Printemps triste'). For his op. 13, Chausson reverted to setting several poets instead of exploring different facets of merely one. 'Apaisement', his first Verlaine setting, is a song of pure delicacy and poetic quality; Jean Lahor's 'Sérénade' and Villiers de l'Isle-Adam's 'L'Aveu' are both interesting and complex, and only Leconte de Lisle's 'La Cigale' is disappointingly dull.

The two *Chansons de Miarka* op. 17 display Chausson's gifts at their most characteristic. Based on poems by Jean Richepin which are in themselves of no great merit but whose imagery has drawn an exquisite response from the composer, these two songs deserve to be more frequently performed. 'Les Morts', though concerned with death and written in a minor key, is by no means depressing or gloomy. Instead, it is gently consolatory. The second song 'La Pluie', is a lyrical description of rain falling. One's first reaction on hearing it is to consider it curiously unlike Chausson. Closer acquaintance leads one to revise this view, though 'La Pluie' lacks that vein of melancholy which generally persists throughout Chausson's songs and chamber music, revealing momentarily a happier disposition.

Chausson's most important group of songs is *Serres chaudes* op. 24, a cycle of five settings of poems by the Belgian symbolist poet, Maurice Maeterlinck. Harmonically more complex than most of the composer's other songs, these capture to perfection the strange, dream-like world of Maeterlinck, and find appropriate musical forms for the images of fear, sadness, religious fervour, mystery and confusion to be found in the poems, which are obscure and which read as though they need music to complete them, or to explain them. In the first song, 'Serre chaude', Chausson goes beyond Maeterlinck's forest imagery to the feeling behind the words, and creates a musical equivalent which seems completely convincing, though often one is unable to trace a rational surface connection between verbal and musical phrase. The second song, 'Serre d'ennui', is simpler in form, though no less closely sympathetic to the poem, and 'Lassitude', dominated by its harmonies, is perhaps the most rewarding song of the five. 'Fauves las' and 'Oraison' may be thought to lack melodic interest, but again repeated hearings eventually reveal to the sensitive listener the common territory behind words and notes which is shared by poet and composer, and which is so originally embodied in these songs. Debussy said of this cycle, 'These songs are little dramas with an impassioned metaphysics. Chausson's music comments on it without making it dull. One would even wish that he had given more freedom to all the palpitations of inner emotion that one hears in his very personal interpretation.'*

Op. 27, *Trois Lieder*, settings of poems by Camille Mauclair, are not of the stature of the *Serres chaudes* but have a freshness and clarity of texture that are immensely appealing. The first song, 'Les Heures', does not assert itself, but subtly underlines and emphasizes the feeling in Mauclair's poem. The poet himself, in his book *La religion de la Musique†* speaks, however, of the power of Chausson's music in this song. 'Ballade' makes brilliant use of rhythm to sustain in music the strength of the poet's imagery, and, in the final song, 'Les Couronnes', the composer adopts the accent of popular song. The following opus number, 28, consists of *Chansons de Shakespeare*, translated by Maurice Bouchor. One of them, 'Chant funèbre' (from *Much Ado About Nothing*), is written for female chorus and piano, but the other three are solo songs. All four are plaintive in mood, and curiously un-Shakespearian in that they emanate a certain fragility that seems wholly French. 'Chanson de Clown' (from *Twelfth Night*) is the most interesting of the three solo songs, though 'Chanson d'amour' (from *Measure for Measure*) is livelier than its fellows. 'Chanson d'Ophélie' (*Hamlet*) is touching, though insubstantial.

In op. 34, *Deux Poèmes*, Chausson returned to Verlaine, the poet he had so beautifully and perceptively set in 'Apaisement' thirteen years earlier. One wishes there were more Chausson settings of Verlaine, for the three that exist are among the composer's finest, most characteristic and personal songs. The mood of 'La Chanson bien douce' is caught to perfection in a setting in which each detail of the poem is made into music which sounds so right that it would, one feels, be an act of vandalism to separate the words from the music. 'Le Chevalier Malheur' is no less effective, a magnificent song by the composer who perhaps could have come closer than any other French musician to capturing the elusive essence of Paul Verlaine in music.

The final solo songs with piano are the two which comprise op. 36, composed in 1898: 'Cantique à l'épouse', a charming setting of Albert Jounet's sweet poem, and 'Dans la forêt du charme et de l'enchantement' (poem by Jean Moréas), an eloquent and effortless song which is rightly one of Chausson's

* Léon Vallas *Les Idées de Claude Debussy* Paris 1927
† Camille Mauclair *La Religion de la Musique* Paris Fischbacher 1909

most popular. Even more popular is the 'Chanson perpétuelle', which in its original form is scored for voice and small orchestra. Its delicate sadness is touching, though the song loses much of its effect when performed with piano accompaniment.

Benjamin Godard (1849–1895) wrote more than 100 songs, in the tradition of Gounod, many of them with a direct trace of the influence of Schumann as well. They have, however, not survived, and even Godard's operas and orchestral works have disappeared from the repertoire. He is remembered only for one of his operas, *Jocelyn*, first produced in Brussels in 1888. The opera itself is not produced nowadays, but one number from it, a berceuse, known in English as 'Angels guard thee', became a popular concert song, and is still occasionally encountered. A number of other late 19th- and early 20th-century French composers produced songs which were popular for a time, among them the female composer, Cécile Chaminade (1857–1944), whose songs and piano pieces, though undeniably charming, are mostly rather pale of character. Alfred Bruneau (1857–1934), whose Wagnerian operas with libretti by Emile Zola were produced in Paris at the Opéra-Comique, wrote a number of songs based on traditional song and dance tunes, such as the *Lieds de France*, on poems by Catulle Mendès, and the six *Chansons à danser*. A pupil of Paladilhe, Georges Hüe (1858–1948) left some skilfully composed songs, though none proved strong enough in personality to survive him. Albéric Magnard (1865–1914), who studied with both Massenet and d'Indy and who also came under the influence of Wagner, wrote a handful of songs, in addition to three operas.

Although Fauré continued to write songs until well into the 20th century, his is essentially a 19th-century art. The first real 20th-century figure in French music is Claude Debussy (1862–1918). Debussy, of course, is as renowned for his piano and orchestral music as for his songs, but it would not be misleading to suggest that poetry is, if not the 'onlie begetter', then certainly a prime inspirer of his art. One has only to think of the *Prélude à l'après-midi d'un faune*, based on Mallarmé's eclogue, and of the titles given to the movements of *La mer*, *Images pour orchestre* and much of the piano music, to realize that Debussy's was a literary mind, and that many of his concepts came in the form of literary images. He himself was an accomplished prose writer, and an intelligent and sensitive appreciator and critic of French poetry. For the texts of his songs, although he occasionally resorted to poets of the past, he made more use of such of his older contemporaries as Baudelaire, Verlaine and Mallarmé. He was, perhaps, not a great innovator in song, for, although his songs allow equal importance to voice and piano, this was at the time no longer contentious. He brought his own individual ear to the task of marrying the French language, its rhythms and stresses, to music, and in doing so produced a number of songs which may lack melodic spontaneity à la Fauré, or passion à la Duparc, but which are masterpieces of musical declamation. He is a French equivalent of the Austrian Hugo Wolf. Though he was not primarily a composer of songs, Debussy's strong affinities with poetry and with the written word generally ensured that this most literate of musicians should devote a great deal of his attention to the problem of setting words to music. To an even greater extent than Fauré, he practised in his settings of French poets extreme fidelity not only to the mood and atmosphere of the poem, but also to its own cadences. One might almost say that a song by Debussy has already been half-composed by the poet. Debussy's vocal line, in the mature songs, follows the inflections of the spoken text as though ruled by it, yet in some strange way transcends it as well.

Debussy's first songs were written when the composer was in his mid-teens, and he continued to produce songs throughout his working life. The very early ones do not sound to us today especially like Debussy : they could be by Fauré, or even Massenet. That they do not exhibit the mature characteristics of their composer is, however, no reason for despising or neglecting them, for they are uncommonly attractive songs. 'Fleur des blés', a setting of André Girod, is perhaps the best of the three earliest songs. The others are the lyrical and nostalgic 'Beau soir' (poem by Paul Bourget) and 'Nuit d'étoiles' (Théodore de Banville) which is less individual. These were the creations of the fifteen-year-old Debussy. Within the next three or four years, he composed several songs in a variety of styles. 'La Belle au bois dormant', a version of the sleeping beauty legend with words by the Montmartre cabaret poet Vincent Hypsa, makes use of the popular round 'Nous n'irons plus au bois' which Debussy was also to introduce into the piano piece *Jardins sous la pluie* in 1903 and into the orchestral *Rondes de printemps* in 1909. 'Mandoline', Debussy's first setting of Verlaine, also dates from these early years. Probably his best known song, this graceful little serenade, lightly amorous, ironic and mocking, fully deserves its popularity. The music is a perfect realization of the mood of Verlaine's poem.

Also dating from the period 1882–4, although they were not published until some years after the composer's death, are four songs dedicated to the singer Madame Vasnier. These are, in a way, transitional pieces from the 19th-century language of the earlier songs to the more modern works that were to follow. 'Pantomime' (poem by Verlaine) is melodious, nostalgic; 'Clair de lune', also a Verlaine setting, contrasts strongly with the more famous 'Clair de lune' which was to come; 'Pierrot' (Théodore de Banville) begins with references in the accompaniment to the popular tune 'Au clair de la lune', and continues gaily; 'Apparition' (poem by Mallarmé) makes use of a wide-ranging vocal line which contrives to be both graceful and exciting.

Of the dozen or more groups of songs which constitute Debussy's mature *œuvre*, the earliest is *Cinq Poèmes de Baudelaire*, composed between 1887 and 1889. These five songs are thought by some to show traces of Wagner. It is true that they were produced during the period of Debussy's visits to Bayreuth, where he heard and greatly admired *Parsifal*, *Die Meistersinger* and *Tristan und Isolde*; but Debussy, as he once wrote to a friend, saw no reason to imitate what he admired, and there is really not anything Wagnerian about these songs, except perhaps that their sensuousness might be thought of as Tristanesque. Wagner, it is sometimes in danger of being forgotten, did not invent sensuousness in music.

The first of the Baudelaire songs, 'Le Balcon', is perhaps the one closest to *Tristan* in its *angst*-laden chromaticism which so well captures the masochistic pleasure of Baudelaire's *malaise*. The second song, 'Harmonie du soir', takes on one of the poet's purest and most self-contained utterances, and is only partially successful in finding musical equivalents for Baudelaire's symbols. 'Le Jet d'eau' is the finest of the five songs. The arpeggios of the accompaniment brilliantly evoke the sparkling fountain of the title, while the delicacy and fluidity of the melodic line are remarkable. Almost equally so is the eloquent and sensitive 'Recueillement' with its air of sweet resignation. The strophic song which concludes the set—in published order, that is, for it was the first to be composed—is 'La Mort des amants', which is imaginative, though apt to sound rather archaic when heard after its companions.

The six songs of the *Ariettes oubliées*, settings of Verlaine most of which were composed in 1888, present a strong contrast with the world of Baudelaire. Just as the poems themselves are more reticent, one might almost say devious, in expression, so is Debussy's melody less straightforward, turning into a kind of recitative charged with melodic suggestions. In the first song, 'C'est l'extase', the fusion of words and music is complete: Verlaine and Debussy seem made for each other. Similarly, throughout the other five songs, one finds the most perfect *rapprochment* between poet and composer. 'Il pleure dans mon cœur' conjures up an achingly sad world of time-dulled pain; 'L'ombre des arbres', more detached and ironic in tone, is no less effective, and contains, too, a wealth of cool Debussian harmonies; and 'Chevaux de bois', less compulsively gripping in its authority than its fellows, nevertheless conveys the authentic Verlaine emptiness behind the whirling gaiety of a village fair. The remaining two songs, contrasting strongly with each other, are among Debussy's finest and most popular Verlaine settings. 'Green', tender and joyous, is as real a response to the poem as Fauré's more delicate setting of the same text, while 'Spleen' cunningly disguises its own art and appears to do no more than heighten the spoken rhythms of the poem, though it is, in fact, a highly organized and formally satisfying piece of music.

After the *Ariettes oubliées*, some of Debussy's songs of the next year or two seem technically less adventurous, though always tasteful and, in the case of the *Deux Romances* to poems of Paul Bourget, unusually tuneful as well. The next important group is that composed in 1891 when Debussy turned again to Verlaine, the poet with whom his musical affinity was closest. The *Trois Mélodies* are less frequently performed than the other Debussy-Verlaine groups (the *Ariettes oubliées* of 1888 and the two sets of *Fêtes galantes* which were still to come), but they are certainly not less successful or interesting in themselves. Two of the three poems were written by Verlaine during his English sojourn. 'La Mer est plus belle' is about the sea off the south coast of England, and its mood is caught to perfection in Debussy's subtle impressionist setting with its fluid arpeggio accompaniment. 'Le Son du cor s'afflige' paints a different kind of picture, a country landscape in winter with its associated sounds, and here the music again subtly and unostentatiously parallels the poet's creation. The landscape of the third song, 'L'Échelonnement des haies' is again an English one: the hedgerows are those of Lincolnshire, and the vocal line hovers above a sensitive and uncluttered accompaniment.

The first of the two sets of *Fêtes Galantes*, each of which consists of three settings of Verlaine, was composed in 1892. (The second followed twelve years later.) The poems in the first set, combining the elegance of a Watteau scene with the muted romanticism which permeates Verlaine's work, inspired Debussy to his most flexible and delicate melodic language. In the first song, 'En sourdine', the composer's feeling, too, remains muted as he lazily and sensuously depicts the poet's 'vagues langueurs des pins et des arbousiers', nor does he react, as Fauré did, to the more impassioned melancholy of the poem's closing lines, 'Voix de notre désespoir, le rossignol chantera'. In 'Fantoches', Scaramouche and Pulcinella are gesticulating wildly under the moon. The doctor from Bologna looks for herbs in the cool meadow, while his daughter slyly creeps across the glade, waiting for her bold pirate lover. Debussy paints his impressionist picture of this *commedia dell' arte* world with a gay and rapid spontaneity. The poem of the final song is the well-known 'Clair de lune' ('Votre âme est un paysage choisi'). The almost serene melancholy of the song's sustained melody is enveloped in the clear moonlit atmosphere evoked by the piano part.

For the four *Proses lyriques* of 1892–3, Debussy provided his own texts, four prose poems which are not so much successful in literary terms as interesting for what they reveal of his aims and interests as a musician concerned with the setting of words. Edward Lockspeiser* has written most interestingly of the *Proses lyriques*:

Just as Verlaine, Régnier and Mallarmé were constantly aware of the unattainable art of music to which their own poetic art aspired, so, contrariwise, Debussy would seem to have been anxious himself to define the poetic imagery which was his source of inspiration. If the results of these curious experiments are less satisfying from a literary than from a musical viewpoint, they must nevertheless be considered successful since one of the purposes of such experiments was apparently to placate and exercise such extraneous influences as were binding down the artist in the pursuit of his fantasies.

This makes the eclectic nature of Debussy's texts for these songs

* Edward Lockspeiser *Debussy* J. M. Dent London 1936

more understandable, for they do appear to be written in a
variety of styles, bound in an uneasy unity by the music, although
it, too, is oddly derivative, with echoes here of Wagner, there of
Massenet. 'De rêve' with its procession of Knights of the Grail,
is the least successful of the songs. The others are 'De grève', a
fanciful seascape, 'De fleurs', strange and compelling, and 'De
soir', decidedly satirical.

The three *Chansons de Bilitis* of 1897 are written to icily
delicate prose poems by the young Pierre Louÿs. Debussy's
Grecian frieze of a setting captures to perfection the pseudo-
classical simplicity of the texts, the deliberate decadence of their
style, their objective sensuousness and gently hedonistic flavour.
These three songs which, even had Debussy produced no others,
would have placed him beside Wolf and Mussorgsky, create
their own atmosphere which is one of antique grace and a vague
and remote beauty. Debussy's music is somewhat in the style of
his *Pelléas et Mélisande*, the opera on which he was then working. The first song, 'La Flûte de Pan', has a most charming air
of simplicity in keeping with the verbal purity of Louÿ's poem,
but also evokes with its modal harmonies the paganism of
ancient Greece. The second song, 'La Chevelure', is quite different in its emotional character : it is disturbed and disturbing,
like the erotic dream which is its subject. In the last song, 'Le
Tombeau des Naïades', Debussy has created a perfect work of
musical impressionism. Over its glacial accompaniment the
voice moves through wonder and anticipation to cold disillusion,
across the winter landscape so magically created by the composer.

In 1904, the second set of *Fêtes galantes* appeared. Again, the
poems of Verlaine brought a subtle and sensitive response from
Debussy. 'Les Ingénus' is a witty pastiche, 'Le Faune' is delicate,
evocative yet slightly menacing, and the final song, the well-
known 'Colloque sentimental', is an extraordinary dialogue
between two ghosts, remembering past happiness. It is frequently
likened to Schubert's 'Doppelgänger', but Verlaine's spirits are
sadder and more melancholy, with nothing of Heine's defiance.
The *Trois Chansons de France*, which appeared in the same year,
are settings of Charles d'Orléans and Tristan Lhermite. The two
settings of rondels by the 15th-century poet, Charles d'Orléans,
are remarkable examples of Debussy's ventriloquial art, for he
speaks here in the voice and spirit of mediaeval times, his
harmonies full of archaic-sounding fourths and fifths, his texture
sparse and almost primitive. The first rondel, 'Le temps a laissé

son manteau', is a welcome to the return of spring after the
rigours of winter; while the second, 'Pour ce que plaisance est
morte', is a lament for the death of pleasure, a sad but stately
pavane which paints a strangely beautiful and sympathetic
picture of life and thought in the Middle Ages.

The Tristan Lhermite song, 'La Grotte', was reissued some
years later with two other settings of the same poet as *Le
Promenoir de deux amants*, when it was re-titled 'Auprès de
cette grotte sombre', which is its opening line. It is more at home
in the later set of songs than when sandwiched between the
Charles d'Orléans rondels. 'Auprès de cette grotte sombre'
catches not only the elegance but also the underlying melancholy
of Lhermite's poem, while 'Crois mon conseil, chère Clymène'
is both subtle and delicate, and 'Je tremble en voyant ton visage',
the last of the three *Promenoir* songs, is Debussy at his most
responsive to the mood and texture of the poem. Whereas, on
hearing some of this composer's songs, one might feel that for
all their sensitivity to words, they are in the last resort perhaps
too subservient to those words, here in this song, Debussy's
method produces a perfect fusion of text and notes.

A firmer attack, harder and more dramatic, characterizes the
Trois Ballades de François Villon, composed during 1910.
Villon's ballades have an earthiness which one would not have
expected to appeal to Debussy, yet he both responds to it and
matches it in these three songs. The 'Ballade de Villon à s'amye'
identifies with the poet's own period, but these Middle Ages
are a different world from that of Charles d'Orléans: they are
tougher and more enduring. The prayer to the Virgin Mary—
'Ballade que feit Villon à la requeste de sa mère pour prier
Nostre-Dame'—is deeply felt and affecting, while, by contrast,
the 'Ballade des femmes de Paris', an ironic compliment to the
women of Paris, has a bounding, propulsive motion, and a racy,
chattering vocal line, qualities which make it a highly engaging
song.

In 1913, Debussy returned to the poems of Mallarmé for the
first time since his solitary song of 1882, 'Apparition', and composed the *Trois Poèmes de Stéphane Mallarmé*. The isolated
images of these enigmatic, often obscure poems, have brought
forth from the composer similar musical images, coldly and
carefully placed. 'Soupir' is a less easy song to approach than
'Placet futile' with its delicate ironies, or 'Eventail', which is
the most enigmatic of all, though musically the most satisfactory,

for music is able delicately to sidestep meaning. For the last song he was to compose, in December 1916, Debussy also wrote the words himself. This is his 'Noël des enfants qui n'ont plus de maisons', written out of compassion for the refugee children in Flanders. Its heart is, of course, in the right place, but perhaps its head is at the wrong temperature, for the song lacks the distinction of even minor Debussy. It is well-made, but disappointingly anonymous in character.

A composer of the same generation whose development as a composer of song was roughly parallel with that of Debussy is Charles Koechlin (1867–1951). Koechlin survived Debussy by more than thirty years, and thus moved from romanticism through expressionism to a style or an eclectic series of styles more characteristic of the years between the wars. Massenet and Fauré were among his teachers, and the latter is a clearly discernible influence in the earliest songs. (Koechlin is also the author of an excellent monograph on Fauré*.) His songs, which number nearly 100, are settings of French poets, including those one would expect to find : Verlaine, Louÿs, Sully-Prudhomme, Leconte de Lisle, Tristan Klingsor, as well as some lesser-known names such as Albert Samain (who was, however, set also by Fauré and two or three other composers, among them Casella and Florent Schmitt). The earliest songs, *Cinq Rondels* op. 1, date from the early 1890s, while the last, a collection of seven humorous songs inspired by Lilian Harvey's film, *Calais-Dover*, and entitled *Chanson pour Gladys*, appeared in 1935. Other groups which contain interesting and attractive material include the *Cinq Chansons de Bilitis* op. 39, and *Cinq Poèmes de 'La Bonne Chanson'* op. 24.

Albert Roussel (1869–1937) composed fewer songs than Koechlin, whom in some respects he resembles. A pupil of d'Indy, he wrote several operas and ballets as well as chamber music. With the exception of his early settings of Henri de Régnier, ops. 3 and 8 which are colourlessly conventional (though 'Le jardin mouillé' from op. 3 sounds less contrived than its fellows), Roussel's songs are among his most successful and characteristic compositions. The *Deux Poèmes chinois* op. 12, dating from 1907, are fascinating, though the so-called Chinese poems are actually French translations of English translations. The music makes use of the Chinese pentatonic scale which restores an eastern exoticism present only rather palely in the

* Charles Koechlin *Gabriel Fauré* Dennis Dobson London 1946

words, and the first song in particular, 'Ode à un jeune gentil-homme', is delightful in its formality, restraint and simplicity. The second song, 'Amoureux séparés', more elaborate in structure, is hardly less charming. Roussel's chief virtues as a composer of songs are, first, the sensitivity to verse which he shares with so many French musicians, and second, the easy individuality of his idiom. He is not a great experimenter, but his language and technique are always equal to the stylistic and interpretative demands made upon them by the texts he chose to illustrate. Among his most attractive and rewarding songs are the *Deux poèmes de Ronsard* written in 1924 for voice and flute. More ambitious are the *Odes anacréontiques* ops. 31 and 32, which followed in 1926. These six odes of Anacreon, in French translations by Leconte de Lisle, cannot have been easy to put to music, but the refined texture of Roussel's harmonies, and the easy charm of his vocal line, combine to create songs which admirably mirror the mood and style of the poems.

For the *Deux Mélodies* of op. 20, Roussel turned to the contemporary poet René Chalupt, on whose 'Sarabande' and 'Le Bachelier de Salamanque' he composed two splendid songs, the first sensuous, the second ironically witty. Unusual, yet characteristic of Roussel's personality, is 'Jazz dans la nuit', a 1928 parody composed on a text by René Dommange, its jazz elements beautifully integrated into the composer's own personal style. Roussel displays his familiarity with the English language in 'A Flower given to my Daughter', a sensitive setting of James Joyce contributed in 1931 to a volume of Joyce songs by various composers. An earlier English song, 'A Farewell' (poem by E. Oliphant), is handicapped by its poor text. The *Deux Mélodies* op. 50, to poems of Chalupt, are attractive, particularly the lively 'Cœur en péril'. Roussel's final songs, written in 1935, are the *Deux Mélodies* op. 55, whose words are by Georges Ville. Though interesting, they lack the melodic ease and naturalness of his most successful works in this genre.

Song plays an important part in the *œuvre* of Maurice Ravel (1875–1937), although the number of his published titles is no more than twenty-five. Ravel, a fastidious and intensely self-critical composer, was not, by the standards of the 19th century, prolific. He chose to leave some of his earliest songs unpublished, but in the others it is rare to find a lapse from his high standards of craftsmanship and poetic response. The first of the published songs is 'Sainte', a setting of Mallarmé which Ravel composed

at the age of twenty-one, matching, in its air of solemn detachment, the poet's deliberately remote and archaic style. It was
followed two years later, in 1898, by the *Deux Epigrammes de
Clément Marot*. As in 'Sainte', a strong influence of Debussy
is discernible in these two settings of the mediaeval poet, again
archaic in style almost to the point of pastiche.

In 1903, commissioned to do so by the poet himself, Ravel
set to music a poem called 'Manteau de Fleurs' by Paul Gravolet,
but the banal text resulted in an uncharacteristically dull song.
For his next song, Ravel wrote his own poem. 'Noël des Jouets'
is an unpretentious poem for children, and the song is pleasant,
undemanding and unmemorable. It was followed, in 1906, by
the first really important work by Ravel for solo voice and piano.
(Three years earlier, he had composed his cycle, *Shéhérazade*
on Tristan Klingsor's poems, for voice and orchestra.) Ravel
was attracted by the prose sketches, *Histoires Naturelles*, written
by Jules Renard, by their 'clear, direct language and deep
hidden poetry' as the composer himself described them in a
biographical sketch.[*] He determined to attempt a musical setting
of Renard's thumbnail sketches of these animals and birds, and
finally chose five of them: 'Le Paon', 'Le Grillon', 'Le Cygne',
'Le Martin-Pêcheur' and 'La Pintade'. When the first performance of Ravel's *Histoires Naturelles* was given by the mezzo-
soprano Jane Bathori (to whom the first of the five songs was
dedicated), with the composer playing the piano, the critic
Pierre Lalo, son of the composer Lalo, wrote in *Le Temps* that
Ravel's music 'is well fitted to the text—it is just as precious,
just as laborious, just as dry and almost as unmusical; a collection
of the most out-of-the-way harmonies, industriously contrived,
and the most elaborate and complicated sequences of chords'.[†]
The description is just, the criticism mistaken, for these five
experiments in vocal declamation and musical characterization
are possessed of a rare wit and precision. In 'Le Paon', the
wedding-day of the peacock is majestically rendered: his
diabolical cry, the spreading of his tail, his proud strutting are
all wittily expressed. 'Le Grillon', the cricket, is perhaps the most
extraordinary of the five character-sketches. Consider, for a
moment, Renard's prose, which certainly does not appear to
invite music:

---

[*] From a biographical sketch dictated to Roland-Manuel in 1928 and
printed in a special Ravel number of *La Revue Musicale* Paris 1938
[†] *Le Temps* Paris 19 March 1907

C'est l'heure où, las d'errer, l'insecte nègre revient de
promenade et répare avec soin le désordre de son domaine.
D'abord il ratisse ses étroites allées de sable. Il fait du bran
de scie qu'il écarte au seuil de sa retraite. Il lime la racine
de cette grande herbe propre à la harceler. Il se repose. Puis
il remonte sa miniscule montre. A-t-il fini? Est-elle cassée?*

How skilfully Ravel has found a musical language for the
chirping of the cricket, for the re-winding of his tiny watch, and
all within the narrowest of dynamic ranges. 'Le Cygne' was
perhaps an easier task, but again the composer closely follows
the dry humour, the easy and natural style of Renard, down to
the final sentence in which the romantic swan is dismissed: 'Il
engraisse comme une oie'. 'Le Martin-Pêcheur', the kingfisher,
is surely the most beautiful of the five pieces, Ravel's harmonies
brilliantly suggesting the bird's rich plumage. The cycle ends
with the amusing 'Pintade', a noisy portrait of the bossy guinea-
hen.

The only other song Ravel wrote in 1906 is 'Les Grands Vents
venus d'outre-mer'. Henri de Régnier's symbolist poem about
the great winds from beyond the sea which invade the town
in winter like an enemy, carrying back towards the sea with
them the disaffected adolescents, has called forth an unusually
dramatic, perhaps over-dramatic response from the composer.
It was followed in 1907 by Ravel's only setting of Verlaine, 'Sur
l'Herbe'. The poem is hardly typical Verlaine, but the song
amusingly and suavely characterizes an abbé who has drunk
rather too much Cypriot wine. A more important composition
of the same year is the 'Vocalise en forme d'Habanera'. Over
the rhythm of the habanera, the singer is called upon wordlessly
to vocalize and to execute various feats of technique. Although
intended primarily as a display of skill, that of the composer
and of the singer, the 'Vocalise' is an attractive piece of music
in its own right.

Ravel's next two groups of songs are really folk melodies
for which he provided accompaniments. He was not, as it
happens, particularly interested in folk song and his *Cinq*

* It is the hour when, weary of wandering, the black insect returns from
his promenade, and carefully repairs the disorder of his dwelling. First he
sweeps the narrow pathways of sand. He makes sawdust which he brushes
to the threshold of his retreat. He files away at the root of this long blade
of grass in order to harass it. He rests. Then he winds up his tiny watch. Has
he finished? Is it broken?

mélodies populaires grecques had to be urged into existence by his friend, the critic M. D. Calvocoressi who had collected the tunes on a Greek island. The task of writing Ravelian accompaniments for them was hardly arduous, and the composer completed it in a few hours. The results are quite pleasing, and the songs are made to sound livelier than they probably would do *au naturel*, though it must be admitted that the texts represent the folk spirit at its most satirizible. The following group, *Chants populaires*, collects folk songs from various countries. Ravel initially arranged seven songs, Spanish, French, Italian, Yiddish, Scottish, Flemish and Russian, for a competition organized by a publishing house in Moscow. The first four songs won prizes and were published, while the remaining three have remained unpublished. The four published *Chants populaires* are considerably more interesting than the Greek folk songs: the 'chanson espagnole' has a suave yet affecting melody, very simply accompanied, while its poem, one of regret for a village boy sent off to fight, who, if he returns at all, will return brutalized by experience, is neat and telling. The 'chanson française', from Limousin, is coyly ordinary, but the 'chanson italienne' is excellent, and again the poem itself, though economic of words, is affecting:

M'affacio la finestra e vedo l'onde,	Leaning from my window, I hear the sea,
Vedo le mi miserie che so granne,	I hear my deepest misery.
Chiamo l'amore mio, nun m'arrisponde.	I call my love, naught answers me.

The finest and most interesting song of the four, is the Yiddish 'Mejerke main Suhn', whose sinuous melody, redolent of the synagogue, is supported unobtrusively but firmly by Ravel's sensitive accompaniment. It is more frequently performed than the other *Chants populaires*, as often as not grouped with the *Deux mélodies hébraïques* of 1914, Ravel's last folk settings. These are two traditional tunes, with Hebrew texts. The first, 'Kaddisch', is obviously based on, or at least descends from, liturgical chant, while the second, 'L'Enigme Eternelle', is a simpler tune with an *ostinato* accompaniment.

Before composing the Hebrew songs, Ravel had set *Trois Poèmes de Stéphane Mallarmé*, but these do not, strictly speak-

ing, come within our definition of solo song, as they are scored
for piano, string quartet, two flutes and two clarinets. The next
real solo song is 'Ronsard à son âme', written in 1924, in com-
memoration of the 400th anniversary of Ronsard's birth. The
beautiful poem is given a self-effacing setting which enhances
its purity. The *Chansons Madécasses* of 1926 are, like the *Trois
Poèmes de Mallarmé*, really chamber music. They are scored
for soprano voice, piano, flute and cello, and thus outside the
scope of this survey. Nevertheless it must be said, if only as an
aside, that these three Madegascan songs rank among Ravel's
most exotic and experimental works, their harmonies cool and
subtle, their vocal writing a quasi-recitative whose violent
rhythms now follow those of speech, now create their own
involved patterns. The best description of the spirit and style
of these songs is to be found in the composer's own words. He
emphasized the extent to which the score insisted on the independence of the different parts, and also saw in the work 'a new
dramatic element—the erotic voice, which was introduced by
the very subject of Parny's poems. The work is a sort of quartet
with the voice in the rôle of principal instrument. Simplicity is
the keynote.'*

'Simplicity is the keynote.' One could say that was the secret
of Ravel's songs. There remain only four still to be mentioned.
'Rêves', its poem by the composer's friend, Léon-Paul
Fargue, is a graceful trifle. Ravel's career as a writer of songs
ended in 1932 with the miniature cycle, *Don Quichotte à
Dulcinée*. These three songs were composed for a film of
Cervantes' *Don Quixote*, which was made with the Russian bass
Feodor Chaliapin in the title rôle. The film company apparently approached several composers simultaneously, among them
also Milhaud, Ibert and Marcel Delanney. Ravel's three songs
were not used in the film. The 'Chanson romanesque' is appealing, the 'Chanson épique' catches something of the religious
exaltation of the deluded knight, and the 'Chanson à boire' is
a rousing and amusing drinking song. All are based on Spanish
dance rhythms. They are not only Ravel's last songs, they are the
last music he ever wrote.

Born in the same year as Ravel, the conductor, composer and
critic Reynaldo Hahn (1875–1947) was a pupil of Massenet.
He wrote a number of songs which, often criticized as mere
salon pieces, nevertheless contain among their number several

* Biographical sketch dictated to Roland-Manuel, op. cit.

works of great charm, exquisite sensibility, and melodic appeal. Hahn is hardly known at all today outside France, although during his lifetime he was a popular figure in the fashionable Parisian salons, where his songs were often performed to his own accompaniment. It would, perhaps, be not entirely unfair to describe Hahn's songs as salon music of the very best quality. At its finest, his melodic gift was considerable, and in consequence his songs were immense favourites with the French singers of his own day. Ninon Vallin used to sing many of them with the style, understanding and affection they require in performance. Hahn himself expressed the belief that 'the rôle of music in a song should never be greater than that of the footlights in a play'. This is the sentiment one might have expected from the lips of Debussy : Hahn's footlights are capable sometimes of gleaming more brightly than the play.

At least a dozen of Hahn's songs deserve to be singled out for attention. The one by which the composer's name is most usually remembered is his sentimental 'Si mes vers avaient des ailes'. Victor Hugo's pretty little poem floats to new life on the wings of Hahn's sweetly appealing melody. Greater composers than Hahn have, as we have seen, composed songs to poems of Verlaine; nevertheless there is something special about Hahn's Verlaine settings, some kind of sympathy between poet and composer that makes the songs sound absolutely right, as though words and music had been conceived by one imagination, one sensibility. 'En sourdine', though slight, has a haunting quality; 'D'une Prison' is deceptively simple, in its beginning almost as unobtrusive as those footlights, but again breathing naturally the air of Verlaine; 'L'allée est sans fin' is one of the most touching of Hahn's settings of this poet, and 'L'heure exquise' is deservedly the best known, a perfect matching of words and music, and, as Lotte Lehmann says, 'a feast of the subtlest *piano* tones [in which] everything falls within the enchanting half light of feeling'.* 'Offrande', quietly blissful, has a withdrawn beauty all its own, even surpassing that of Debussy's 'Green', which is a setting of the same Verlaine poem.

'Paysage' (poem by André Theuriet) is remarkable for the ease with which its vocal line combines naturalness of intonation with graceful melody; 'A nos morts ignorés' (Hennevé) is deeply felt, affecting and effective in performance; the graceful, charm-

* Lotte Lohmann *More than Singing. The interpretation of Songs* Boosey & Hawkes New York 1945

ing 'Pholoé', a setting of de Lisle, deserves to be better known. Another and equally fine song whose poem is by de Lisle is 'Phillis', a rhapsodic avowal of love. 'Le Rossignol des Lilas' (poem by Léopold Dauphin) in its lightness and ease of movement could almost be by Fauré, while 'Trois jours de vendange', which sacrifices the urgency of Alphonse Daudet's poem for detail of characterization, is, in a sense, uncharacteristic of Hahn, though an excellent song. Typically Hahn, however, is the gently nostalgic 'Infidélité' (poem by Théophile Gautier).

Erik Satie (1866–1925), though nearly ten years older than Ravel and Hahn, did not begin to make a reputation for himself until he was in his forties, and even then it was a reputation for his eccentricity as much as for his undeniable qualities as a composer. His songs, which include *Trois Poémes d'amour* to words by the composer, *Quatre Petites Mélodies*, whose poems are by Lamartine, Cocteau and Raymond Radiguet, and a cycle of five songs, *Ludions*, settings of Leon Paul Fargue, are ironic, witty, inconsequential, and sometimes impenetrably arcane. They are important less in themselves than in the influence they exerted on a younger generation of composers, specifically those who for a time banded themselves together as 'Les Six', under the artistic leadership, one might almost say the entrepreneur's banner, of Jean Cocteau. These were Durey, Honegger, Milhaud, Taille-ferre, Auric and Poulenc.

Louis Durey (b. 1888) aligned himself with Les Six for only a comparatively brief period between 1916 and 1921, during which time he produced three songs on texts from André Gide's *Voyage d'Urien; Images à Crusoë* (a song-cycle depicting the feelings of Robinson Crusoe on his return to civilization, to poems by Saint-Léger Léger); *Trois Poèmes de Pétrone*; *Epigrammes de Théocrite*; and *Le Bestiaire*, this last a setting of animal poems by Guillaume Apollinaire all of them works which combined natural taste with strong individuality. The songs Durey composed after his period with 'Les Six' seem reticent, even arid, by contrast. Those of Arthur Honegger (1892–1955), whose relationship with Les Six was always somewhat tenuous, are less strongly individual, though invariably pleasing melodic-ally. They include a group of six from Apollinaire's *Alcools* settings, *Six Poésies de Jean Cocteau*, three songs to poems of Paul Claudel, and, in 1941, *Cinq Mélodies-minute* from Jean Giraudoux's 'Suzanne et le Pacifique'. Honegger's sparseness of texture and objectivity of expression are largely typical of the attitude of Les Six and their contemporaries to what they felt to be an over-ripeness, verging on decadence, in the work of their immediate predecessors.

The same qualities of reaction against convention are to be found in the songs of Darius Milhaud (1892–1974). Milhaud, a most prolific composer of songs, produced more than 200, though it cannot be claimed that they are of uniformly high quality. Almost all are easy to listen to, but far too many are rather light. Milhaud's choice of poets is extremely catholic, and includes Francis Jammes, Claudel, Tagore, Coventry Patmore, Mallarmé, traditional Hebrew poetry, Cocteau, René Chalupt, Cactullus, Francis Thompson, Jules Supervielle, Rimbaud, and a variety of lesser-known French poets. The *Four Poems* by Léo Latil of 1914, the eight *Poèmes juifs* of 1916 and a cycle of fifteen songs, *Le Voyage d'été*, to poems of Camille Paliard, are among the most successful and likeable of Milhaud's songs. Germaine Tailleferre (b. 1892), unlike Milhaud, has written comparatively few songs, concentrating instead on orchestral and chamber music, and producing unmemorable works of quiet charm.

Georges Auric (b. 1899) has in recent years busied himself with providing musical scores for films, but he has also produced some easily accessible songs to texts of Cocteau, Radiguet, Éluard, Gérard de Nerval and others, many of them light in idiom, and jazz-influenced but others more lyrical.

By far the most considerable song-writer of Les Six is Francis Poulenc (1899–1963). Not only is he extremely prolific, having written nearly 150 songs, he has also a most enviable gift of melodic invention and ease, and a lively, personal and immediately recognizable style. His earliest songs were settings of Apollinaire, a poet he was to return to over and over again. These first songs were settings of six of the poems in Apollinaire's *Le Bestiaire*, striking miniatures which, according to Marie Laurencin, have 'the very sound of Apollinaire's voice'.* The version for voice and piano is an arrangement of the original, whose accompaniment was scored for flute, clarinet, bassoon and string quartet. *Cocardes*, three settings of Cocteau which date from the same year, 1919, were also first written for voice and various instruments, and arranged for voice and piano twenty years later. These three Cocteau songs, in ironic imitation of the style of popular song, owe much to Satie. The five *Poèmes*

* Henri Hell *Francis Poulenc* John Calder London 1959

de Ronsard (1924) are disappointing, but the eight *Chansons gaillardes*, composed in 1926 to anonymous 17th- and 18th-century texts, are immensely engaging : bucolic, high-spirited, yet full of melodic charm. Poulenc's skill in musical characterization is displayed brilliantly in such pieces as the 'Chanson à boire' and 'Couplets bacchiques', his sense of parody in the brief 'Madrigal', and his fresh lyricism in 'Invocation aux parques' and the final 'Sérénade'.

The first performance of the *Chansons gaillardes* was given in 1926 by the young baritone Pierre Bernac, for whom, after 1935, Poulenc was to write most of his songs, and whom he was frequently to accompany in recital. It has even been said that Poulenc learned how to write songs by accompanying Bernac : certainly he benefitted considerably from his close association with so distinguished a singer and musician, just as Benjamin Britten has benefitted from his friendship with his admired interpreter, Peter Pears.

Among Poulenc's songs of the 'twenties are the four *Airs chantés*, whose poems are by Jean Moréas, a dully conventional symbolist poet. Despite the unpromising texts, these songs are attractive, exhibiting both Poulenc's lyricism and his rough country humour. The composer himself, however, has repudiated the *Airs chantés* in an amusing and typical comment in his *Journal de mes Mélodies* :

> I am constantly astonished at ever having thought of writing these songs. I have no gift for paradox : an expression of paradox in music requires the mastery of a Ravel. The fact is that I loathe these poems of Moréas and I chose them for this very reason, namely that I thought they deserved to be torn to shreds. In the 'Air champêtre' I underlined a certain aspect of the prosody. Have I been punished for such vandalism ? I fear I have, for this unlikeable song has won ill-deserved success. The 'Air grave' is surely the worst of my songs, conventional in the extreme. As for the joyous explosion which is the 'Air vif', this has turned out to be a typical example of meretricious success. The outcome of all this is that I simply turned away from writing songs altogether for a long time to come.[*]

The 'long time to come' was no longer than two years, after

[*] Quoted in Henri Hell op. cit.

which Poulenc returned to song and to his favourite poet, Apollinaire. The *Trois Poèmes* which he set in 1931 are ascribed to one Louise Lalanne, but the lady never existed: she was Apollinaire. The first two songs, 'Le Présent', and 'Chanson', are products of Poulenc the joker, while the third, 'Hier', is from the pen of Poulenc the almost Schubertian lyricist. In the same year there appeared *Quatre Poèmes* (also by Apollinaire), songs in which the composer's ironic and lyrical veins are made to blend remarkably well. 'L'Anguille' is an exercise in the art of gentle parody, 'Carte postale' an affectionate cameo bordering on pastiche, 'Avant le cinéma' a wittily brief song which has an air of sudden improvisation, and '1904' a gay conclusion to the tiny cycle.

It is surprising that the *Cinq Poèmes* of 1931 are, apart from the secular cantata for voice and instrumental ensemble, 'Le bal masqué', Poulenc's only settings of Max Jacob (1876–1944); for Jacob's sardonic humour, shot through with flashes of a sweet lyricism, might almost be thought of as a verbal equivalent of Poulenc's chief qualities. The five Max Jacob songs are highly attractive, and make one wish there had been many more of them. Poulenc was, understandably, at his best when setting those poets with whom he felt a special affinity. He confined himself almost exclusively to contemporary poets, and, among them, to those few whose outlook and style were particularly sympathetic to him. Jacob was one such poet, Apollinaire another, and a third was Paul Eluard, the surrealist, of whom Poulenc wrote: 'Eluard is responsible for having bestowed real lyricism on my music. Every composer eventually discovers what he considers to be his own source of greatness. I have found it in the poetry of Paul Eluard.'* The first of Poulec's Eluard settings were the *Cinq Poèmes* of 1935, dedicated to Pierre Bernac, and given their first performance by Bernac and the composer at the first of their joint public recitals. Poulenc himself came to consider these songs inferior to his later Eluard settings, and in this instance perhaps he was not being unfair to himself, for the songs, though not unattractive, are curiously uncertain in manner. More successful is the single Ronsard song of 1935, 'Ronsard à sa guitare', with its strumming guitar-like introduction and conclusion on the piano, and its simple, appealing melodic line.

By far the most valuable of the Eluard–Poulenc compositions

* Poulenc op. cit.

is the cycle, *Tel jour telle nuit*, nine short songs which, when they were first heard in 1937, were hailed by many critics as the French equivalent of Schumann's *Dichterliebe*. The comparison is by no means far-fetched, and in fact is rather interesting in that there is something of Heine's wit, bitterness, passion and clarity in Eluard's remarkably vivid poems. Another point of similarity with Schumann's cycle is that Poulenc's nine songs are not really performable separately: they are movements related to each other by key, mood and tempo to form a unity. The first song, 'Bonne journée, begins in a mood of bleak melancholy, a mood which achieves a certain ambiguity as the vocal line moves onwards to acquire a tenuous confidence. 'Une ruine coquille vide' strangely combines a kind of objectivity with infinite tenderness, contrasting with the desperation of 'Le front comme un drapeau perdu'. The grimly dramatic recitative of 'Une roulotte couverte en tuiles' similarly contrasts with the swift hurricane of 'A toutes brides'. 'Une herbe pauvre' has an air of pure simplicity, while 'Je n'ai envie que de t'aimer' introduces a sensuous note into the cycle, and 'Figure de force brûlante et farouche' a mood of wild frustration. 'Nous avons fait la nuit' reveals both the poet and the composer at their most serious. This moving love song ends the cycle both appropriately and beautifully.

Of the many songs written in 1938, 'Dans le jardin d'Anna' (poem by Apollinaire) is one of the finest and most original. In his study of Poulenc, the French critic Henri Hell says of it: 'It runs through the whole gamut of irony and parody, and borders on eroticism. Not only is this song a brilliant musical counterpart of Apollinaire's baroque verve: every nuance of humour and tenderness is faithfully portrayed.'* 'Dans le jardin d'Anna' is the first of *Deux Poèmes*. The second, also by Apollinaire, is 'Allons plus vite', a song of quiet melancholy. Dating from the same year is 'Le portrait', a lively and confident setting of Colette.

At the beginning of the war, Poulenc composed the cycle *Fiançailles pour rire*, on poems by Louise de Vilmorin, three of whose poems he had already set in 1937. The cycle, intended as a tribute to the poetess who was imprisoned in a castle in Hungary, is disturbingly empty of real feeling. Far more successful is *Banalités*, five settings of Apollinaire which were composed in 1940. *Banalités* has become one of the most popular

* Hell op. cit.

of Poulenc's groups of songs, and not surprisingly, for the composer has brought his most persuasive lyrical style and his gift for
penetrating characterization to these songs. The most moving
of the poems is 'Sanglots', but the lighter ones are equally
memorable. 'Voyage à Paris' has the sweetness and immediate
melodic appeal of a Parisian music-hall song, and 'Hôtel' a
lazy Mediterranean charm. Also in 1940 Poulenc wrote a
charming waltz, to words by Jean Anouilh, for the operetta star
Yvonne Printemps to sing in Anouilh's Léocadia.

Another deservedly popular cycle dating from the war years
is Chansons villageoises, first written for baritone and orchestra,
the accompaniment later arranged for piano. The poems by
Maurice Fombeure are genial pastiches of folk poetry, and
Poulenc's six songs possess both the spirit and something of the
style of popular French song. The composer has said that he
allowed himself to be influenced here by the manner of Maurice
Chevalier. In the following year, 1943, Poulenc returned to the
poetry of Louise de Vilmorin for the three songs of
Métamorphoses of which the best is 'Paganini', and also composed two more songs on texts of Aragon, the well-known 'C',
which is both beautiful and moving, and the cynical 'Fêtes
galantes'. In the same year, there appeared two sensitive
Apollinaire songs, 'Montparnasse' and 'Hyde Park'.

'Paul et Virginie' (1946) is a graceful miniature, whose poem
comes from Raymond Radiguet, the novelist who died very young.
In 1947, two more Eluard songs were written. '. . . Mais mourir'
in which the poet's fragmented images are gathered up into a
lyrical line of feeling and sensitivity, and 'Main dominée par le
cœur'. Less successful in finding musical terms for Eluard's simple
philosophizing. The 1948 cycle Calligrammes appeared to be
Poulenc's farewell to Apollinaire; these seven songs are not
among the composer's best, and he was no doubt right in feeling
that he had already extracted from Apollinaire all that he was
likely to extract. The solemn 'Hymne' (words by Racine) of
1949 is impressive, and closer in manner to Poulenc's choral
religious music than to any of the other songs, while the cycle
of Eluard poems La Fraîcheur et le Feu, composed in 1951,
reveals the composer still at the peak of his powers. This subtle,
spontaneous work is dedicated to Stravinsky whose piano
'Serenade' of 1925 is quoted briefly in the third song. The next
few years were largely devoted by Poulenc to the composition of
the opera Dialogues des Carmélites, but in 1954 he returned to

Apollinaire with a beautifully lyrical setting of the poet's 'Rosemonde'. Two years later came the brilliant and engaging cycle *Le Travail du Peintre*, settings of poems by Eluard from the collection *Voir*, in which various contemporary painters are described and celebrated. The seven painters of Poulenc's cycle are Pablo Picasso, Marc Chagall, Georges Braque, Juan Gris, Paul Klee, Juan Miro and Jacques Villon. Also dating from 1956 are the *Deux mélodies* to poems of Apollinaire and Laurence de Beylié. 'Souris', Apollinaire's sweetly sad little poem about the beautiful days, 'souris de temps' gnawing away at his life, is sympathetically set by Poulenc, and 'Nuage' develops the same theme in a longer lyrical line. 'Dernier Poéme', a setting of the last poem of Robert Desnos, is an exquisite example of Poulenc's meditative lyricism.

Among French composers born in the 20th century, Henri Sauguet (b. 1901) is worthy of mention as a composer of songs not unlike those of Poulenc, though lacking the older composer's powerful personality. Although he was never a member of Les Six, Sauguet associated with the composers of that group, and was, like them, a disciple of Erik Satie. He has set Eluard, Baudelaire, Mallarmé and Cocteau, but has also ranged more widely in his choice of poets, to include Shakespeare, Schiller, Heine, Rilke, Hölderlin and Swinburne. Among the most interesting of Sauguet's songs are the *Six Mélodies sur des poèmes symbolistes* (two each by Mallarmé, Laforgue and Baudelaire), *Force et faiblesse* (seven songs to poems of Eluard) and *Deux mélodies* (Paul Valéry). André Jolivet (b. 1905) has written songs of undeniable originality, though mostly for voice and orchestra. Those of Jacques Leguerney (b. 1906) are less original, though always gracefully and confidently written for the voice. Among them are settings of La Pléiade, the 16th-century group of poets which included Ronsard, Du Bellay, Jodelle and Dorat. More important is Olivier Messiaen (b. 1908) whose music, much of it for organ or piano, is harmonically rich, highly coloured, and intensely personal in style. His songs include *Deux Ballades de Villon* (1912), *Poèmes pour Mi* (1936), *Chants de terre et de ciel* (1938), these last two typical of Messiaen's mature style, and *Harawi, Chant d'amour et de mort* (1945). *Harawi*, like most of Messiaen's mature compositions, is strikingly remote from the influence of earlier composers, and owes more to the composer's own theories, in explaining which Messiaen is highly articulate if also extremely dogmatic. His music, he has said, exists to illustrate his mystical and religious ideals. The word *Harawi*, in the Quechua language, which is the ancient language of Peru, means a love song which ends with the death of the lovers, in fact a *Liebestod*. Messiaen's cycle of twelve songs, the words of which are his own, is intended as an exploration of the Tristan and Isolde myth in terms of Peruvian folklore.

It would be perhaps unkind, though not entirely inaccurate, to refer to Jean Françaix (b. 1912) as a kind of sub-Poulenc, for his music is pleasant, witty, and technically proficient. Among his elegant though hardly memorable songs are the cycle *L'Adolescence clémentine* (poems by Clément Marot) and *Cinq Poésies de Charles d'Orléans*. René Leibowitz (1913–1972), leader of the French twelve-note composers, studied with Schoenberg and Webern, and his works display the strong influence of the former master. Leibowitz's songs include a group of six for the bass voice, and three settings of poems by Picasso, for soprano. Pierre Boulez (b. 1926) is, at the time of writing, in mid-career. Until the mid 1960s, when his activities as a conductor of other men's music began to increase, it was an extremely single-minded career, based on rigidly adhered-to rules of the composer's own devising. The human voice plays an important rôle in the compositions of Boulez, though he is more interested in combinations of voice or voices and orchestra than in the simple solo song with piano. Jean-Michel Damase (b. 1928) has written graceful and charming songs which have featured in the recital programmes of current French singers; however, ten years after the death of Poulenc, it does not seem as though the true successor to that master of lyrical art has yet emerged. The mid 20th-century French song retains a suavity which German song perhaps lost with Schumann; but it no longer possesses that confident and sensitive response to poetry which had been one of the glories of the French *chanson* in the 19th and early 20th centuries.

III

RUSSIA, SCANDINAVIA AND
EASTERN EUROPE

SOLO SONG IN Russia emerged in the early 19th century
from the country's store of folk music. The earliest of the
composers whose songs are known and sung today is Mikhail
Ivanovich Glinka (1804–1857), renowned as the creator of the
first great Russian operas *A Life for the Tsar* and *Russlan and
Ludmila.* He was an initiator, though hardly in any sense an
experimenter, whose interests were primarily Western, and not
Russian. As a child, Glinka received a few piano lessons from
the Irish composer and pianist, John Field; as a young man he
studied singing with Belloli, an Italian teacher in St Petersburg;
and in his twenties he travelled to Italy where he studied for
three years in Milan and also met Bellini and Donizetti. Small
wonder, then, that Glinka's songs, of which he wrote more than
seventy, are Italianate in style, graceful *bel canto* melodies of
charm rather than of forceful character. The earliest songs were
written in the mid 1820s, when both Schubert and Bellini were
at the height of their powers, but they are much closer to the
simple tunes of the Italian than to the more highly organized
Lieder of the Viennese composer. The last songs, composed in
the mid 1850s, though contemporaneous with those of the young
Brahms, appear not to have developed at all significantly from
the earlier ones. Nevertheless, Glinka's works deserve their place
in any survey of European song, however uncharacteristic
of the Russian spirit they may be, many of them, despite the
old-fashioned style of their musical language, are exceptionally
beautiful.

Some of the songs, such as the gentle 'Oh, you sweet, lovely
girl', possess the unadorned simplicity of folk song. Others, like
'Tell me why', a setting of a poem by Golitzin, with its conventionally pretty accompaniment supporting and framing a somewhat more sophisticated melody, are, by contrast, far removed

from folk style. In the 1820s Glinka composed a number of songs and arias on Italian texts, though by far the majority of his songs are settings of Russian poets. In addition to Golitzin, his poets included Pushkin, Alexei Kiltsov, who was a kind of Russian Robert Burns, the elegant Baron Delvig, the elegiac Vasily Zhukovsky, and Mikhail Lermontov.

The strophic 'Venetian Night' (poem by Kozlov), composed in 1832, its accompaniment depicting the gently lapping water of the canals, is one of Glinka's most attractive songs, and even more attractive is the 1838 setting of Pushkin's 'I remember that magical moment', its tune exquisitely moulded to the contours of the Russian language, its feeling unforced and lyrical. This song and 'Doubt' are probably Glinka's best-known outside Russia, for they turn up not infrequently in recital programmes. 'Doubt' (poem by Kukolnik) in its original version was written for contralto, harp (or piano) and violin, but its sad, appealing melody loses little by being heard supported by piano alone. That these songs are not simply imitations of Italian models is evident from the quality of Glinka's melody, which is curiously Russian, and always slightly melancholy even when illustrating an ostensibly carefree text. The melodies of 'How happy I am with you' (poem by P. Ryndin) and 'I love you, dear rose' (Samarin) could only have been written by a Russian for the Russian language. The twelve songs of the cycle *Farewell to Petersburg*, whose poems are by Kukolnik, include some remarkably fine things. Composed in 1840, the year of Schumann's great cycles, this one hardly deserves its almost complete neglect. Perhaps the most impressive of its songs are no. 1, 'David Rizzio's Song' (David Rizzio being the Italian secretary of Mary Stuart, murdered at Holyrood House in 1566); no. 5, the sweetly beguiling 'Lullaby'; no. 6, a lively outburst, 'This song travels with us', its tempo unusually fast for Glinka; and no. 10, 'The Lark', with its flowing Italianate cantilena. 'Gretchen's Song', composed in 1848, uses a translation by E. I. Huber of 'Meine Ruh ist hin' from Goethe's *Faust*. In its fashion, it is as appealing a setting as the more familiar one by Schubert, tuneful yet full of character.

Combining both lyrical and dramatic elements, 'Do not call her divine' (poem by N. Pavlov) is another of the many Glinka songs which, if taken up by singers with a knowledge of Russian, would surely become popular with audiences outside Russia. To mention only three other songs of similar potential : 'Oh, if

I had known before' is an arrangement of an old gypsy song, 'The Gulf of Finland' (poem by P. Obodovsky) has an unusual and arresting melody, and Pushkin's 'Adele' an engaging and infectious quality of happiness. A Glinka song which is already indisputably established in the West is the dramatic but uncharacteristic 'Midnight Review (poem by Zhukovsky) which Chaliapin used to sing.

Alexander Sergeyevich Dargomizhsky (1813–1869) was no less prolific a song writer than Glinka, though his life's main work was in the field of opera (*Esmeralda, Russalka, The Stone Guest*). In his earthier realism and robust humour, he was decidedly more Russian than Glinka, and his songs are both more dramatic and less influenced by Italian ideas of melody. Something of the spirit of Gogol is to be found in many of Dargomizhsky's humorous character-songs, satirizing petty officialdom, while in certain other songs, such as 'O Maid, my Rose' and 'An Eastern Song', the spirit of the old Eastern Russia pervades his melody. 'The Paladin', 'The Worm' and 'I think that thou wert born for this' are among the stronger, more successful songs, while 'I am grieving' and 'Little Cloud in the Sky' (poems by Lermontov), which successfully combine an elegiac, lyrical line with a fidelity to speech rhythms, are two of the most beautiful. Dargomizhsky's essays in folk style certainly sound authentic, but tend to lack melodic individuality, though the wistful 'Sixteen years old' (poem by Delvig) is ingratiating. His contemporary, Anton Rubinstein (1830–1894), pianist and composer, wrote more than a hundred songs, many of which, such as the *Twelve Persian Songs* op. 34, were, in their time, very popular. Rubinstein's gift for romantic, Lisztian melody is displayed at its finest in the passionate 'Night', a setting of Pushkin which is better known in English as 'If you are but a dream'.

The next five composers to be considered are those who, as a group, came to be known in Western Europe as 'The Five'. The Russian nickname of these strongly nationalist artists was *Moguchaya Kuchka*, 'the mighty handful'; their aim was to rescue Russian music from baleful Western influences by their example, and to fight against the ultra-conservative elements in Russian musical life. The Five—Borodin, Cui, Balakirev, Mussorgsky and Rimsky-Korsakov—born in the 1830s and '40s, derived their inspiration from Dargomizhsky, who was twenty years senior to the eldest of them, and gained the support of the influential critic Vladimir Vassilievich Stassov who, firm in his belief that the Russian genius was essentially Eastern, made himself the spokesman for nationalism not only in music but in the arts in Russia generally. The Five, and those other composers who became their supporters, were political liberals, interested in and inspired by such important reforms as the liberation of the serfs in 1861. They carried their aims and ideals into music by devoting themselves to subjects derived from Russian life, therefore they tended to make use of folk song, either by way of direct quotation or by adopting a folk idiom. All of them were interested in song, and most of The Five composed a good many songs, often political in intent, either covertly or overtly.

The most senior of The Five, Alexander Porfirevich Borodin (1833–1887), composed fewer songs than the others—no more than sixteen—but those few include some of his boldest musical ideas. His sixteen songs divide themselves naturally into two groups : four early works, written when Borodin was about twenty years of age, and the remaining twelve, composed in his maturity, between the ages of thirty-four and fifty-two. The very first song, 'Why art thou so early, dawn?' (poem by Soloviev) is of little interest. Its three companions all have 'cello obbligati, and Borodin's writing for the 'cello in these songs seems more assured than his writing for the voice. 'The fair young maid no longer loves me' is less sentimental than its text (by Vinogradev) would seem to suggest, and is certainly the most attractive of these juvenile exercises. 'Friends, hear my song' (poem by Von Kruse) is more folkish in manner than the others. The fourth song of this period differs from the others in being a setting not of minor Russian verse but of Heine, a poet to whom Borodin was to turn twice again in later years. 'The beautiful fishermaiden' is an unsuitably hearty interpretation of Heine's 'Das schöne Fishchermädchen', though again the 'cello part contributes a freshness and charm to the song. A version omitting the 'cello obbligato also exists.

The first of Borodin's mature songs, 'The Sleeping Princess', is also the first of several for which the composer wrote the words himself. Ostensibly a variant of the well-known French fairy tale, the poem allegorically describes the land of Russia herself failing to awaken to the ideas of the new liberalism. As the Soviet critic Serge Dianin said of it, from his own specifically Marxist viewpoint, 'The Princess can only signify Borodin's native land, Russia, which was still sleeping under the heavy spell of bondage and the oppressive "bewitchment" of tsarist autocracy. At the time that Borodin was writing his song, there was no organized revolutionary movement in Russia, and not the least sign of one for years to come. But Borodin felt that Russia would have to awaken when the fateful hour struck, even though he viewed with scepticism the revolutionary groups and insurrectionists of his own day.'*

Musically, the song is quite simply organized, its lethargic sleep theme, with major seconds in the accompaniment to denote drowsiness, alternating with the urgent sounds of those forces which would awaken the princess. The song ends with the princess still sleeping, impervious to the outside world. One's impression is that she will sleep for ever, though the ambiguous final line is 'And no one knows when she will awaken'. 'The Sleeping Princess' was dedicated to Rimsky-Korsakov who later orchestrated its accompaniment.

More direct in its methods is 'The Song of the Dark Forest'. Borodin's poem tells of a forest which sings a song of the past, a past when men cared for freedom, and when a mighty force rose up against its oppressors. The music is hypnotically powerful, and Borodin made use of it later for Galitsky's seditious speech at the end of Act I of *Prince Igor*. (The Russian composers of the 19th century appear to have been unable to keep their hands off one another's works: after Borodin's death an arrangement of this song was made for male chorus and orchestra by Glazunov.) 'The Sea Princess' seems to possess no political undertones: Borodin's poem, this time a reference to the Lorelei myth, is lyrical and impressionistic, and the song itself is appealing, with its typical dissonant seconds, and its attractive harmonic background.

The words of the short, but deeply felt 'False Note' are again by the composer. These five lines of disenchantment with a woman's avowal of love are given a dully aching setting only seventeen bars long, with a repeated dissonant F natural in the accompaniment symbolizing the false note struck by the disharmonious relationship. 'My songs are filled with poison', a setting of a Russian translation of Heine's 'Vergiftet sind meine Lieder' catches, even in translation, the authentic voice of Heine, and at the same time carries echoes of Schumann, that poet's supreme interpreter. 'The Sea', with words by Borodin, is a ballad about a sailor who is drowned while returning home

* Serge Dianin *Borodin* O.U.P. London 1963

to his native country and his beautiful wife. According to Stassov, the original text told a slightly different story, of 'a young exile banished from his country for political reasons who, full of impassioned and burning hopes, returns home only to meet a tragic death in a storm within sight of the shores of his native land'.* This text, Stassov asserts, was rejected by the censor. Borodin himself wrote of this highly dramatic ballad, with its graphic opening in G flat minor depicting a raging sea, and its excited and exciting narrative, 'It's a good piece, it has charm, fire and sparkle, and is tuneful as well.'†

'From my tears', a setting of Heine's 'Aus meinen Tränen' translated by Borodin himself, is a song underrated by Russian critics from Stassov onwards, a gentle, affectionate and faithful rendering into music of the mood of the poem. It was written in 1871, and a gap of ten years separates it from Borodin's next song, years during which he devoted himself entirely to opera, and worked on *Mlada* and *Prince Igor*. In 1881, disillusioned for a time with *Prince Igor*, he turned again to songs, and produced three during the year, a year in which he wrote very little other music. The 'Arab Melody', for which Borodin provided words turning it into a declaration of love, was a tune he came across when examining Arabic *qasids* or odes in the St Petersburg Public Library with a view to adapting some of them to his own use. This authentic Arabic tune, collected by the Russian orientalist, Christianovich, makes an exotic love song, its harmonies subtly attractive. 'At home among real people', its poem by Nicolai Nekrassov, the leading Russian poet of the second half of the 19th century, is a comic song which makes its effect through clear and pointed setting of the words, rather than by musically attempting to compete with the verbal humour. Having composed it with piano accompaniment, Borodin himself then orchestrated the accompaniment. The third song of 1881 is 'Far the shores of your distant homeland', still the most popular Borodin song in Russia, and understandably so, for its melody has a natural beauty and grace, and carries Pushkin's poem with admirable clarity and sincerity. This song disconcerted several of Borodin's friends who thought it classical and Western, and Stassov even suspected the composer of succumbing to the dangerous un-Russian influence of Schubert. There exists an effective orchestration of the song by Glazunov.

* V. V. Stassov *Life of Borodin* St Petersburg 1889
† Dianin op. cit.

After 1881, Borodin wrote only two more songs. 'Pride' (poem by Alexei Tolstoy) is an excellent piece of musical satire in the style of a folk ballad crossed with one of Mussorgsky's character-sketches, and 'The Marvellous Garden' (a translation of the poem 'Septain' by the Belgian, Georges Collin) is a delicate impressionistic evocation of an elegantly beautiful scene. The width of range and musical character of Borodin's sixteen songs is out of all proportion to their number: this is the impression that remains strongly with one after hearing them.

César Antonovich Cui (1835–1918) composed more than 200 songs, as well as eleven operas and orchestral and instrumental pieces. He is generally regarded as the least original talent among The Five, and is certainly the least Russian of them, his music owing more to Chopin and Schumann than to Russian folk song; it is perhaps worth remembering that Cui's father was French and his mother Lithuanian. He was Russian by nation-ality rather than by race, and many of his songs were composed to French texts, and a few to Polish texts. The best of them are extremely beautiful, though they lack the Russian feeling of Borodin or the individuality of the other members of The Five. Of Cui's earliest songs, some of those in op. 5 and op. 7, each consisting of six songs, are attractive, in particular op. 5 no. 2, 'A dead man's love' (poem by Lermontov) and the almost Schubertian 'Forget those lost days', a setting of a tender love lyric by Nekrassov. Some of the French songs, such as 'La tombe et la rose' (Victor Hugo), tend to sound rather colourless, though others, for instance 'Ici-bas' (the Sully-Prudhomme poem better known in Fauré's setting), have an unexpected intensity that puts one in mind of Duparc. Cui's 'Ici-bas' was composed in the 1890s, some years after Duparc had completed his *œuvre*. Cui's taste in French verse is hardly impeccable. In 1890 he completed a group of twenty songs (op. 44) on the poems of Jean Richepin (1849–1926), a poet, vastly overrated in his own day, who has now fallen into oblivion. The Richepin songs include some excellent pieces of characterization, such as 'Le Hun' in which Attila sings of his own exploits, and a few pleasant and more lyrical settings, among them 'Les Songeants' and 'Le Ciel est transi', though the latter is marred by faulty accentuation. Among Cui's Russian songs, the most interesting are his settings of Pushkin and Lermontov. An early Lermontov song has already been mentioned. Of the mature ones, 'The Imprisoned Cavalier' op. 55 no. 7 is unusual for the force and determination the composer has injected into the poet's despondent lines, and 'The Prophet' op. 55 no. 8 is particularly effective in the way its vocal line treads cunningly between the demands of characterization and lyricism. The Pushkin songs include the short, beautiful 'Statue at Tsarkoye-Selo', and 'Desire', one of Cui's most simple and effective melodies, both of them from op. 57, which consists of twenty-five settings of the poet. In 'The Conjuring', a desperate lover conjures up the spirit of his dead beloved : Cui is at his best when the poem he is working on is strong enough in feeling and language to require little more than the slightest melodic support, as is the case here. 'In memory of Stassov' (poem by N. Klark) was written on the death in 1906 of the critic who had been both spokesman and soul of The Five. 'No, he is not dead at all, for he will live forever', the poem confidently begins, and the mood of Cui's tribute remains one of heightened, ennobled grief : a touching hymn, not on the death of the great critic, but on his life.

Unofficial leader of The Five, certainly teacher and adviser to his four colleagues, Mily Balakirev (1837–1910) himself learned much from Glinka about Russian song, and wrote forty-five songs, predominantly lyrical, which derive and develop from the earlier composer. Balakirev's earliest efforts, composed when he was eighteen, but not published until 1908 when they appeared as *Three Forgotten Songs*, are very similar in style to those of Glinka, especially 'Thou art so captivating' (words by Golovinsky). The remainder of Balakirev's songs can be divided into two groups, the first consisting of twenty songs composed between 1858 and 1865, the second consisting of the remaining twenty-two songs, written in 1895 or later. In other words, during the thirty years of his maturity, from his twenty-eighth to his fifty-eighth year, Balakirev wrote no songs. He composed only intermittently during this period, being occupied with an administrative post, and troubled for some years by a spiritual and mental crisis from which he emerged an eccentrically superstitious Orthodox Christian with little or no interest in music. Gradually, over the years, his interest in music and in composing revived.

Koltsov and Lermontov were Balakirev's two favourite poets; his first group of twenty songs contains seven settings of the former poet and five of the latter. Balakirev's finest songs are to be found among this group, songs in which lyrical fervour and classical restraint are perfectly balanced. The songs written after

1895 are, in general, considerably less good. 'Cradle Song' (poem by Arsenev), no. 4 of the twenty early songs, is a miniature masterpiece of great beauty and simplicity. There exists a version of this song for voice and orchestra, made by Sir Henry Wood for use at a Promenade Concert. 'The Bright Moon' (no. 5, poem by Yatsevich), equally fine, is in ternary form with a simple, though highly effective accompaniment. 'The Knight', no. 7, is a lively, dramatic ballad (words by Vilde) about a knight who returns from the wars to find his beloved has died. The subject is hackneyed, but Balakirev's setting is swift and to the point, and the galloping rhythm in the piano part is natural and unforced. Two love songs to poems by Koltsov, 'My heart is torn' and 'Come to me', are both charming and individual, but it is no. 11 of this group, 'Selim's Song', the first of the Lermontov settings, which really captures one's interest. In its combination of economy and lyrical simplicity with great dramatic effect, 'Selim's Song' is positively Schubert-ian. 'Hebrew Melody' is a setting in B flat minor of Lermontov's free translation of Byron, a highly attractive song in two verses, in each of which a largo introduction gives way to a passionate allegro melody of great character and individuality. Another magnificent song is Lermontov's 'Song of the Golden Fish', in which a mermaid lures her enchanted victim down to the depths of the sea into a dream world existing beyond time. Balakirev's setting has a remote and strange beauty, in part due to the almost Debussian chromaticism of his harmonies, and in part to the sheer beauty of his vocal line. Of the remaining early songs, 'When I hear thy voice' (Lermontov) is particularly charming and Pushkin's 'Georgian Song', which Balakirev later orches-trated, is another minor masterpiece, a mournful, oriental melody of great appeal, heard twice, separated by an agitated recitative section.

Twenty years later, Balakirev returned to song composition with ten pieces written in 1895–6. In general, these are of less interest than the earlier songs, though there are certainly some excellent touches in several of them. They appear to have been composed with considerably less ease than the songs of Balakirev's youth; much is contrived, the melodic ideas are lacking in freshness, and the earlier simplicity has lost its spontaneity. 'The Wilderness' (poem by Zhemchuzhnikov), with its deliberately monotonous sound-picture of the desert traveller trudging along (a repeated C sharp pedal in the bass), its mood becoming livelier, richer in harmony, at the prospect of an oasis, is effective, though perhaps rather superficial. 'When the yellow cornfield waves' (Lermontov) is not unattractive. Three of these ten songs are considerably better than the others : 'The Pine Tree' (Heine, translated by Lermontov) is a somewhat Schubertian exercise in nostalgia, of undeniable charm; 'Nachtstück' (Khomiakov) seems to have tapped a deeper spring of feeling in its composer, a feeling which can be excitingly communicated in performance by a first-rate singer; and 'The Putting Right' (Mey) is an excellent Mussorgskian character-sketch of a drunkard.

A gap of a further eight years separates these songs from the next, another group of ten, composed in 1903–4. This latter group contains a higher number of successes than those composed in 1895–6. The first song, 'Prologue' (poem by Mey) exhibits the mournful simplicity of Russian folk song, while the second, 'Dream' (Lermontov), a dramatic ballad of death and delusion, is conceived on a heroic scale, with a superb accompaniment. 'Starless midnight coldly breathed' is a setting of a poem by Khomiakov which lends itself admirably to musical treatment. An exile imagines himself soaring through the winter night to Prague where, in the cathedral, he hears the old Russian Orthodox Easter chant, 'Christ is risen from the dead'. The fourth song, '7th November' (Khomiakov), a dramatic master-piece, describes the opening of Napoleon's tomb at St Helena. The opening and closing sections are marched along by the piano, and the voice recounts the grim proceedings in near-recitative. This is a song for a singer who is also an accomplished actor. 'I came to thee with greeting' (Fet), despite its simple charm, contrives to be one of the least compelling songs of the group, but 'Look, my friend' (Krasov) is an engaging love song, with two attractive and contrasting melodies. No. 7, 'A whisper, a timid breath' (Fet), is a delicate, impressionistic miniature masterpiece, its accompaniment both sensitive and subtle. No. 8, 'Song' (Lermontov), in Balakirev's folk song style, is rather pleasant, but the following Lermontov setting, 'Under the mysterious mask', sounds contrived. The final song, 'Sleep' (Khomiakov) is an evocative and ambitious account of the sleep of a child, an adult and an old man, a song of powerful atmosphere and unique inspiration. After another interval of five years, Balakirev wrote a final pair of songs only months before his death : 'Dawn' (Khomiakov), and 'The Rock'

(Lermontov). Neither is among his best, though 'Dawn' contains some attractive passages. Throughout his life, Balakirev also collected a number of Russian folk songs, and these he arranged with piano accompaniments. A collection of forty songs was published in 1866 and a further *Thirty Songs of the Russian People* in 1898.

Modest Mussorgsky (1839–1881) was surely the greatest song composer of The Five, and probably the strongest creative personality. His masterpiece, the opera *Boris Godunov*, with its realistic portrayal of scenes of Russian life, is composed in a style which owes little to earlier composers but is based on the speech rhythms of the Russian language, rarely attempting to take lyrical flight from the implicit restrictions of such a style. The same can be said of Mussorgsky's songs, the majority of which are miniature character-sketches, often declamatory in manner, though frequently close to Russian folk song as well. Mussorgsky's genius is, in a way, more clearly revealed in his sixty-six songs than in *Boris Godunov* which is still known to most people only in the version heavily edited and disfigured by the well-meaning Rimsky-Korsakov. Many of the songs were similarly 'touched-up' by Rimsky-Korsakov after Mussorgsky's death. The authentic Mussorgskian texts are to be found in the Russian edition of the complete works, edited by Paul Lamm.*

Mussorgsky's earliest surviving song, 'Where art thou, little star?', a setting of a poem by Nicolai Grekov, is one of his most lyrical, a delightful and somewhat uncharacteristic piece which he wrote at the age of eighteen, and which was not improved when he re-wrote it for voice and orchestra the following year. Most of the other very early songs are decidedly less attractive than 'Where art thou, little star?', though 'Sadly rustled the leaves' is not without merit, and Russian singers still find 'Tell me why' and the drinking-song 'Hour of Jollity' (poem by Koltsov) worth performing. Another Koltsov setting, 'I have many palaces and gardens', is one of the first really to reveal the young composer's individuality, and in the same year, 1863, 'Old Man's Song' made it clear that this individuality was on the way to blossoming into genius. The words of 'Old Man's Song' are a Russian translation of the Harper's song, 'An die Türen will ich schleichen', from Goethe's *Wilhelm Meister*; Mussorgsky has turned the old man into a Russian beggar, expressing himself in a musical language which the composer

* Moscow 1930

was to perfect in *Boris Godunov*. A remarkable feature of this
song is the use made of the piano to add to the dramatic picture.
'King Saul' (from Byron's 'Hebrew Melodies' translated by
Pavel Kozlov), also composed in 1863, in two versions, the
second of which is inferior to the first, is a fine and powerful
song. The remaining song of that year, 'But if I could meet thee
again' (Kurochkin), is disappointingly weak.

The accents of *Boris Godunov* are heard again in 'The wild
winds blow', a powerful evocation of nature, composed in 1864.
Two further songs composed during this year each exist in two
versions. The musical differences between the two versions of
'Night', a Pushkin setting of great beauty, are insignificant, but
the textual differences are curious, for, having first set the poem
virtually as it stands, Mussorgsky then almost completely re-
wrote it, by no means improving upon Pushkin in the process.
This apparent inability to regard any work as at last completed
was to remain with Mussorgsky throughout his comparatively
brief life. 'Kalistrat', a setting of Nekrassov's poem about a
peasant musing on the lullaby his mother used to sing to him,
incorporates a folk tune to do duty for the remembered lullaby.
The two versions, one for tenor, one for baritone, differ only
in matters of detail.

The songs mentioned so far are those designated as from the
'Years of Youth' in the definitive Lamm edition. The remaining
songs of these years are of little interest : Mussorgsky's setting
of Lermontov's famous 'Prayer' is dull, and his 'experiment in
recitative', 'The Outcast' (text by Ivan Goltz-Miller) pointless.
However, the *Seven Romances and Songs*, most of which date
from 1866, contain some of the composer's finest mature works.
'Desire', a translation by Mikhail Mikhailov of Heine's 'Ich
wollt' meine Schmerzen ergössen', is pleasant though unmemorable, but most of the songs to original Russian texts are first-rate.
The popular 'Hopak', a lively peasant dance, is a character
piece in which an old man sings and dances, telling the story of a
girl and her Cossack husband, 'old and weak and ailing'. The text
is a translation by Lyov Mey from Taras Shevchenko's *The
Haidamaks*. The almost equally popular 'Lovely Savishna',
whose text is by Mussorgsky himself, is an extraordinary sketch
of an idiot stammering out his confession of love to the village
beauty. The critic Stassov has left an account of how the song
came to be written :

As [Mussorgsky] himself told me later, he conceived this piece in the country at his brother's farm at Minkino in the summer of 1865. He was standing at the window, and was struck by a commotion that was taking place before his eyes. An unfortunate simpleton was declaring his love to a young peasant woman whom he liked, imploring her, all the while ashamed of his own ugliness and unfortunate situation; he himself understood that nothing on earth, especially the joys of love, could exist for him. Mussorgsky was deeply moved; the figure and the scene fell powerfully on his soul; in an instant appeared the particular forms and sounds for the clear embodiment of the images that had stunned him, but he did not write down the song at once; first of all he wrote his 'Peasant Lullaby', full of oppressive sadness, and completed and wrote down 'Lovely Savishna' only some months later.*

The cradle song, or peasant's lullaby (text from Alexander Ostrovsky's *Voyevoda*) is indeed a sad little piece. 'You drunken sot' (words by the composer), a tirade addressed to a drunkard, began life as a private joke but was later to provide a moving passage for *Boris Godunov*. "The Seminarist', another setting of Mussorgsky's own words, is an amusing sketch of a theological student whose mind is simultaneously preoccupied with Latin texts and amorous thoughts.

The *Thirteen Romances and Songs* of the Russian collected edition are miscellaneous songs composed between 1867 and 1871, most of them in the former year. 'Hebraic Song', its text from Mey's translation of the *Song of Solomon*, is one of Mussorgsky's most beautiful lyrical utterances. Its melody, distinctly oriental in contour, is not specifically Hebraic. (It is contemporaneous with Rimsky-Korsakov's 'Hebraic Song' op. 7 no. 2 (q.v.) which is dedicated to Mussorgsky. The two songs have certain melodic similarities, and it is probable that they represent some kind of joint project.) 'The White-Flanked Magpie', a gay scherzo subtitled 'a joke', uses a text made up from two poems by Pushkin : 'A chattering magpie' and 'Little bells tinkle'. 'Gathering Mushrooms' (text by Mey) is a superb example of the kind of song Mussorgsky virtually invented : a heightened rendering of Russian speech flattened out into even crotchets. In it, a woman gathering mushrooms muses on the possibility of feeding a poisonous species to her husband.

* V. V. Stassov *Modest Petrovich Mussorgsky* St Petersburg 1881

Similar in style is 'The Feast', Koltsov's description of a peasant gathering. 'The Naughty Boy' (or 'The Ragamuffin'), its words by the composer, is another scherzo character-sketch, this time of an urchin hurling insults at an old woman in the street. 'A worldly fable' is how Mussorgsky describes 'The He-Goat', another song for which he provided the words. The verbal satire —a bearded old goat frightens a young girl, but her bearded old bridegroom does not—though obvious, is sharply pointed, but the music in this case seems almost an afterthought. Nevertheless, the piece can be made to sound amusing in performance by a singer who can act with his voice. The same can be said of 'The Classicist', another satirical song, written 'in answer to Famintzin's notice on the heresies of the Russian school of music', in which, according to a note on the score, the composer's text is intended to be declaimed by a classical musician hostile to 'new-fangled contrivances'. At the mention of the abhorred new music, the classical poise of the melody is interrupted by a quotation from Rimsky-Korsakov's *Sadko* in the accompaniment. A pleasant musical joke, but a purely topical in-joke of its time. 'On the Don the gardens bloom' (poem by Koltsov) is a charming and delicate lyric, fresh, unsentimental and delicate. 'The Little Orphan Girl' (text by Mussorgsky) and 'Child's Song' (Mey) are excellent, and 'Yeremushka's Cradle Song' (Nekrassov) is no conventional cradle song, but another superb character-sketch, this time of a peasant nurse brooding on the future of the child in her care. 'Evening Song', a setting of a poem by Alexei Pleshcheyev, exhibits a simple but real charm, and the ballad 'Forgotten', its text by Arseni Golenishchev-Kutuzov, the poet of Mussorgsky's great cycles, *Sunless* and *Songs and Dances of Death*, is a magnificent forerunner of the latter cycle. Both the grim poem and its finely appropriate music were inspired by a painting by the war artist Vasili Vereshchagin, which was exhibited in St Petersburg, and which depicted the body of a Russian soldier, forgotten and left behind on a battlefield in Turkestan.

'Peepshow', a lengthy parody directed against the enemies of The Five, is of little musical interest. A Prelude, sung, says the composer, by 'myself', invites the audience to step up and enjoy the peepshow of great musicians, after which the victims to be satirized are introduced one by one: the theorist Zaremba, to a paraphrase of two choruses from Handel's *Judas Maccabaeus*, 'Sing unto God' and 'See, the Conquering Hero Comes'; the critic F. M. Tolstoy, made to sing the praises of the soprano Adelina Patti to a waltz tune based partly on the gypsy melody, 'Dark eyes'; the conservative composers Famintsin and Serov are next caricatured with quotations from their own music; finally, the goddess Euterpe, invoked in a song based on a tune from Serov's opera *Rogneda*. Mussorgsky's text is witless and, today, incomprehensible, and his composition no more than ephemeral musical journalism.

Mussorgsky's greatest achievements in song are his three cycles, the first of which, *The Nursery*, consisting of seven songs written to the composer's own texts, was composed at various times between 1868 and 1872. *The Nursery* is a remarkable achievement in that it explores the psychological make-up of a child in a series of accurately observed and remembered vignettes of child behaviour; specifically Russian child behaviour, one is tempted to add, for the Russian peasant nurse is a vastly different figure from the English nanny, and the superstitious peasant-lore with which middle-class Russian children used to be impregnated formed a significant background to their adult culture. In the first song, 'With Nurse', the little boy, Mishenka, asks his nurse to tell him again some of the fairy tales he already knows so well. Here, and throughout the cycle, the apparent ease with which Mussorgsky has wed a lyrical vocal style to a quasi-realistic declamation of the Russian language is a hallmark of genius. Every inflection of the child's chatter is impeccably caught as regards both pitch and rhythm, yet the songs stand up musically as well, and are given formal coherence by the piano parts. The second song, 'In the corner', is in the form of a dialogue between child and nurse, and the third, 'The Beetle', describes, under the guise of an encounter with a large black beetle, the child's first experience of death. 'What is "dead"?', he asks his nurse casually. The charming 'Doll's Lullaby' is crooned by a child to its doll; and in 'Evening Prayer', the child himself falls asleep almost before he has finished the prayer which he repeats parrot-fashion with some prompting from the nurse. This song displays the composer's skill in lyrical declamation at its most beguiling. 'Sailor, the Cat' recounts an exciting adventure in which the family's caged bird is saved at the last moment from the family cat. The child's not altogether innocent part in the proceedings is clearly revealed in the highly articulate vocal line. The cycle ends with 'The Hobby-Horse' an equally impressive reconstruction of the exhilaration and tears of childhood.

Mussorgsky's second cycle, *Sunless*, makes use of the gloomy and pessimistic verses of his friend and distant relative, Count Arseny Golenishchev-Kutuzov. 'Apart from Pushkin and Lermontov', the composer once wrote to Stassov, 'I have not discovered elsewhere what I find in Kutuzov'.* And indeed these poems do appear to have released into musical expression a pessimism which this usually objective musical dramatist has concealed in most of his other works. These six introspective songs are linked not by narrative but by mood and style. Largely declamatory, they manage to impress themselves on the memory as though their melodic content were higher, such is Mussorgsky's skill in writing for the voice. That these songs are more subjective than the majority of his other songs, and that Mussorgsky should have turned to these texts, is understandable when one remembers that they were composed during a time when he was suffering from the brutally hostile criticism directed against his opera *Boris Godunov*. In the first song, 'Within Four Walls', a patient in a hospital soliloquizes on his condition. 'You did not recognize me in the crowd' and 'The idle, noisy day is ended' are both exercises in bitterness, regret and solitude. The passage in the latter song where the text speaks of 'spring-like passions of the past returning as phantoms in dreams' was later quoted by Debussy in the 'Nuages' movement of his *Nocturnes* to express a similar mood. The gloomiest of the six songs is 'Boredom' with its air of unrelieved bitterness and tedium. A lighter, more lyrical mood is introduced with 'Elegy', despite the piano's funeral knell near the end, but the final song, 'On the river', reminds us that these useless self-communings will soon be ended by death.

The final cycle, *Songs and Dances of Death*, though its poems, again by Golenishchev-Kutuzov, can hardly be called cheerful, is considerably less depressing than *Sunless*, perhaps because the mood of bitterness is here given some kind of objective correlative by the personification of Death as a malevolent, deceitful figure. The correct order of the four songs is 'Lullaby', 'Serenade', 'Trepak' and 'The Field-Marshal', not the altered order decided upon by Rimsky-Korsakov when he published the songs after Mussorgsky's death. The 'Lullaby' that the mother attempts to sing over her sick child in the first song is completed by Death, who enters the hut at dawn and lulls the suffering child to death

* Ed. Jay Leyda and Sergei Berlensson *The Mussorgsky Reader* London 1947

with the most gently beguiling melody. The dialogue in the
second song is between Death and a maiden, and, although it is
not easy to put Schubert's Claudius song, 'Der Tod und das
Mädchen', out of one's mind while hearing it, Mussorgsky's lyric
response to Kutuzov's words is hardly less compelling, except at
the very end, when Death's melodramatic cry of 'You are mine!'
substitutes Russian theatricality of gesture for Austrian
Todesahnung. 'Trepak', a fantastic 'Dance of Death', is one of
the most compelling of all Mussorgsky's songs, in which Death
dances with the drunken peasant who has lost his way in a
snowstorm. The final song, 'The Field-Marshal', was written
two years later than the other three, in 1877. The scene is a
corpse-strewn battlefield by night, over which the moon rises
to reveal the figure of a skeleton on horseback surveying the
field. He is Field-Marshal Death, the only real victor in battle.
To the dead, he announces 'In life you were always in conflict.
Death will unite you.' The concept is perhaps too overtly
theatrical, but there can be no doubting the powerful inventiveness of Mussorgsky's response to the poet's grim scene-painting.

A final group of *Ten Romances and Songs* contains
Mussorgsky's last songs, most of them written in 1877. For one
of them, 'The Vision', he again turned to Golenishchev-Kutuzov
for his text, but five are settings of Alexei Tolstoy : 'Not like
thunder, trouble struck', 'Softly, the spirit flew up to heaven',
'Pride', 'Is spinning man's work?' and 'It scatters and breaks'.
Unfortunately, none of these is first-rate, nor is 'The Sphinx', for
which Mussorgsky provided his own words. But 'On the Dnieper',
its text by Taras Shevchenko, a Ukrainian nationalist poet, is a
masterpiece, a song of political protest calling for a free Ukraine.
It was actually composed as early as 1866, and revised by the
composer in 1879. Mussorgsky's last two songs are, uncharacteristically, settings of German verse in translation : 'The Wanderer'
and 'Song of the Flea'. 'The Wanderer' is Rückert's 'Abendlied
des Wanderers' in a somewhat pedestrian setting, but the 'Song
of the Flea', Mephistopheles' song from Goethe's *Faust*, though
not very Mussorgskian, is a splendid piece of musical satire.
Ironically, it is the only Mussorgsky song known to the wide
musical public, having been taken up by several bass singers,
from Chaliapin on. The best of Mussorgsky, the musical realist,
is to be found in the cycles and a handful of the earlier songs,
songs original in achievement and fresh in voice, wide-ranging,
yet rooted in native Russian soil.

The youngest of The Five or 'Mighty handful' is Nicolai Rimsky-Korsakov (1844–1908). No less Russian than his four colleagues in sentiment, he nevertheless was not, as a musician, as deeply influenced by the folk spirit as they were. A master of harmony and orchestration, and an over-enthusiastic and insensitive editor of other men's music, his finest work is to be found in his operas, among them *The Snow Maiden, Sadko* and *The Golden Cockerel*. Rimsky-Korsakov's songs, of which there are more than eighty, are quite charming, and lyrical in style. A certain melodic blandness is compensated for by the unusually strong piano parts of many of the songs. His favourite poets were Lermontov, Pushkin, Mey, Maikov and Alexei Tolstoy, but he also set a few of Heine's most popular lyrics, and three poems of Byron. Among the most interesting songs are the six Pushkin settings of op. 8; the Tolstoy cycle, *By the Sea*, op. 46; the four Maikov translations of modern Greek poets op. 50; and the cycle *In Spring*, op. 43, three of whose four poems are by Alexei Tolstoy. It is not easy to sound a note of genuine enthusiasm about Rimsky-Korsakov's songs, despite their attractive lyricism and picturesque harmonies, for they lack any strong creative individuality. There is no one song of which one could say that it simply had to exist.

It is with the great Russian melodist, Peter Tchaikovsky (1840–1893) that Russian song reached its zenith in the 19th century. Harmonically and melodically, Tchaikovsky's songs admit Western influences, for their composer was no fierce nationalist but, musically, a cosmopolitan. Often his accompaniments will reflect something of Schumann, and occasionally his melody will reveal an Italian flavour, yet such is the strength of Tchaikovsky's creative personality that his songs very rarely sound as though they could have been written by anyone else. His declamation may be less accurate than that of The Five, but these powerful songs with their wide emotional range are composed with a confident authority and a lyrical fervour that place the best of them far above the achievements of his contemporaries. Tchaikovsky was, of course, held in disfavour by The Five, and in his book, *Russian Song*, Cui, though he paid tribute to Tchaikovsky's craftsmanship, asserted that his talent 'lacks the flexibility required for real vocal music. . . . He did not acknowledge the equal rights of poetry and music. . . . Having chosen texts with no artistic value, Tchaikovsky treated them without ceremony . . . more often than not his development consists of

repetition and variation.'* Cui shows a just appreciation of
Tchaikovsky's defects but lacks the sympathy to appreciate his
positive qualities which far outweigh those defects. The charge
that his texts had little artistic value used also to be made against
Schubert. Even if it were proved to be true, has there been a
greater genius of song? Tchaikovsky's genius may not have been
of the order of Schubert's, if one can measure these things, but
he was the same kind of composer, continually in search of
artistic truth, rather than the truth of reality. As he himself said,
'The two are completely different. . . . For people to confuse
them when contrasting speech and song is simply dishonest.'† It
is true that Tchaikovsky was cavalier in his attitude to his poets,
but the poets he chose were those also set by The Five, namely
Pushkin, Alexei Tolstoy, Mey, Fet, Lermontov, Khomiakov and
so on. He wrote more than 100 songs, an *œuvre* important
enough to be considered in some detail, for it is through
Tchaikovsky that Russian song is best known outside Russia.

Preceding the first published songs with opus numbers are
four pieces of juvenilia, composed by Tchaikovsky in his late
teens. The earliest is 'My genius, my angel, my friend' (poem
by Fet), a simple, melodic setting of a sentimental poem.
'Zemphira's song' (Pushkin), only a little more ambitious, could
almost be minor Schumann, except for its operatic climax; 'Who
goes?' (poem by Apukhtin) is uninteresting; and 'Mezza notte',
to anonymous Italian words, seems hardly more than an exercise.
The first published group, the six songs of op. 6, written at the
age of twenty-nine, show a considerable advance on these first
four attempts. In the first song, 'Do not believe, my friend',
Tchaikovsky imposes his own passionate interpretation upon
Tolstoy's love poem, a passion tinged with a sadness lacking in
the words of the poem. 'Not a word, O my friend', its poem by
Pleshcheev from the German of M. Hartmann, introduces the
sweetly lyrical vein of yearning which was to pervade so much
of the composer's mature work. 'Painfully and sweetly' (poem
by E. P. Rostopchina) is relatively colourless, but Tolstoy's 'A
tear trembles' is interesting in a rather operatic style. 'Why?' is
a setting of Mey's translation of Heine's 'Warum sind denn die
Rosen so blass?', a song of great emotional force. The group
concludes with Tchaikovsky's best known song, 'None but the

* César Cui *La Musique en Russie* Paris 1880
† Modest Tchaikovsky *Life and letters of Peter Ilyich Tchaikovsky*
(trans. and ed. Rosa Newmarch) London 1906

weary heart', Mey's translation of Goethe's 'Nur wer die Sehnsucht kennt'. In the heart-felt expressiveness of its melody, it comes as close to Goethe as do the various German language settings, if not closer.

The single song, 'To forget so soon' (poem by Apukhtin; no opus number), relies less on Tchaikovsky's lyrical genius than on his equally great gift of psychological penetration, as remarkable as that of Hugo Wolf. The poet's lament on the transience of happiness, of love ('. . . To forget how the full moon looked upon us through the window, how the blind gently swayed . . . to forget so soon, so soon') has found an eloquent response in Tchaikovsky's impassioned monologue.

The six songs of op. 16, written in 1872 when the composer was thirty-two, include among their number more than one masterpiece. Maikov's gentle 'Cradle Song' is a perfect fusion of words and text, and Grekov's 'Wait', its words inspired by the Shakespeare of *Romeo and Juliet* and *The Merchant of Venice*, is a most beautiful evocation of night, peace and love, the charm of its melody irresistible. 'Accept just once' (poem by Fet), less compelling, nevertheless has a fine melodic impulse; 'O sing that song' (Pleshcheev, after Mrs Hemans) and 'Thy radiant image' (words by Tchaikovsky) are both highly attractive lyrics. The final song, 'New Greek Song' (words by Maikov), turns a strange and remarkable ballad into a flawless piece of music. 'In dark Hell beneath the earth, the sinful shadows are languishing', begins the singer, and goes on to describe a scene of infernal torment. The song is a variation on the theme of the 13th-century 'Dies Irae', brilliantly organized, harsh and compelling. The melody passes from voice to piano and back again in a manner unusual in Tchaikovsky, and the musical language is assured, original and convincing. Even Cui had no fault to find with this song.

The next two songs, without opus numbers, although pleasant, do not call for especial comment: 'Take my heart away' (Fet) has more character than 'Blue eyes of spring' which is a setting of a translation of Heine. The six songs of op. 25 are considerably more interesting. The first of them, 'Reconciliation' (poem by Shcherbina), owes something to Russian gypsy music, to its rhythms and cadences upon which Tchaikovsky has imposed his unerring sense of form. 'As o'er the burning ashes' (Tuchev) fails to cohere or convince, but the same poet's translation of Goethe's 'Kennst du das Land?' is given a setting of naïve charm that perhaps is more suited to the poem than Wolf's great song. Two songs to poems by Mey, 'The Canary' and 'I never spoke to her', are rather dull, though it should be noted that Ernest Newman thought highly of 'The Canary'. 'It is striken humanity that finds a voice here', he wrote, 'not the canary in the Sultana's cage.'* The final song of the group is a setting of a poem by Mey which twenty years later was to be very effectively put to music by Balakirev: 'As they kept on saying, "Fool"'. (Balakirev's song is called 'The Putting Right' (q.v.).) The drunkard addresses the river. 'How', he asks, 'can I drown my anguish which is like a serpent?' Tchaikovsky's village drunk is clearly a superior type of fellow to Balakirev's lout. The song is unique in Tchaikovsky's output, and quite lively, though hardly one of his greatest successes. Two single songs were written between op. 25 and op. 27: 'I should like in a single word', an innocuous setting of Heine translated by Mey, and Grekov's 'We have not far to walk'. The six songs of op. 27 vary both in style and standard, the best of them being the beautiful 'Do not leave me' (poem by Fet), 'Evening' with its simple but evocative accompaniment, the poem a translation by Mey from the Ukrainian of Shevchenko, and the light-hearted 'My spoiled darling' (Mey, from the Polish of Mickiewicz). 'To Sleep (poem by Ogarev) is typically Tchaikovskian in its mournful, yearning andante.

Op. 28, consisting of six songs, begins with 'No, I shall never tell', a graceful setting of Grekov's translation of de Musset's 'Chanson de Fortunio'. The second song, 'The Corals', is a magnificent musical account of a ballad by the Polish poet and politician Syrokomla in which a young soldier returns to his village with the gift of corals which his sweetheart has asked for, only to find she has died in his absence. In its drama, and its persuasive melody, 'The Corals' stands high in the list of Tchaikovsky's songs. 'Why did I dream of you?' (Mey) and 'He loved me so much' (Anon.) are romantic, and somewhat gypsyish in colour and rhythm, while 'No response or word of greeting' is almost defeated by Apukhtin's poem. 'The Fearful Moment', whose words are by the composer, is verbally fearfully melodramatic in its passion, though musically effective in its restraint.

The next songs, the six of op. 38, were composed three years

* Quoted in a sleeve-note to a gramophone record (ALP 1793) of Tchaikovsky songs sung by Boris Christoff

later, in 1878, and are the only songs of that year. With the exception of a windily rhetorical musicalization of Lermontov's 'Love of a Corpse', these are all first-rate songs, especially the four settings of Alexei Tolstoy. The first of these, 'Don Juan's Serenade', a serenade of great theatrical gesture, its 3/4 rhythm exhilarating and lusty, has retained its popularity throughout the years. 'It was in the early spring', a song of wistful charm and insinuating melody is as attractive as its better-known companion, 'Mid the din of the ball', which is lyrical, sensitive, and deservedly one of Tchaikovsky's best known songs in translation into several languages. 'Oh, if thou couldst for one moment' imposes a typically Tchaikovskian melody upon a Schumannesque accompaniment. The final song of 1878, the tuneful 'Pimpinella', for which the composer provided his own words, is based upon an Italian popular song which he heard a ten-year-old lad singing in a street in Florence. Tchaikovsky made use of the same tune in the waltz movement of his Fifth Symphony.

It was not until two years later that the next songs appeared, the seven which comprise op. 47. The first song of the group, 'If I'd only known', is the dramatic lament of a peasant girl, the stylized repetition of her cry bringing both intensity of expression and coherence of form to the musical material. Curiously, the song is framed by fifteen bars of a rather gay allegro moderato in the piano part, which appears both as prelude and postlude, perhaps to give a kind of distancing effect to the girl's sad song, and to Alexei Tolstoy's words. Four of the seven songs of op. 47 are Tolstoy settings: no. 2 is his 'Softly the spirit flew up to heaven', one of Tchaikovsky's most affecting melodies. 'Dusk fell on the earth' (words by N. V. Berg, from the Polish of Mickiewicz) is excellent, though less compelling than the two Tolstoy songs which follow: 'Sleep, my poor friend' and 'I bless you, forests', also known as 'The Pilgrim's Song'. The former is most effectively constructed from the repetition of a melodic fragment, highly charged with feeling; the 'Pilgrim's Song', from Tolstoy's poem 'John of Damascus' in which John, escaping from the palace of Damascus, greets nature in a great paean of praise, is a magnificent song, and one of great humanity, its spirit akin to that of Schubert's 'Die Allmacht'. No less remarkable is 'Does the day reign?' (poem by Apukhtin), another passionate outpouring of love. The final song of op. 47 utilizes a translation by Surikov of Shevchenko's Ukrainian poem, 'Was I not a little blade of grass?', to voice its mood of lament.

Op. 54 is a set of sixteen *Songs for Children*, the majority of them composed to poems of Pleshcheev in 1883. These charming little songs range from the delightful 'Cuckoo' to the grave and poignant 'Legend' of the infant Christ and his garden. One of the finest is the last of the set, 'Child's Song' (poem by K. S. Aksakov). In the following year, Tchaikovsky wrote his op. 57, six songs to texts of various poets. Sologub's 'Tell me, what in the shade of the branches' is formally very satisfying, and 'On the golden cornfields' (Alexei Tolstoy) is a fine psychological study of loneliness and separation. In this song, the piano begins by suggesting the melancholy ringing of bells heard across the fields at twilight, while the voice brings its personal drama to the landscape of restless longing. In 'Do not ask', a translation by Strugovshchikov of Goethe's 'Heiss mich nicht reden', one of Mignon's songs, Tchaikovsky does not quite capture the mood of the poem, though his song is both exciting and beautiful in itself. Two Merezhkovsky poems, 'Sleep' and 'Death' result in curiously unaffecting songs, but 'Only thou' (poem by Pleshcheev after A. Kristen) shows the composer in full command again, his melody affecting, his sense of form masterly.

The twelve songs of op. 60, composed in 1886, are uneven in quality. 'Last night' (Khomiakov) has a fine melodic and rhythmic impulse, and 'I'll tell thee nothing' (Fet) a naturalness of expression, but Pleshcheev's 'O, if you knew' is somewhat conventionally treated. Pushkin's 'The Nightingale', from the Serbian of Stefanovic, is attractive in the purity of its folk style, but 'Simple words' (the words are the composer's own) is uncomfortably stilted in manner. 'Frenzied Nights' is an extraordinary song. Apukhtin's poem about the guilt and despair caused by wasteful living has found a sensitive and not overdramatic response in Tchaikovsky. 'The Gypsy's Song' (Polonsky) is a pleasant genre-piece, and Nekrassov's 'Forgive' very poetic in expression. Of three further settings of poems by Polonsky, 'Night' is the least successful, its voice part too declamatory for the lyricism of the poem. 'Behind the window, in the shadow' is lively, and 'The Mild Stars Shone For Us' attractively romantic. The drama of 'Exploit' (poem by Khomiakov) is externalized and not very convincing.

Tchaikovsky's song output in 1887 consists entirely of the six settings of love poems by the Grand Duke Constantine which make up op. 63. 'I did not love thee at first' is somewhat pedestrian, and 'I opened the window' hardly an improvement. Tchaikovsky recovers his form in 'I do not please you', the self-pitying sentiment being something which came easily to him. He also makes something interesting, albeit also eccentric, of 'The First Tryst'. 'The fires in the rooms were already extinguished' treads, none too confidently, a dangerous line between delicacy and dullness, but the final song, 'Serenade', has an unforced lyrical charm that is greatly appealing. The 1880 songs again number six: they are the *Six French Songs* of op. 65, their texts from minor French poets. 'Aurore' (E. Turquety) is light and attractive, 'Déception' (Paul Collin) is, on the contrary, heavy-handed, failing to achieve the tragic stature it aims for, and the other Collin settings, 'Sérénade', 'Poème d'octobre' and 'Rondel', either forced or lacking in character. 'Les Larmes' (A. M. Blanchecotte) seems more deeply felt, and also more natural.

Tchaikovsky wrote no more songs for five years, and then, in 1893, the last year of his life, composed a cycle of six songs, op. 73, to poems by D. M. Rathaus, a student at Kiev University, who had sent his poems to the composer. In these songs Tchaikovsky not only recovered completely the confidence and ease of his best work, but appeared to be renewing himself in a series of exquisite mood pieces which are small impressionistic masterpieces. The passionate recollection of 'We sat together', the deep melancholy of 'Night', the evocative 'In this moonlight' and 'The sun has set': these, and 'Mild sombre days', are among Tchaikovsky's finest achievements in song. The remarkable 'Again, as before, alone', an outburst of desolate pessimism, which ends the cycle, is both psychologically penetrating and lyrically inspired.

The younger generation of Russian composers continued the division between nationalism and Europeanism, the more interesting talents tending to range themselves on the side of nationalism. Alexander Grechaninov (1864–1956) devoted himself to church music and to song, producing more than 250 songs, many of them strongly influenced by 'The Five' and, in particular, by Mussorgsky. Alexander Glazunov (1865–1946) wrote fewer songs, and those few in the manner of Rimsky-Korsakov, with whom he had studied. The next Russian song composer of importance is Sergei Rachmaninov (1873–1943) whose ideals were closer to those of Tchaikovsky than to The

Five. Though Rachmaninov is best known for his piano concertos, some of his finest music is to be found in his songs, all
of which were composed before he left Russia at the time of the
Revolution. They are close to Tchaikovsky in style, conservative
in musical language, but sincere in their romanticism. As a
virtuoso pianist, Rachmaninov naturally wrote interesting and
independent piano parts in his songs, though never merely for
the sake of pianistic display. The earliest group, op. 4, consists
of six songs which the composer wrote in his teens. 'Oh stay,
my love', a setting of Dmitri Merezhkovsky, is highly romantic
and Tchaikovskian in manner; it is also an attractive and
memorable song. Three of the other songs in this juvenile group
are as fine as anything Rachmaninov composed in his maturity.
They are 'In the silent night' (poem by Fet) which explores a
vein of ecstasy that was always to come easily to Rachmaninov,
'Oh never sing to me again', a Pushkin poem perhaps better
known in the translation which begins, 'O cease thy singing,
maiden fair', and 'The Harvest of Sorrow' (Alexei Tolstoy). The
Pushkin poem, in which a Georgian maiden is asked not to sing
the songs of her homeland, for they fill the listener with a
nostalgia and yearning too sad to be endured, becomes itself
unendurably sad in Rachmaninov's setting. 'The Harvest of
Sorrow' is similarly affecting, its very Russian melodic line
somehow evocative of the vast fields of corn, external symbols
of the poet's thoughts, just as easy to scatter, just as difficult
to destroy.

In his twentieth year, Rachmaninov composed six songs, their
texts taken from Pleshcheev's translations of Heine, Goethe
and the Ukrainian, Shevchenko. They are not especially interesting, though Shevchenko's 'Brooding' is rather more successful
than the others. Three years later, in 1896, came the twelve
songs of op. 14, most of them settings of the kind of poets whom
Tchaikovsky had also admired and set: Fet, Rathaus, Apukhtin,
Alexei Tolstoy and others. A curiosity, though no more than
that, is 'The Little Island', a setting of Shelley translated by
Balmont. The finest songs in the group are Apukhtin's 'Oh, do
not grieve' and Tyuchev's 'Spring waters'. The former im-
presses as much by the restraint of its beginning as by the excitement of its climactic high notes, while the latter has achieved
an understandable popularity for the thrust and impulse of its
picture of spring breaking through the winter snows, in an
allegro vivace torrent.

All but one of the twelve songs of op. 21 were written in 1902. The most impressive among them are 'The Answer' (Victor Hugo, translated by Mey), which combines Rachmaninov's typical energy with his lyrical gift; the delicate 'Lilacs' (poem by Kathleen Beketova); Apukhtin's desperate 'Loneliness'; and the beautiful "How fair this spot' (poem by G. Galina). The best of the fifteen songs of op. 26, composed in 1906, combine the ardour of the young Rachmaninov with a greater degree of subtlety. The dramatic 'Christ is risen' (Merezhkovsky) is unusually strong and spare, Khomiakov's 'To the Children' has a gentleness and sensitivity that help to disguise its musical monotony, while Galina's 'Before my window' is an exquisite miniature, somewhat reminiscent of 'How fair this spot'. 'When yesterday we met' (Yakov Polonsky) is a simple but effective setting of a poem of farewell.

Six years separate the songs of op. 26 from those of op. 34, composed in 1912. In general, the fourteen songs of the later set tend to be more dramatic in manner than the earlier songs, though the composer's lyrical, romantic manner is also in evidence. In Pushkin's 'The Storm', the voice part competes in recitative with the raging storm of the piano. Balmont's 'Day to night comparing', though quieter, indeed rarely rising above piano, similarly uses the voice almost as an accompaniment to the instrumental part. Voice and piano achieve a real and equal partnership in Pushkin's 'Arion'. One of the most beautiful lyrical songs in the set is Tyuchev's 'The morn of life', and perhaps the most impressive dramatically is Khomiakov's 'The Raising of Lazarus'. The final song is a 'Vocalise', an attractive molto cantabile melody, sung on a vowel sound, its range taking the tenor or soprano from C sharp to the high C sharp two octaves above.

In 1915, Rachmaninov set Chapter 15, verse 13 from the Gospel according to St John, and in the following year he composed the six songs of op. 38, and his last. With the possible exception of 'Daisies' (poem by Igor Severyanin), these make a disappointing end to his career as a song writer. He has had no followers, except for Reinhold Glière (1875–1956) whose 120 or more songs exhibit his own brand, not a sufficiently individual one, of the rhapsodic style of melody we usually associate with Rachmaninov.

Among Russian composers of the 20th century, an important though neglected name is that of Nicholas Medtner (1880–1951).

Neo-classical in style, his music, most of it for piano, has not found a large audience; but to those who can hear beyond the surface unfashionableness of its language it has much to offer. Medtner, who left Russia when he was in his forties to live in Germany and France and, finally, in England, composed 100 songs during the first half of the century, some to Russian texts, and some to German. (He was of German descent on his father's side.) Pushkin and Goethe were his preferred poets, though he set several other 19th-century texts, including a good many which had already been made into splendid and well-known songs by Mozart, Schubert and Schumann. Medtner's op. 6, nine songs to poems of Goethe, contains for instance a 'Wanderers Nachtlied' and an 'Erster Verlust', while his op. 15, twelve Goethe poems, includes 'Meeresstille', 'Nähe des Geliebten' and 'Gleich und Gleich'. These German settings are, in any case, less successful than the Russian songs, and certainly do not succeed in making one forget their famous predecessors.

The Pushkin settings are another matter. Although Medtner's vocal line lacks lyrical warmth, and his piano parts tend to be over-elaborate, the best of the Russian songs do enter fully into the spirit of their poems, creating a kind of musical parallel in mood. The seven Pushkin songs of op. 29, composed in 1913, as well as three later Pushkin cycles, op. 32 (six songs), op. 36 (six) and op. 52 (seven), contain the best of Medtner. 'The Muse', op. 29 no. 1, 'The Angel', op. 36 no. 1, and 'The Waltz', op. 32 no. 5 ought certainly to be rescued from their temporary oblivion. At one time, the songs of Medtner were taken up by a few English-domiciled Russian and German singers, including Oda Slobodskaya, Tatiana Makushina and Elisabeth Schwarz-kopf, none of whom, however, succeeded in popularizing them.

Igor Stravinsky (1882–1971), who seems to us now to be our century's towering musical genius (though time may come up with the rival names of Britten or Shostakovich), devoted very little of his attention and talent to the art of song. 'Pastorale', a song without words for soprano and piano, composed in 1907, and two songs for mezzo-soprano, to poems by S. Gorodetzky (1907–8) are his earliest, not very interesting attempts, though his teacher Rimsky-Korsakov complained of their 'contemporary decadence'. Two poems of Verlaine for baritone and piano, 'Un grand sommeil noir' and 'La lune blanche', are settings of the original French words, composed in 1910 for the composer's brother to sing. When one considers that these songs are contemporary with *Petrushka* and *Firebird*, they seem curiously lacking in personality. Two poems of K. Balmont, 'The Flower' and 'The Dove', composed in 1911, reveal, as Eric Walter White points out in his *Stravinsky*,* a considerable advance on the Verlaine songs; and *Three Japanese Lyrics*, tiny poems about the coming of spring, are delicately beautiful. These, and most of Stravinsky's songs, exist also in instrumental versions usually made by the composer shortly after the voice and piano versions. With 'Pribaoutki', in 1914, the process was reversed: these popular Russian jingles were first composed for voice with flute, oboe, clarinet, violin, viola, 'cello and double-bass, and a reduction for voice and piano was made later by Stravinsky. Though the tunes sound folkish, they are, in fact, original.

The four *Cat's Cradle Songs* are, in Eric Walter White's words, 'further essays in the popular Russian idiom already used in "Pribaoutki", but here the utterance is even terser and more epigrammatic'.† Again, Stravinsky composed them first with an ensemble accompaniment, this time three clarinets, and then made his own reduction for piano. The *Three Tales for Children*, in the same idiom, have proved popular, especially the first, 'Tilimbom'. The *Four Russian Songs* written in 1918 and 1919 are somewhat fragmentary and disjointed, and it has been suggested that they were hurriedly put together from an assortment of sketches, at the request of a singer. Stravinsky then abandoned the composition of songs until 1953 when he wrote three Shakespeare songs for mezzo-soprano, flute, clarinet and viola. Though the composer made his own reduction for voice and piano, the songs are considerably more effective in their chamber music versions. It has to be admitted that the combination of voice and piano appears not to have interested Stravinsky very strongly. The Shakespeare songs were his last.

Sergei Prokofiev (1891–1953) moves from a French-influenced yet also characteristically Russian astringency to a rather weak lyricism in his songs. 'The Ugly Duckling' (1914) is the best known of the earlier pieces, though the five songs to poems by Anna Akhmatova, op. 27 (1916) are musically of considerably greater interest. After Prokofiev's return to Russia, when his music tended to toe a party line, it became increasingly banal. The *Seven Songs of the Masses* (1938) are typical of his Soviet

---

* Eric Walter White *Stravinsky: The Composer and his Works* Faber & Faber London 1966
† op. cit.

output. A Soviet composer who has found it easier to compose to order without seriously compromising his artistic principles or standards is Dmitri Shostakovich (b. 1906), though he has been able to achieve this only by an almost total avoidance of song. He has, of course, written the propaganda pieces and the popular songs required of him, but it is frustrating that so gifted a melodist should not have given the world great songs, as well as the superb series of symphonies he has produced. Aram Khachaturian (b. 1903) is the most gifted of those Soviet composers able to produce popular songs at the apparent behest of the masses, and Dmitri Kabalevsky (b. 1903) has also composed songs of various kinds.

In the Scandinavian countries, the most important composer of songs in the 19th century was the Norwegian Edvard Grieg (1843–1907). Grieg's lyric talent was ideally suited to the genre, and his agreeable melodic gift and feeling for the piano as an accompanying instrument enabled him to produce a great many first-rate settings of poems, not only in his own language but also in Danish and German. His first songs, written when he was around the age of twenty, were based on the model of the German *Lied*, and the poets he chose were Chamisso and Heine, thus underlining the similarity of his approach to that of Schumann. In 1864, at the age of twenty-one, he produced his op. 5, *Four Danish Songs*, to texts of Hans Christian Andersen, amongst them the one song by which Grieg is known the world over, 'Jeg elsker dig', a melody of great charm, familiar in English as 'I love thee'. These Andersen settings, and also those of op. 15 and op. 18, are among the finest of Grieg's 131 songs, for there seemed to be a real affinity of spirit between the Norwegian composer and the Danish poet. Of Grieg's several settings of the Norwegian Bjørnstjerne Bjørnson, 'Prinsessen' (The Princess) stands out for the ease and simplicity of its plangent melody, 'Dulgt kjaerlighed' (Hidden love) op. 39 no. 2 for the skill with which its narrative is projected so lyrically, and 'Lok' ('Farmyard Song') op. 61 no. 3 for its childlike gaiety. Op. 25, a collection of six Ibsen songs, includes the well-known 'En svane' (A swan), graceful and also strikingly original, and the charming 'Med en vandlilje' ('With a Waterlily'). All of the five songs to texts of Julius Paulsen, op. 26, are remarkable for their romantic charm and natural ease of expression, the most beautiful of them being 'Med en primula veris' ('With a primrose'). Op. 33, two volumes each of six songs to poems by the peasant poet, Aasmund Olafsen Vinje, contains some particularly interesting songs, one of which, the nostalgic 'Vaaren' (Spring) has become popular in the orchestral version Grieg made of it for his op. 34, *Two Elegiac Melodies*. (The other song orchestrated was 'Den Saarede' [The Wounded One].) The popular song known in English as 'A Dream' is 'Ein Traum', op. 48 no. 6, the last of six settings of German poets. Its poem, by Friedrich Martin von Bodenstedt, drew from Grieg one of his most beautiful melodies. Less well known, though they are remarkably fine songs, are the late cycles, *Norge* (Norway) op. 58 and *Elegiske Digte* (Elegiac Poems), op. 59, both to poems by Paulsen, and *Haugtussa* (words by Arne Garborg), op. 67.

Greig's Norwegian successor, the neo-Romantic Christian Sinding (1856–1941), composed more than 200 songs, many of them charming, but of no great originality. He is known today principally for his piano piece, 'Rustle of Spring'. Sweden has produced a number of minor song composers equal in stature to Sinding, though none of them has made much effect outside Scandinavia. The following are mentioned here because occasionally an internationally-known Swedish singer will include one or two of their songs in a recital programme. John Söderman (1832–1876), a strong influence on most of the others to be mentioned, was Sweden's leading opera and song composer of his time, a pioneer of the romantic movement, and strongly nationalist in sentiment. Wilhelm Peterson-Berger (1867–1942) took his inspiration from nature and from folk melody, in his four operas as well as his songs. Hugo Alfven (1872–1960), similar in temperament to Peterson-Berger, was also well known in Sweden as a violinist and as a choral conductor. Svante Leonard Sjöberg (1873–1935) was an organist who, in addition to songs, composed a number of orchestral works. The Swedish tenors Jussi Björling and Nicolai Gedda both included his song, 'Tonerna' (Vision) in their repertoires. Ture Rangström (1884–1947), composer, conductor and critic, wrote a large number of songs which remain extremely popular in Sweden because of their romantic qualities and their celebration of the beauties of the Swedish landscape. Gustav Nordqvist (1886–1949), organist and teacher of composition, is best known for his 200 songs, mainly settings of Swedish poets.

The Danish Carl Nielsen (1865–1931) wrote a number of

songs which are greatly admired in his own country, but the
two modern Scandinavian composers whose songs have pleased
audiences abroad are both Finnish: they are Sibelius and
Kilpinen. Jean Sibelius (1865–1957), the great symphonist,
wrote nearly 100 songs, melodic in style, sometimes highly
intense in mood. The language of his poets is usually Swedish,
as this was the literary language of Finland for much of the
19th century. Among the titles best known in translation are
'Black roses' (poem by Ernst Josephson), 'Sigh, sigh, reeds'
(Gustav Fröding) and 'The Tryst' (Runeberg).

As a song writer Sibelius is rather uneven. The qualities which
make him so fine a symphonist are not necessarily those con-
ducive to success in the smaller forms, but in the best of his
songs, for which he has resorted to a form of melodic declamation, one is made to respond to his strength and integrity of
purpose. As Astra Desmond points out in her excellent chapter
on the songs in a volume on Sibelius,* 'to anyone familiar with
his orchestral music it will not be surprising that his best songs
are conceived directly or indirectly with nature and her moods.
Love lyrics do not seem to attract him unless there is a secondary nature theme'. The majority of Sibelius's songs are, it must
be admitted, disappointing, but to the well known and first-rate
titles already mentioned should be added 'March snow' op. 36
no. 5 (poem by Wechsell), both songs of op. 35, 'Jubal'
(Josephson) and 'Teodora' (Gripenberg), and a Swedish translation of 'Come away Death' (op. 60 no. 1) from Shakespeare's
Twelfth Night.

Yrjö Kilpinen (1892–1959) wrote songs to Finnish, Swedish
and German texts. His German settings of Rilke and Christian
Morgenstern show the same close attention to detail as those
of Wolf, with whom he has often been compared. He wrote
well over 700 songs, the Finnish settings being generally more
lyrical, less terse and concentrated than his German *Lieder*.

Turning from Scandinavia to Eastern Europe, we find that there
are very few composers of song to be compared with the greatest
of the French and Germans. In Poland, the famous national
and cosmopolitan figure Frédéric Chopin (1810–1849), renowned
primarily as pianist and composer for the piano, composed

* Gerald Abraham (ed.) *Music of the Masters* Lindsay Drummond
London 1945

nineteen songs during the course of his short life, all of them to Polish texts. Seventeen of these were published, shortly after his death, as op. 74, and two more were found and published in 1910. The two separate songs are of lesser interest than the op. 74 group: 'Czary' ('Charms'), a strophic setting of a poem by Stefan Witwicki, dates from the composer's twentieth year, and would probably not have achieved publication had it not been by Chopin. 'Dumka' ('Dirge'), its poem by Bohdan Zaleski, though it was written ten years later, is almost equally disappointing, and very slight.

The op. 74 songs begin with 'Zyczenie' ('The Wish'), another poem by Witwicki, but this time a gay, delightful song in the rhythm of the mazurka. No. 2, 'Wiosna' ('Spring'), paints a quiet lyrical scene and No. 3, 'Smutna Rzeka' ('The Sad Stream'), intrudes a touch of drama into the landscape. The poems of the first five songs of op. 74, also nos. 7, 10, 14 and 15, are by Witwicki. No. 4 'Hulanka' ('Drinking Song'), is a gay, lively invitation to drink; and no. 5, 'Gdzie lubi' ('There where she loves') is nondescript; but no. 6, 'Precz z moich oczu' ('Out of my sight'), interestingly combines dramatic narrative with an almost Bellinian singing line. The poem is by Adam Mickiewicz. No. 7, 'Posel' ('The Messenger'), suffers from its coy text and its dull tune; but no. 8, 'Sliczny chlopiec' ('Handsome Lad'), its poem by Bohdan Zaleski, is delightful. Chopin's accompaniments to these songs are surprisingly modest, and the songs themselves are in no way unusual formally, with the exception of no. 9, 'Melodya' ('Melody'), a song of exile based on a poem by Zygmunt Krasinski which begins and ends in recitative which encloses a mournful middle section of melody. 'Wojak' ('The Warrior'), no. 10, has a more important piano part than most of the others; in fact the piano is largely responsible for conveying its atmosphere of the battle field. No. 11, 'Dwojaki koniec' ('Twofold End'), a poem by Zaleski, tells a tragic story simply but affectingly; and 'Moja pieszczotka' ('My Darling'), no. 12, is a particularly charming mazurka setting of a Mickiewicz love poem. No. 13, 'Nie ma czego trzeba' ('I want what I have not'), poem by Zaleski, is another mournful song of exile; and 'Pierscien' ('The Ring'), no. 14 is a not too serious lover's lament. No. 15, 'Narzeczony' ('The Bridegroom'), has an unusual dramatic force; no. 16, 'Piomska Litweska' ('Lithuanian Song'), its poem by Ludwika Osinskiego, tells a folk tale charmingly; and the final song, no. 17, 'Spiew grobowy' ('Hymn from the tomb'), is the longest of the songs, a fervent song of exile and patriotic feeling, to words by Wincenty Pol.

A Polish composer of the 20th century whose early works are strongly influenced by Chopin, Karol Szymanowski (1882–1937) later won his way through to a personal style with its roots nevertheless in strong national feeling. This he expressed not only in his larger-scale works but also in a number of songs. The earliest ones, settings of such Polish and German-language poets as Kazimierz Tetmaier, Waclaw Berent, Richard Dehmel and Gustav Falke, are post-romantic in style. Later, Szymanowski went through a period of infatuation with the East, and produced the *Love Songs of Hafiz* and settings of Rabindranath Tagore. But the songs of his last years, settings of Polish poets, including some delightful children's songs, and the five James Joyce songs of 1925, reveal this composer as one of this century's most interesting and least appreciated talents.

In Czechoslovakia, Bedřich Smetana (1825–1884) devoted himself primarily to operatic composition, and left only a handful of solo songs. The earliest of these are settings of German verse, four of them composed in 1846, and a fifth, 'Liebesfrühling' (Rückert) in 1853. The first four songs are disappointingly colourless, considering that they were, after all, written when Smetana was in his mid twenties, but the Rückert setting displays a certain individuality and confidence. In 1867, Smetana wrote a song for the tragedy *Baron Goertz* by Bozdech, apart from which his only songs are the five which make up the cycle *Večerní písně* (*Evening Songs*), to verses by the poet and journalist Vítězslav Hálek. The style of these songs is not basically dissimilar to that to be found in the vocal writing in Smetana's operas. That they are enjoyable to hear is undeniable, but they can hardly be considered as anything more than side-products of the composer's essentially operatic talent.

Antonin Dvořák (1841–1904) was much more interested in the art of song. He wrote approximately seventy songs, stylistically related to the German *Lied*, although his poems were usually Czechoslovakian. The four songs of op. 2, composed in 1865 but revised seventeen years later, are settings of Gustav Pfleger-Moravsky. They possess that easy gift of melody which was one of Dvořák's greatest assets, but in op. 2 the melody is somewhat stiffly accompanied. Most impressive is the third song, 'Nought to my heart can bring relief'. 'The Orphan', op. 5, its

poem by Karel Jaromir Erben, is a dull, awkwardly composed
ballad, and the *Four Serbian Songs* op. 6, are little better. As
Alec Robertson writes in his *Dvořák*,* 'The accompaniments are
very lumpish and the composer is even deserted by his usual
copious outpouring of melody. Interest lies only in the curious
tonality of the opening phrase of the first song and in the un-
conscious humour of the English translations, which quite unseat
the Rev Dr Troutbeck.' ('Wrangling full long and sore thus
each did each implead; until the Judge deemed parting their
only remede.') But it is hardly fair to blame Dvořák for the
translations of an English edition. These songs fall down in their
own right. Much better, fortunately, are the six songs of op. 7,
settings of poems from the Königinhof manuscripts discovered
in 1818, which were later denounced as forgeries. The simple
folkish charm of these songs is refreshing after the dullness of
the Serbian songs. The *Evening Songs* op. 3 and op. 31, eight
of them to texts of Vítězslav Hálek, mark a further advance in
Dvořák's mastery of the art of song-writing. The *Three Modern
Greek Songs* op. 50, for baritone, are first-rate ballads, using
poems written on Greek themes by the Czech poet Václav
Nebeský.

The *Gypsy Songs* op. 55, seven settings of poems by Adolf
Heyduk, represent Dvořák's finest achievement in solo song. His
melody is at its most free-ranging and spontaneous, and his piano
accompaniments, though hardly Wolfian in their ambition, are
excellently judged. The first song, 'I chant my lay', sets the tone
of the cycle with its sensitivity and charm, and the other songs
contain much that is beautiful, particularly no. 3, 'Silent Woods',
and no. 4, 'Songs my mother taught me', which has achieved a
well-deserved fame out of context. Our hackneyed ears may find
it difficult to hear this lovely song freshly, but it is worth making
the effort. The last three songs of the cycle are all first-rate,
especially the final one, 'The cloudy heights of Tatra'. Dvořák's
next few songs were settings of Czech folk poems, two of them,
'Lullaby' and 'Disturbed Devotion' composed during a visit to
London in 1885, and the other four, op. 73, written the following year at the request of the composer's publisher. These four
are among Dvořák's most attractive and singable lyrics:
'Goodnight' has great tenderness and charm, 'The Mower'
though slighter, is delightful, 'The Maiden's Lament' is a great

* Alec Robertson *Dvořák* J. M. Dent London 1945

and moving song, and only the fourth, 'Loved and Lost' perhaps fails to reach the level of its fellows.

The next four songs, op. 82, settings of the poetess Ottilie Malybrok-Stieler, were written to the original German words, and only later provided with Czech texts. 'Springtide', no. 3, is enchanting, but the others are comparatively mundane. We come now to Dvořák's last achievement in song (except for the disappointing 'Smith of Lešetín', a colourless ballad). This is the cycle of *Biblical Songs* op. 99. The texts of these ten songs are taken from the Czech Protestant Bible. Alec Robertson thinks them influenced by 'the simplicity and inner urge of the Negro spiritual',* but, despite Dvořák's American experience, there seems no reason to attribute the striking simplicity of these songs to anything other than the composer's own lyrical response to the familiar Biblical words. The songs veer towards sentimentality rather than spirituality, perhaps, but sentimentality was an essential part of Dvořák's nature, and these sweetly appealing songs make an appropriate end to his essays in this genre.

In the 20th century, the only Czech composers to make their voices heard internationally have been Janáček and Martinu. Leoš Janáček (1854–1928) lived most of his life in the 19th century, but the majority of his operas were written in this century. His most remarkable vocal work falls outside the scope of this volume, for *The Diary of One Who Vanished* is written not for solo voice, but for contralto, tenor and three female voices; its language, personal, and closely related to speech rhythms, can be heard too in Janáček's solo songs, even those based on folk song. Bohuslav Martinu (1890–1959) was a less strong creative personality, but wrote some interesting songs, while Vítězslav Novák (1870–1949), whose work is hardly known at all outside Czechoslovakia, though it has been widely influential within his own country, was a prolific writer of songs.

The most important and influential Hungarian composer of the 20th century, Béla Bartók (1881–1945), despite his intense interest in folk song, did not himself write a great many original songs. Some German settings, dating from his seventeenth year, and including Heine's 'Im wunderschönen Monat Mai', remain unpublished, as do five children's songs, and a number of other settings of Hungarian verse. The *Five Songs* op. 16, to poems of Endre Ady, and the cycle of five *Village Scenes* to folk texts

* op. cit.

complete Bartók's song output. His colleague Zoltán Kodály (1882–1967) produced more than fifty songs, but where these are not closely related to folk song they are disappointingly academic. Kodály's pupil, Mátyás Seiber (1905–1960), a more cosmopolitan figure, wrote songs to Hungarian, German and French texts, as well as, in 1953 after settling in Great Britain, a cycle *To Poetry*, utilizing verse by Goethe, Shakespeare, Dowland and John Dunbar.

IV

ITALY, SPAIN AND THE
REST OF EUROPE

S O L O   S O N G   I N Italy emerged with the troubadors of the
15th and 16th centuries, with the songs of such composers as
the lutenist Marchetto Cara (d. 1527); the singer and composer
Giulio Caccini (1545–1618) whose *Euridice* was one of the first
operas, and whose song 'Amarilli' is perhaps the oldest still to
retain a place in the modern concert repertoire; the lutenist
Andrea Falconieri (1586–1656) and many others. If some of
the songs and arias of these composers still find a place in modern
recital programmes, this is largely due to their inclusion in the
collection of *Arie antiche* published by Alessandro Parisotti.
However, many of these pieces now so frequently used by singers
to begin their recitals are not really songs but arias from operas
or cantatas. Among the most frequently encountered of them are
'Le violette', 'Gia il sole dal Gange' and 'O cessate di piagarmi'
by Alessandro Scarlatti (1660–1725), 'Vittoria! Vittoria!' by
Giacomo Carissimi (1605–1674), the passionate 'Come raggio
di sol' by Antonio Caldara (1670–1736) who spent the most
fruitful years of his life as Court Composer in Vienna, the gay
'Danza, danza, fanciulla gentile' by Francesco Durante (1684–
1755) and 'Nina' ('Tre giorni son che Nina in letto senesta'),
once thought to be by Giovanni Battista Pergolesi (1710–1736)
but now usually attributed to Vincenzo Ciampi (1719–1762)
whose authorship of this melodious and graceful song is, however,
by no means certain.

The great composers of Italian *bel canto* opera in the 18th-
and early 19th-centuries all composed a number of songs,
frequently at the request of singers for special occasions.
Gioacchino Rossini (1792–1868) is the earliest whose songs have
remained in the repertory. He compared a great many, most of
them written for his own pleasure after he had brought his career
as an opera composer to a close in 1829 with *Guillaume Tell*. The

majority are to be found in the collections *Soirées musicales* and *Péchés de vieillesse*. The *Soirées musicales*, published in 1835, consists of eight songs or ariettes and four duets with piano accompaniment. The songs are, in general, graceful or lively tunes with appropriate accompaniments. Rossini's piano parts are always full of character, and his melodic gift has a distinct personality of its own. The solo songs of the *Soirées musicales* are superior to most of those which Rossini wrote later in life : among the most attractive of them are 'La gita in gondola', a limpid barcarolle, 'L'orgia', a drinking song of lightness and charm, and the gay 'Pastorella delle Alpi', a tongue-in-cheek piece of Tyrolean pastiche. The tarantella, 'La Danza', is too well known in its original form and in countless arrangements to require comment. Five of the *Soirées musicales* pieces, including three solo songs, 'La Pastorella delle Alpi', 'L'Invito', a bolero whose piano part is more inventive than its vocal melody, and 'La Danza', were orchestrated by Benjamin Britten in 1936 in his suite *Soirées Musicales* which subsequently was used for a ballet.

Péchés de vieillesse (*Sins of old age*) is the title Rossini gave to several volumes of miscellaneous short compositions, vocal, choral and instrumental, written at various times during his years of so-called retirement. Many of the songs included in these volumes have their share of Rossini's melodic gift, but too many more seem closer to doodling than to composition. 'L'esule' is a sympathetic little song of real feeling, and the three songs of 'La regata veneziana', sung by a young lady to encourage her lover to win the gondola race, are highly engaging. There are a few oddities, such as the duet for two cats which is sung to the word 'Miaou', and 'La chanson du bébé', in which the baby cries to its mummy and daddy that it urgently requires to make 'pipi' and 'caca'! Also odd is the fact that Rossini produced several hundred settings of a few lines by Metastasio, 'Mi lagnerò tacendo della mia sorte amara . . .' His obsessive interest in this rather ordinary piece of verse did not result in songs of great worth, rather in formal little exercises, though usually quite tuneful ones. Rossini, we are continually reminded by these pieces, is the man who told Wagner to his face that he was delivering the funeral oration of melody.

Gaetano Donizetti (1797–1848) wrote at least 200 songs, and probably many more, for by no means all of his songs were published in his lifetime. Many remain in manuscript today. In addition to those which were published individually, several collections were issued during the composer's lifetime and immediately after his death. *Donizetti per camera* is the title of a collection of twelve solo songs and four duets published in Naples. The solo songs, mostly in Neapolitan dialect, include 'Lu trademiento' in which Donizetti's vein of pathetic melody is rather appealing; however, most of the songs are unmemorable, their accompaniments minimal, usually simple chords marking the rhythm, their tunes machine-made. Italian singers today occasionally offer 'Giuro d'amore', an unconvincing little love song. *Matinées musicales* is the title of a collection of solo songs, duets and quartets, dedicated to Queen Victoria. The most considerable song in it is 'Preghiera', a large-scale prayer which would not sound out of place in one of Donizetti's operas. *Nuits d'été à Pausilippe* contains six songs which are rather more interesting than the general run of Donizetti's attempts at the genre. 'La Conocchia' is an agreeable little Neapolitan piece, Victor Hugo's 'Le Crépuscule' has inspired the composer to a more impassioned melody than the Neapolitan texts have wrung from him, 'Il Barcajuolo', its text by Leopold Tarantini, has a distinguished, quasi-operatic melody, and 'A Mezzanotte' is a lively serenade. *Soirées d'automne à l'Infrascata* consists of four solo songs and a duet. The songs include 'Amor marinaro', also known by the opening words of its text, 'Me voglio fa 'na casa', a charming little arietta which is still popular, and 'Amore e morte', a tearful, sentimental piece which is nonetheless undeniably appealing. Among the collections which appeared posthumously are *Dernières Glânes musicales* and *Fiori di sepolcro*. The finest solo number in the former is 'La Chanson de l'abeille' (poem by Hippolyte Lucas), and, in the latter, 'L'Amor mio', a graceful setting of lines by the famous opera librettist Felice Romani.

Vincenzo Bellini (1801–1835) lived for a much shorter time than Rossini or even Donizetti, and he was not by nature a prolific composer. During his thirty-four years, he produced ten operas and fewer than twenty songs, in addition to an oboe concerto, a few *sinfonie* and some church music. In general, it can be said of his songs that they display the same individual, languid grace in their melodies as do Bellini's operas. Vigorous energy is not what one looks for in Bellini, though this is not to say that passionate intensity is lacking. The earliest song, 'La Farfaletta', dates from his twelfth year: a gay and engaging piece, it is hardly typical of his mature style, that is to say the style of his twenties and early thirties. 'Dolente immagine', an arietta for soprano and piano accompaniment, written in 1821, sounds more Bellinian, but is hardly one of his more inspired tunes, and little more can be said for 'Sogno d'infanzia' which followed three years later. The cream of Bellini's songs is to be found in the collection, *Sei ariette*, which appeared in 1829. All six songs are, in their way, highly attractive. 'La Malinconia' is expressively melancholy indeed, but by no means depressing; 'Vanne, O rosa' is typically appealing, 'Bella Nice' a graceful love song, and 'Almen se non poss' io' has the high style and poise of an aria from *La Sonnambula*. 'Per pietà, bel idol mio' displays a vitality of tempo and expression rare in Bellini, and 'Ma rendi pur contento' shows the composer at his most elegant. Of the remaining songs of Bellini's last years, 'L'Abbandono' deserves mention for the originality of its vocal lines and for an accompaniment more interesting than is usual for this composer, and 'Vaga luna che inargenti' for possessing most of the Bellinian virtues already described.

The songs of the brothers Ricci, Federico Ricci (1809–1877) and Luigi Ricci (1805–1859) are simple, and of no more than slight interest, though Federico, a pupil of Bellini, possessed a more fluent melodic gift than his brother. Luigi Gordigiani (1806–1860) composed more than 300 songs, pleasantly sentimental melodies which achieved an immense popularity both in Italy and abroad.

Italy's greatest composer, Giuseppe Verdi (1813–1901) was, in general, not given to setting pen to paper unless a contract had been signed, and so his song output is not large. What exists, however, is interesting not only in its own right but for the light it casts on the operas, or, to be more exact, for its adumbrations of themes which were to reach their finest form in the operas.

Verdi's earliest published work was an album of six songs, published in 1838 when the composer was in his twenty-fifth year. There is no trace in them of Verdian energy; in fact, they are distinctly Bellinian in mood and manner. 'Non t'accostare all' urna', a setting of a self-pityingly melancholy poem by Jacopo Vittorelli, is a graceful and attractive andante with an allegro middle section. Actually, the feeling of both words and music in this song is not so much Bellinian as akin to that of Beethoven's 'In questa tomba oscura' written thirty years earlier. 'More, Elisa, lo stanco poeta', a sad, gentle adagio whose poem is by Tommaso Bianchi, is in the same vein. The third song in the album, 'In solitaria stanza', contains a quite startling anticipation of a phrase from Leonora's first act aria in *Il trovatore*. 'Nell' orror di notte oscura' sounds more obviously immature than its fellows, but 'Perduta ho la pace' is both simple and touching. The poem is a translation, by Luigi Balestra, a friend of Verdi's early days, of Margarete's lament, 'Meine Ruh' ist hin', from Goethe's *Faust*, and Verdi's response to the poem is sensitive and appealing. The final song in the collection, 'Deh, pietoso, oh Addolorata' is another *Faust* setting. The poem is Margarete's prayer to the Virgin, and Verdi has given it a beautifully limpid vocal line which puts one in mind of part of the second act finale of his third opera, *Nabucco*, composed three years later. The resemblance of the song's andante cantabile tune to the descending phrase that Saint-Saëns was to use nearly forty years later to begin the refrain of 'Mon cœur s'ouvre à ta voix' in *Samson et Dalila*, though distinct, does not obtrude itself in Verdi's context.

Two songs were published separately in 1839, the year in which Verdi's first opera, *Oberto*, reached the stage. 'L'esule' is a setting of a poem by Temistocle Solera (one of Verdi's librettists) describing the feelings of an exile in a foreign land as the sun sinks to rest. This is the most extended of Verdi's early songs, a scena which opens with a piano introduction descriptive of the melancholy of sunset. The voice enters in recitative which leads to an andante, and a lengthy and varied concluding allegro. It contains a musical phrase, to the words, 'Ed il pianto all' infelice', which appears again, years later, to express a similar feeling of exile in the lines 'Ritorna al suo natio, ti seguira il mio cor', which Elizabeth sings to her lady-in-waiting in *Don Carlo*. The second song of 1839, 'La Seduzione', is a setting of an original but rather awful poem by Luigi Balestra, Verdi's Goethe translator of the earlier songs. A beautiful virgin is seduced and, of course, dies. Verdi's song is sweetly sentimental, but hardly memorable. A solitary song of 1842, 'Chi i bei dì m'adduce ancora', is a translation, probably by Balestra, of Goethe's lyric, 'Erster Verlust', which Schubert had set so memorably. Considerably more florid in style than Verdi's two earlier Goethe songs, it contains a phrase anticipating the famous love theme, 'Di quell' amor' from *La traviata*.

Verdi's second album of six songs, published in 1845, consists entirely of settings of contemporary Italian poets. The nostalgic poem of 'Il tramonto', by the composer's friend Andrea Maffei, describes the sun sinking to rest over a calm sea. The song has a modest charm. 'La zingara' (poem by S. M. Maggioni) is rhythmically lively, and 'Ad una stella' (Maffei) is elegant. 'Lo spazzacamino', the most popular Verdi song, is still heard in recitals by Italian singers. Maggioni's poem tells of the little chimney-sweep who calls up to the windows, 'Ladies, gentlemen, I will save you from fire for a few pennies'. Verdi's three stanzas with their catchy waltz refrain are delicious: they are preceded by an unaccompanied bar consisting of the child's cry of 'Lo spazzacamin'. The lightness and rhythmical élan of the music put one in mind of Oscar in *Un ballo in maschera*. 'Il mistero' is somewhat more ambitious than the other songs in the album, but not entirely successful. The overwrought verses are by the famous librettist, Romani. The poem of 'Brindisi' is by Maffei. Verdi's autograph copy of this song differs somewhat from the version published. Both are in F major, but the tessitura of the published version is lower, and Verdi's second thoughts in general seem improvements. But the song is not, in either version, a very distinguished piece of music. It is, in fact, rather sluggish.

In 'Il poveretto' (poem by Maggioni), written in 1847, a starving ex-soldier begs from passers-by. The song is gently affecting, and the accompaniment, though simple, is skilful. This is a rather beautiful little song of its unpretentious kind: the three bars of piano prelude are no mere marking of time, but a real contribution to the whole. It was at the request of the republican leader Mazzini whom he had met in London in 1847 that Verdi wrote 'Suona la tromba', a setting of patriotic verses by the young poet of the Risorgimento, Goffredo Mameli, who was killed during the fighting in Rome in 1849, at the age of twenty-two. The song, intended to be sung on the battlefields of Lombardy, was composed in October 1848 while Verdi was also at work on his propaganda opera, *La battaglia di Legnano*, and is in the popular style of the patriotic music from that opera. Verdi sent the song to Mazzini with a letter expressing his fear that he may have tried to be too popular and facile, and suggesting that Mazzini burn the manuscript if he thought it not good enough. Mazzini published it, but, since the fighting was over by the time the song arrived, it was never heard on the battlefields of Lombardy.

'L'Abandonnée' was composed in Paris for Giuseppina Strepponi at the time when she and Verdi were living together there, and was published as a supplement to the magazine *La France Musicale* in 1849. An andante with, for Verdi, a somewhat over-decorated vocal line, it is more valuable as a guide to the kind of singer Strepponi may have been than in its own right. But 'Fiorellin' che sorge appena' (words by Verdi's librettist Piave), written in Trieste in 1850 while *Stiffelio* was being prepared for production, is quite charming. 'La preghiera del poeta' dates from 1858, the time of *Un ballo in maschera*. The remaining Verdi songs, none of them as attractive as the 1838 or 1845 albums, are 'Il brigidin', written in 1863 to a poem by Dell' Ongaro; 'Tu dici che non m'ami', a stornello or Tuscan folk poem (1869); and 'Pietà, Signor', which Verdi and Boito contributed to a publication for the benefit of victims of an earthquake in Sicily and Calabria in November 1894, its text adapted by Boito from the 'Agnus Dei' section of the mass.

Luigi Arditi (1822–1903), violinist, conductor and composer, settled in London in his mid thirties as conductor of opera at Her Majesty's Theatre. None of his operas has survived, and, of his many songs which were so admired by the Victorians, only the waltz 'Il bacio' is still heard. The songs of Paolo Tosti (1846–1916) have fared better. Unusually for an Italian composer, Tosti showed no desire to excel in the field of opera, and concentrated on the composition of songs, of which he wrote a great many. He had a flair for Italianate vocal melody, less elegant than that of his bel canto predecessors, more plebeian in style, and owing a great deal to popular Neapolitan song. Among the best of the songs which are still frequently performed by Italian singers (though Tosti wrote to French and English texts as well) are 'Ideale', 'A Vuchella' (poem by D'Annunzio), 'Addio' (Goodbye for ever'), 'Vorrei morire' and 'Marechiare'.

Another Italian composer who, like Tosti, showed little interest in opera was Luigi Denza (1846–1922). He did, in fact, produce one opera : as a pupil of Mercadante this was no doubt expected of him. But his principal activity was the composition of songs, of which he wrote more than 500. His name survives today, however, because of one of them, 'Funiculi funiculà', written to celebrate the opening of the funicular cable car service that runs up to Vesuvius. More than half a million copies of the song were sold upon publication, and translated versions appeared in virtually every civilized language. Richard Strauss, under the impression that it was a Neapolitan folk song, quoted from it in his orchestral suite *Aus Italien*.

Giacomo Puccini (1858–1924), the only Italian opera composer of real stature since Verdi, left no more than a handful of songs, mostly to texts of Ghislanzoni, such as 'Malinconia', 'Allor ch'io sarò morto' and 'Spirto gentil'. The most attractive of the songs is 'E L'uccellino', to words by Renato Fuccini, contemporary with *La Bohème* and indeed somewhat Mimi-like in its utterance. 'Malinconia', written much earlier, in 1881, for voice and strings, was made use of by Puccini in the love duet of *Le Villi* three years later. Ruggiero Leoncavallo (1858–1919), Puccini's exact contemporary and rival, is remembered for no more than one opera and one song: the opera, *I Pagliacci*, and the song 'Mattinata' which he composed specially for Caruso to record for the gramophone. The recording, with Leoncavallo accompanying the tenor, was one of Caruso's most popular, and the song a lilting and easily memorized tune, was enthusiastically taken up by most other tenors.

If song did not flourish in Italy in the 19th century to the extent that it did in Germany, France and England, this was no doubt due to the immense popularity of opera in that country. Since the days of the *verismo* composers of the turn of the century, the popularity of opera has declined in Italy, and it would have been reasonable to expect the Italian melodic flair now to have manifested itself in song. This has happened, though not to any very significant extent: smarting under the imagined sneer of the central Europeans and their great symphonic tradition, Italian composers of the 20th century have tended to move, not only away from opera, but towards instrumental music. No one has made his reputation in Italy in this century as a composer of songs. Perhaps the most distinguished example of the general trend can be found in the work of Ferruccio Busoni (1866–1924) who, in parentage as well as upbringing and training, was as much Austrian as Italian. Busoni was sufficiently Italian, and sufficiently 19th-century, to compose four operas, but his orchestral and instrumental music comprises an equally important part of his *œuvre*. His songs do not number more than twenty or so, but they are interesting and unusual because of the diversity of influences they reveal, and also because of the breadth of Busoni's literary culture. He set Italian, German and English texts with equal facility. His two earliest songs, written when he was a child, are both settings of the 'Ave Maria', but the next published songs, op. 15, take their texts from Byron : 'I saw thee weep' and 'By the waters of Babel'. The German songs of the same period, written around 1880 when Busoni was in his teens, although they are late romantic in style, begin to show traces of individuality, especially the two songs of op. 27, 'Wer hat das erste Lied erdacht' (poem by Blüthgen) and 'Bin ein fahrender Gesell', (two titles which today sound to us quasi-Mahlerian). At the age of fifteen, Busoni wrote his Italian songs, all four of them published as an *Album vocale*, op. 30. The poems are from various sources, including Busoni's own father and Boito. The later songs revert to German texts, except for a second shot at Byron's 'By the waters of Babel', which is really a revision of the earlier song. In his later years Busoni turned to Goethe, and the last four and in many ways the finest of his songs are settings of Germany's greatest poet: two songs for baritone voice, 'Lied des Unmuts' and 'Lied des Mephistopheles', one for mezzo-soprano, 'Die Bekehrte', and, in the final year of his life, 'Schlechter Trost'.

The few songs of Franco Alfano (1876–1954), the opera composer who completed the third act of *Turandot* after Puccini's death, are suitably Puccinian. They include a cycle, *Il giardiniere*, to poems of Tagore.

The songs of Stefano Donaudy (1879–1925) are deliberately archaic throwbacks to the era of the *arie antiche*. Some of these pastiches are nevertheless highly attractive songs in their own right. The most popular of them are 'O del mio amato ben', 'Luoghi sereni e cari' and 'Vaghissima sembianza'.

Ottorino Respighi (1879–1936), more modern in style, and owing something to Austro-German influences, nevertheless reveals in his more than fifty songs a leaning towards cool neo-classicism. Strikingly free of 19th-century operatic mannerisms, Respighi's songs are among the most original and sensitive to have emerged from Italy in the first half of the 20th century: sensitivity to the mood of a poem, rather than to subtlety of verbal inflection, for Respighi, having distilled the essence of the poem he is setting, then plays upon the language almost instrumentally. Among the early songs, the well-known 'Nebbie', the poised, atmospheric 'Notte' and the haunting, lyrical 'Stornellatrice' are some of the most successful. In the twenties and thirties, Respighi's lyricism flowed less easily; nevertheless the *Quattro liriche armene* of 1921 and the *Tre vocalizzi* of 1933 are impressive. Balancing Respighi's neo-classicism in the twenties and thirties was the neo-romanticism of the songs of

Ildebrando Pizzetti (1880–1968). Primarily a composer of opera, Pizzetti carried his dramatic style over into his songs, the best of which have a strength and solidity more appealing to Italian audiences then the delicacy of Respighi. The most widely known of Pizzetti's songs is 'I pastori', written in 1908 on a poem by D'Annunzio, but equally fine are the three Petrarch sonnets of 1922, 'Oscuro è il ciel', from the *Altre cinque liriche* of 1932, which also exists in a version with orchestral accompaniment, and the *Tre liriche* of 1944.

Francesco Pratella (1880–1955), the first of the Italian futurist composers, did not always adhere to his futurist principles in his songs, some of which are engagingly lyrical in a traditional language. Gian Francesco Malipiero (1882–1973) brought his austere neo-classical style to the creation of a number of songs to texts by various Italian poets including D'Annunzio, as well as three vocalizes and a setting in English of the French poet Jean-Aubry ('Keepsake'). Riccardo Pick-Mangiagalli (1882–1949), Czech by birth but Italian by naturalization and life-long domicile, wrote songs which are late romantic in manner. The songs of Alfredo Casella (1883–1947) reveal a variety of styles, the later ones sounding more natural and spontaneous in expression than the early settings of French verse. Of the French songs, the *Trois Lyriques* of 1905, to poems by Verlaine, Samain and Richepin, 'L'Adieu de la Vie' (Tagore translated by André Gide) are the most impressive, while the Italian songs include several of interest, such as 'La sera fiesolana' (d'Annunzio) and *Quattro favole romanesche* (poems by Trilussa). Giorgio Ghedini (1892–1965) has, like most other Italian composers of song, produced settings of Rabindranath Tagore : in his case, the *Tre liriche di Tagore* of 1919. These and his songs to texts by Italian poets are, in general, lacking in any strong personality.

Much more rewarding is Mario Castelnuovo-Tedesco (1896–1968), an Italian Jewish pupil of Pizzetti who has composed a great many songs, from the popular 'Ninna-Nanna' and the excellent song-cycles of his youth, *Stelle cadenti* and *Coplas* (both to folk texts, in the latter case Spanish), to the sensitive settings of Elizabeth Barrett Browning, *Three Sonnets from the Portuguese*. During the 1920s, Castelnuovo-Tedesco produced nine books of Shakespeare songs, containing settings of all the songs in the plays. Much later, in 1945, there appeared his 27 *Shakespeare Sonnets*. Castelnuovo-Tedesco's songs are noted for their individuality, their musical language which is both modern and accessible, and for the composer's delicate response to Italian and English verse. The Shakespeare songs, in particular, are a remarkable achievement, re-creating in contemporary musical terms the spirit and impulse of the Elizabethan verses. Luigi Cortese (b. 1899), a pupil of Casella, has written numerous songs which are widely admired, while Mario Pilati (1903–1938), equally industrious in song, might well have challenged Castelnuovo-Tedesco in the range and vitality of his *œuvre*, had it not been cut short by his early death.

Goffredo Petrassi (b. 1904), composer of several choral and orchestral works in a neo-classical style, has composed songs at most periods in his career, though without, one feels, ever having offered his most personal gifts to the genre. The *Tre liriche antiche italiane* of 1929 sound like intellectualized Donaudy, and the *Tre liriche* of 1944 for baritone voice elicit admiration rather than enthusiasm. A more engaging talent, though perhaps he would frown at the adjective, is that of Luigi Dallapiccola (b. 1904), whose acquaintance with Alban Berg led to his adoption of the twelve-tone method of composition in several of his works. A gifted melodist, Dallapiccola has written more extensively for voice and small orchestra than for voice and piano, but both in the chamber music works and in his songs (such as the three *Fiori di Tapo* of 1925, and the Machado settings, *Quattro liriche* of 1948) he brings an expressive warmth and melodic charm to his writing for the voice. Among other contemporary composers who have written songs worthy of note are the following: Adone Zecchi (b. 1904); Giovanni Salviucci (1907–1937) whose 'Salmo di David' for tenor or soprano and piano, composed in 1933, has been much admired; Riccardo Nielsen (b. 1908), of Scandinavian descent, most of whose mature work is in the twelve-note idiom; Riccardo Malipiero (b. 1914), nephew of Gian Francesco Malipiero, exponent of the twelve-tone technique, and critic; and Mario Zafred (b.1922) whose political commitment to Soviet-style Communism has led him, one gathers, to 'compose down' to the people.

In Spain, the art of song was not widely cultivated in the 19th century, though there has been a revival of interest in this century. The repertoire is becoming more widely known abroad through the recitals of such Spanish singers as Victoria de los

Angeles, Teresa Berganza and Montserrat Caballé. The 19th-century composers of *zarzuelas*, the Spanish near-equivalent of operetta, of course composed songs which were widely popular; one of them, Joaquin Valverde (1846–1910) produced the catchy 'Clavelitos' which is widely used as an encore piece by Spanish recitalists. The 20th-century composers had their attention drawn to the popular music of the 19th century, and the folk tunes of the 18th century and earlier, by Enrique Granados (1867–1916) who not only created modern Spanish piano music but also, with his collections of songs and arrangements, especially the *Colleción de canciones amatorias* and the *Colleción de tonadillas, escritas en estile antiguo*, rejuvenated Spanish song, and opened up a wide vein of material for later composers to draw upon. Manuel de Falla (1876–1946), composer of imaginative and evocative instrumental and orchestral music, left only two groups of solo songs, settings of three Gautier poems in 1909, and the famous *Siete canciones populares españolas*, arrangements of folk songs, in 1922. Joaquin Nin (1879–1949), Cuban, but musically educated in Spain, did even more valuable work than Falla in editing and publishing Spanish folk songs.

The essentially lyrical gifts of Joaquin Turina (1882–1949) found ideal expression in his many songs, composed throughout his career. Favouring the traditional type of Spanish song, to which he brought a sensitive response to poetry and a flexible melodic line, Turina produced, in the *Poema en forma de canciones*, composed in 1918 to texts of De Campoamor, and the *Tres arias* of 1923, some of the most attractive modern Spanish songs. The first of the *Tres arias*, 'Romanza', and two of the three songs of *Triptico* (1929) are settings of the Duke of Rivas, the 19th-century romantic playwright whose play *La fuerza del sino* was the starting point of Verdi's *La forza del destino*. Among the more important of Turina's later songs are the *Tres sonetos* of 1930, the sonnets being by Francisco Rodriguez Marin, and the Lope de Vega setting of 1935, called 'Homenaje a Lope de Vega'. The Basque composer Jesús Guridi (1886–1961), famous for his *zarzuelas*, brought his fluent melodic gift to the art of song, and also collected and arranged a great many folk songs, whereas Oscar Esplá (b. 1886), just as interested in folk song but more intellectually inclined, has written songs less obvious and immediate in their appeal, lyrical yet austere. The strongest contrast to Esplá is offered by Federico Mompou

(b. 1893), a self-taught primitive whose simple direct style is yet highly evocative of his own Catalan world. As Emile Vuillermoz wrote of him, his music, 'which is so gentle and peaceful, reaches out to unexplored regions of the subconscious'.* Many of Mompou's songs have their basis in folk song, but they are original works, not simply arrangements. Mompou possessed the art of producing instant folk music.

Roberto Gerhard (1896–1970) left his native Spain to settle in England after the defeat of the Republicans in the Civil War. A pupil of Schoenberg in Vienna and Berlin, Gerhard came to regard himself in later life as an English composer, though the musical character of his work remained essentially Spanish. In addition to arrangements of Catalan folk songs of voice and piano which he also orchestrated, his songs include 'L'Infantament meravellós de Shaharazade' and a collection of *Servenillas*. Another emigré, Rodolfo Halffter (b. 1900), who settled in Mexico in 1939, wrote a number of songs, as did his brother Ernesto Halffter (b. 1905). Other 20th-century Spanish composers worthy of mention are Joaquin Rodrigo (b. 1902) whose *Canciones sobre textos castillanos* are said to be extremely faithful to the cadences of the language, and Xavier Montsalvatge (b. 1912), the lyrical charm of whose *Cansciones negras* has ensured these delightful songs a wide popularity with foreign as well as Spanish singers. One of them, the 'Canción de Cuña Para Dormir a un Negrito' ('Lullaby for a Black Baby'), features regularly in the recitals of Victoria de los Angeles.

Of the Latin-American composers who have contributed to the literature of song in our century, those of Brazil have been more indefatigable than their colleagues in neighbouring countries. Heitor Villa-Lobos (1887–1959), in addition to producing original songs, was a great collector and arranger of Brazilian folk song, and he has had several followers, among them Ernani Braga (b. 1888), composer of many songs which are popular in his own country. (He is not to be confused with the 19th-century Italian Gaetano Braga (1829–1907) of the famous and much-arranged 'Serenata'.) The Mexican Manuel Ponce (1882–1948) deserves a mention for his arrangements of Mexican folk songs, as well as for his own charming and tuneful songs, one of which, 'Estrellita' (1913), achieved world-wide popularity,

* Emile Vuillermoz *Musique d'aujourd'hui* Paris 1923

and was used again by its composer nearly thirty years later as the theme of a movement in his violin concerto.

In Switzerland, the folk song arrangements of Emile Jaques-Dalcroze (1865–1950), adjuncts to his teaching methods, were never intended for the concert-hall. The leading Swiss composer of his time, Frank Martin (b. 1890) has written more tellingly for voice and orchestra than for voice and piano, though mention should be made of his 'Dédicace à Jaques-Dalcroze', a Ronsard setting for tenor voice. In Holland, the foundations of 20th-century Dutch song were laid by Julius Röntgen (1855–1932), with his arrangements of folk songs. Sem Dresden (1881–1957) is among the Dutch composers who have made important contributions to the song repertoire, together with Willem Pijper (1894–1947) who has exercised a considerable influence on his contemporaries and followers with his settings of Dutch poets, as well as of French texts. His pupils include Karel Mengelberg (1902–1951) and Henk Badings (b. 1907). The Belgian Jan Blockx (1851–1912) was a prolific composer of songs to Flemish texts, while the work of Paul Gilson (1865–1942) revealed Russian and even Oriental influences. The brothers Jongen, Joseph Jongen (1873–1953) and Léon Jongen (b. 1884), wrote several songs to Flemish texts, and the more modern-sounding Jean Absil (1893–1974) has also written songs, some of them in the twelve-tone system. August Baeyens (b. 1895), the leading Belgian expressionist composer, set poems by such Flemish expressionist poets as Paul van Ostaeven and Gaston Burssens. The surrealist, and more recently Schoenbergian, André Souris (1899–1970) has written interestingly for the voice, but most of his accompaniments are for various combinations of instruments. In Greece, the most important modern name is that of Peto Petridis (b. 1892) whose earliest song, 'Lullaby', was composed while he was working in London in 1917. Most of his songs, to English as well as modern Greek texts, are French and almost Debussian, in manner.

V

THE ENGLISH LANGUAGE

THE EARLIEST ENGLISH songs which still retain their
power to delight a general, non-specialist musical audience are
those of John Dowland (1563–1626), the English lutenist who
travelled and studied on the continent, who was for some time
lutenist to King Christian IV of Denmark and, towards the end
of his life, in the service of the Duke of Wolgast in Pomerania.
A virtuoso performer on the lute, and apparently an excellent
singer of his own songs, Dowland can lay claim to being the
first great English composer, and indeed one of the very few
great English composers of song in any period. His solo songs to
lute accompaniment stand at the beginning of a line of descent
that leads, through the classical song of the 18th century, to the
great flowering of the German *Lied* in the 19th century. It is
thought that some of his tunes may be based on folk song; he
was certainly a remarkable melodist, and far in advance of his
time in that he had no inhibitions about sharing the melodic
interest of a song between singer and accompanist in a manner
that, to modern ears, can sometimes sound startlingly Schubertian.
In recent years, Peter Pears and Julian Bream have done much
in their joint recitals to popularize the songs of Dowland, and to
remind modern listeners of the pure genius of one of the finest
composers for the human voice. Such songs as 'Sorrow, stay',
'Flow, my tears' and 'Weep you no more, sad fountains' are as
accessible and direct in their effect as any of the masterpieces of
19th-century German song.

The songs of Henry Lawes (1596–1662) differ from those
of Dowland and his contemporaries in several ways. By the time
of Lawes, the composer of song had ceased to be his own poet,
and looked to the court poets of his age, such as Herrick,
Suckling and Carew, for suitable material upon which to compose. Lawes was less prodigally gifted a melodist than his great
predecessor, but he turned this lack into a virtue by the scrupulous

care with which he set word to note. He chose his texts from the
finest poets of his age, including Milton, and set them in a
style of heightened recitative whose declamation was always
true to the metre and accent of the verse, as well as to its sense.
A 17th-century Wolf, to follow the 16th-century Schubert.
Dowland's tunes, like those of Schubert, lose little of their musical
appeal when played on instruments, without words, whereas
the declamatory style of Henry Lawes produced music which
often largely depended for its effect upon its words, just as in
the songs of Hugo Wolf. But there is no valid reason why one
should attempt to divorce the music of a song from its words.
If the music does stand up on its own, that is a bonus. Though
popular in his lifetime, Lawes was criticized by later generations,
and his aims misunderstood. One of his brothers, William Lawes
(1602–1645) was considered in his time to have been as gifted
a composer as Henry.

The development of English song during the 17th century
was, of course, deflected by the political and social events of the
period, by the years of Cromwell's rule and then by the Restora-
tion. By the time of Purcell, solo song had in general become
absorbed into opera, though songs from the operas continued
to be published separately as well. John Blow (1649–1708), who
taught Purcell, wrote songs with accompaniment for harpsichord
or spinet, as well as songs for insertion into plays such as Tate's
The Loyal General and Aphra Behn's *The Lucky Chance*.
Blow's finest vocal music is to be found in his opera, *Venus and
Adonis*, perhaps the first real English opera, and a significant
precursor of Purcell's *Dido and Aeneas*.

With Henry Purcell (1659–1695), English song reaches a level
of truthfulness in declamation and expressiveness in melody
which it has not to this day surpassed. Though the best-known
examples of Purcell's melody are to be found in the songs from
his operas and masques, notably *Dido and Aeneas* and *King
Arthur*, it should not be forgotten that, in a large number of
secular songs with continuo accompaniment, he has left a body
of work which constitutes the real beginning of English song as
we know it today. It was Purcell who transformed the recitative
style of Henry Lawes into the arioso, retaining the direct
expressiveness of recitative while taking advantage of some of
the discipline of melodic form. Purcell himself was a singer, a
counter-tenor, which helps to explain how he came to write so
gratefully and, as it seems, instinctively for the voice. In his

sureness of touch and his unfussiness of style, he reaches across the centuries to the greatest living English composer, Benjamin Britten, whose style of vocal writing in part derives from Purcell, and who has proved so expert and sympathetic an editor of Purcell for modern performance. It is sad that, though lip service is paid to Purcell as the father of English music, singers have not been at all adventurous in exploring the delights and treasures of his songs. In addition to the better known titles, such as 'Ah, how pleasant 'tis to love', 'On the brow of Richmond Hill', and Herbert's magnificent elegy on the death of Queen Mary, 'Incassum, Lesbia, rogas', so memorably set by Purcell, there are more than 100 other songs, among them some of the finest settings of English verse ever composed. These include all three settings, composed at various times, of 'If music be the food of love', a poem whose first line alone quotes from *Twelfth Night*; the brilliant study in madness, 'Bess of Bedlam'; and the charming 'Lucinda is bewitching fair'.

After Purcell's death, a number of his songs and extracts from his stage works were collected by his widow, and published under the title of *Orpheus Britannicus*.* A publisher's note to the second edition of this great collection aptly describes the nature of Purcell's art: 'The Author's extraordinary Tallent in all sorts of *Music* is sufficiently known; but he was particularly admir'd for his *Vocal*, having a peculiar *Genius* to express the Energy of *English Words*, whereby he mov'd the Passions as well as caus'd Admiration in all his Auditors.'

Perhaps the most popular composer of song among Purcell's contemporaries was John Eccles (1668–1735) who, in 1710, published a collection of almost 100 songs, several of them having first been heard in plays and masques. The bass singer, Richard Leveridge (1670–1758), in his younger days a noted performer of Purcell and Blow, later a mainstay of the Italian opera at the Haymarket and Covent Garden, composed a great many individual songs as well as masques and songs for insertion in the plays of Farquhar, Vanbrugh and others. One of the most popular of them was 'The Roast Beef of Old England'. Of totally different background was Maurice Greene (1695–1755), organist and academic, whose songs were correspondingly less operatic in manner than those of Leveridge, though no less attractive. Henry Carey (1687–1743), poet, playwright and

* Volume I was published in London by Henry Playford in 1698, and volume II in 1702

composer, wrote hundreds of songs for popular performance. The words and music of 'Sally in our Alley' are his, though the tune to which the words are sung today is earlier than Carey.

The most important English composer of the 18th-century, and a popularizer of opera through his own operas composed in the Italian style but in the English language, Thomas Arne (1710–1778), made an important contribution to the song literature with the gay and entertaining songs he composed for performance at the various pleasure gardens of London, such as Vauxhall, Ranelagh and Marylebone Gardens, and equally with his settings of Shakespeare, written for productions of the plays at Drury Lane. The songs from *As You Like It, Twelfth Night, The Merchant of Venice, The Tempest* (including the delightful 'Where the Bee Sucks'), *Much Ado About Nothing, Romeo and Juliet* and *Cymbeline*, engagingly and successfully bring an 18th-century formality of melody to the Elizabethan lyrics. Many of Arne's non-Shakespearian songs appeared in a collection entitled *The Monthly Melody, or Polite Entertainment for Ladies and Gentlemen*. The famous patriotic song, 'Rule Britannia', comes from one of Arne's masques.

Another excellent composer, Arne's exact contemporary William Boyce (1710–1779) was a pupil of Maurice Greene. He, too, wrote for performance at the pleasure gardens, and his songs display the same freshness and ease as those of Arne, though perhaps not the same individuality. Like Arne, he too is remembered today by a wide public for one particular song; in Boyce's case, 'Hearts of Oak'.

Among the composers of the second half of the 18th-century who wrote agreeable songs for the pleasure gardens, or for amateur performance at home, are Charles Dibden, James Hook and William Shield. Charles Dibden (1745–1814) acted and sang in his own operas and entertainments, for which he wrote such songs as ' 'Twas in the Good Ship Rover', 'Saturday Night at Sea' and 'Tom Bowling'. 'Tom Bowling' has recently had a new lease of life in Benjamin Britten's arrangement. Dibden's sea songs, which gained for their composer the title of 'the Tyrtaeus of the British Navy', continued to be popular throughout the 19th-century, and some of them are still to be found in popular song albums. James Hook (1746–1827), organist and teacher of pianoforte, was exceedingly prolific in a variety of forms. For the Vauxhall gardens he composed more than 2,000 songs, many of them in a pseudo-Scottish vein of melody. His

'Within a Mile of Edinboro' Town' was, and still is, frequently mistaken for a genuine Scottish folk song, and his charming 'Lass of Richmond Hill' has survived to sound as fresh and appealing now as when it was written. William Shield (1748–1829) wrote popular songs such as 'The Thorn', 'The Ploughboy' and 'The Post Captain', as well as a number of bravura pieces designed to display the vocal agility of the soprano, Elizabeth Billington. The name of Henry Bishop (1786–1855) should be added here, for, although his songs were written in the 19th century, their idiom and musical language are distinctly 18th-century. In 1830, Bishop became Musical Director at Vauxhall, in which capacity he wrote numerous songs of easy charm, though slightly archaic, or at least old-fashioned. 'Lo, here the gentle lark' and 'Bid me discourse' are still occasionally heard, but the song which keeps Bishop's name alive today, 'Home, Sweet Home', comes from his opera *Clari, or the Maid of Milan*, composed in 1832. Its pleasant, sentimental tune was made use of by Donizetti seven years later in *Anna Bolena*, perhaps in the belief that it was a traditional English tune, and from there it made its way into Verdi's *Nabucco* in 1842, as 'Dio di Giuda'.

Of the composers born in the 19th century, the earliest of note is John Hatton (1809–1886) who was mainly self-taught. He wrote two operas, one of which was produced in Vienna, and nearly 200 songs, the earliest of which were published under the pseudonym of 'Czapek'. The songs vary in quality, many are extremely bland, and it would not be unfair to categorize them, in the main, as drawing-room ballads, though this is not to deny them their own distinction of vigorous and attractive melody. Hatton's setting of Herrick's 'To Anthea' achieved a wide popularity through being taken up by the famous baritone, Sir Charles Santley. Edward Loder (1813–1865), born in the same year as Verdi and Wagner, has certain affinities with the Italian composer. The melodic impulse of his opera *Raymond and Agnes* is at times distinctly Verdian. However, Loder began to write operas not out of any dramatic conviction but to provide suitable frameworks in which his songs could be heard. The songs, which include such titles as 'The Brave Old Oak' and 'Invocation to the Deep', are first-rate. One of them 'The Brooklet', a setting of an English translation of 'Wohin?', the poem by Wilhelm Müller best known for its inclusion in Schubert's *Die schöne Müllerin*, has a melodic charm not unworthy of Schubert. Grove calls it one of 'the most beautiful songs in existence'. Among Loder's early compositions is a set of *Twelve Sacred Songs*, which he dedicated to Sterndale Bennett. William Sterndale Bennett (1816–1875), a friend of Mendelssohn and Schumann, possessed a demure and fastidious talent which might have blossomed into greater personality had it not fallen so completely under the influence of Mendelssohn. Bennett's songs, in particular, are sub-Mendelssohnian, though the best of them, such as 'Maiden Mine' and 'Resignation' are undeniably charming.

For the purpose of this survey, Arthur Sullivan (1842–1900) must be cruelly wrested apart from his collaborator William Gilbert, although his finest music undoubtedly was composed for the operettas written to Gilbert's texts. Sullivan, it is obvious, was a highly gifted melodist; nevertheless his talent was an extremely eclectic one. The most enjoyable tunes in the operettas are those in which he deliberately set out to compose in someone else's style—Mendelssohn, Donizetti, Verdi, Mozart, Schubert; Sullivan produced amiable, attractive and affectionate parodies of them all. He had their styles at his finger-tips, but he did not find it so easy to discover his own style, and in fact was still, in his so called 'serious' music, pondering the nature of his own talent when he died. His songs had a vogue in their day, and indeed there are some very fine ones amongst those written in the 1850s and '60s before Sullivan became almost exclusively occupied with the composition of operettas in collaboration with Gilbert. The group of five Shakespeare songs dating from 1863-4 includes the delightful 'Orpheus with his lute', probably Sullivan's finest song. Other excellent songs include 'The Arabian Love Song', 'O Fair Dove', 'Thou'rt Passing Hence' and 'The White Plume'. *The Window, or The Song of the Wrens*, a cycle of twelve settings of Tennyson, though completely unknown today, is well worth resuscitating. Sullivan's most popular single song was, and remains, the sentimental 'Lost Chord', composed in 1877, and therefore contemporaneous with *The Sorcerer*. The later songs are rather poor, and 'The Absent-Minded Beggar', a setting of Kipling which Sullivan composed in 1899 during the Boer War, sounds unfortunately like the work of someone whose talent is completely played-out.

Hubert Parry (1848–1918) is usually thought of as the Victorian choral composer par excellence. In such choral works as 'Blest Pair of Sirens' and the famous unison setting of Blake's 'Jerusalem' for children's voices, one finds the same felicitous care in accentuation that is displayed in Parry's songs. In the songs it is allied in masterly fashion with a strong and individual lyric gift which was this composer's most valuable asset. Confining himself to settings of the English language, he began with Thomas Moore, Thomas Hood, Tennyson and Shelley, and then, in his mid twenties, produced the excellent *Garland of Old Fashioned Songs*, half of them on texts of Shakespeare. He also set three 'Odes of Anacreon', in Moore's translations, after which his songs tended to appear as volumes of *English Lyrics*. Twelve sets of these were published, the last two posthumously. The first set, dating from the early 1880s, consists of four well-known poems : 'My true love hath my heart' (Sidney), 'Good-night' (Shelley), 'Where shall the lover rest ?' (Scott) and 'Willow, willow' (Shakespeare); and, throughout the remaining volumes, Parry's intention continued constant. It was to provide tuneful and attractive settings for some of the best-loved English lyrical verse, from Lovelace and Suckling to Mary Coleridge and Christina Rossetti. His technique was not adventurous, but the best of his songs, such as the Mary Coleridge settings of Set IX of the *English Lyrics*, succeeded because of the strength and sincerity of his creative personality. Parry's less successful songs, though unfailingly skilful, suffer from a certain pallidness of spirit, or want of creative personality. Their musical manners are good, so good that at times one longs for a dash of more wayward eccentricity.

One of Parry's great strengths as a writer of songs was his literary taste which, though hardly adventurous, was confident and well-judged. Another, purely musical strength was the delicacy and professionalism of his craftsmanship. His emotional range is wider than might at first be supposed, and his melody, admittedly notable more for its dramatic truthfulness than for its spontaneity, has a lyrical quality which never degenerates into sentimentality.

Parry's songs appealed very much to the singers of his day. The famous bass-baritone Harry Plunket Greene wrote of them : 'To Parry the words were everything. I never heard him profess any creed or reveal the foundations of his belief, but his passionate devotion to words cries out in every song he wrote. He knew that a song is a message, that from time immemorial we have given our messages by speech or its symbols, that the more human you make it the better the singer can deliver it, and that music is the torch to read it by. Of all the great song-writers that I know, no one has made it easier for the singer; and that is the highest testimony a singer can give.'*

Charles Villiers Stanford (1852–1924), with whom Parry's name is sometimes coupled, was in some ways the finer composer. He too composed oratorio, as every respectable Victorian did, but his talent was essentially a dramatic one, and it is likely that some of his best music lies buried in such operas as *The Veiled Prophet of Khorassan* which was produced in Hanover in 1881, *Savonarola* (Hamburg, 1884) and *Shamus O'Brien* (London, 1896). Stanford's skill and versatility in word-setting are revealed in more than 100 songs which are not only as attractive as those of Parry in terms of vocal melody, but are frequently additionally interesting as well for their well-judged and natural sounding accompaniments. If Stanford, in his songs, does not actually reach 'a degree of perfection which . . . puts him level with the greatest song-writers of his day', which is the claim that Grove's Dictionary† makes for him, he nevertheless is capable of giving real delight both with his narrative songs and his lyrical settings. His op. 1 in 1877 was a collection of eight songs from George Eliot's *The Spanish Gypsy*. The next two groups are sympathetic, if Schumannesque, settings of Heine, after which, with one or two exceptions, Stanford was to confine himself to English language verse. The six songs of *An Irish Idyll* (poems by Moira O'Neill) reveal an especially delicate charm and imagination. The most popular song of the six with singers used to be 'The Fairy Lough', a delicate and natural berceuse. Stanford was Irish by birth, and responded naturally to Irish poetry in such later cycles as *Cushendall* (J. Stevenson), *Six Songs from The Glens of Antrim* (Moira O'Neill) and *A Sheaf of Songs from Leinster* (Letts). Harry Plunket Greene (also Irish), enumerated Stanford's qualities as 'Lilt, rhythm, sense of words, sense of atmosphere, musical imagery and illustration, directness of purpose and—guiding them all— imagination, humour and economy',‡ which seems a fair summing up of one of the most remarkable talents in English 19th-century song. Maude Valerie White (1855–1937) is hardly to be mentioned in the same breath as Stanford, though she did

* Charles L. Graves *Hubert Parry: his life and works* Macmillan London 1926

† *Grove's Dictionary of Music and Musicians* (5th edition) Macmillan London 1954

‡ Harry Plunket Greene *Charles Villiers Stanford* E. Arnold London 1935

compose some delightful songs, to poems of Herrick and Shelley as well as of French and German poets, two of the best of which are 'My soul is an enchanted boat' from Shelley's 'Prometheus Unbound', and another Shelley setting, the stately yet impassioned 'To Mary'.

By far the greatest English composer of his time, and the only one worthy of comparison with the best of his foreign contemporaries such as Mahler and Debussy, Edward Elgar (1857–1934) displayed no great interest in solo song. He began his career in the approved Victorian manner as a composer of oratorio, and indeed created some of his finest works in this form, including *The Dream of Gerontius* in 1900, before going on to produce his masterpieces of the Edwardian era, the decade he has in retrospect come to symbolize, in the two symphonies and the violin concerto. Though, with the exception of the stirring, quasi-national anthem 'Land of Hope and Glory', which is an arrangement of part of an earlier composition, none of his songs is among his best works, Elgar did at least persevere with the genre throughout his life. His earliest song, still unpublished, is 'The Language of Flowers', known to have been written when he was fifteen. A number of songs composed around the age of thirty, but not given opus numbers, include 'Queen Mary's Song' (Tennyson) and 'Song of Autumn' (Adam Lindsay Gordon). The three songs of op. 16 include the attractive 'Shepherd's Song'. Perhaps the worst Elgar song is the arch 'Pipes of Pan' (1900 : words by Adrian Ross). Of those written during the Edwardian decade, 1901–11, the best are 'Pleading', its words by Arthur Salmon, and Elizabeth Barrett Browning's 'A Child Asleep'. A late curiosity is 'It is nae me', a setting of a poem by Sally Holmes, composed in Elgar's old age in 1930. The plain truth is that, *Gerontius* notwithstanding, Elgar was generally insensitive to poetry, and apparently also incapable of characterizing in music. As so much of the work of Elgar's contemporaries and followers of the next generation was influenced by English folk song, mention should be made here of Cecil Sharp (1859–1924) who was largely responsible for the revival of interest in folk song through his enthusiastic collection of English songs and dances. He sought these out assiduously not only in the British Isles but abroad in the Empire, and even in the Southern Appalachian mountains of the United States. His editions of English folk tunes led to their infiltrating into the work of several British composers in the first years of this century.

Frederick Delius (1862–1934) was no more strongly devoted to song than Elgar was. But, in addition to the orchestral tone poems and the choral works which made his reputation, he nevertheless composed several sets of songs. Two of the earliest, *Five Songs from the Norwegian* and *Seven Songs from the Norwegian*, dedicated to Grieg's wife Nina, contain settings of Ibsen, Bjørnson and others. These spring from the composer's friendship with Grieg whom he met in Leipzig when he was studying there. Not surprisingly, these songs sound somewhat like Grieg who, in praising them, uttered an apt warning to Delius: 'Yet there are other things which don't appeal to me— I don't mean in the ideas themselves, for nowhere do you lack invention, but in the handling of the voice. A Norwegian tune and a Wagnerian vocal line—these are dangerous things to bring together.'*

One of the songs which the young Delius had sent Grieg was 'Quicker, my horse', a setting of a poem by Geibel. Grieg thought highly of it, and it became known in performances in French translation as 'Plus vite, mon cheval'; however, after a few years, it was withdrawn by the composer. What Grieg most admired in Delius's songs was that they were 'so beautifully felt'.† This, rather than any originality, is certainly their strength. Although Delius was to find his own personal style in his orchestral music, the songs viewed as a whole reveal a frank eclecticism. For instance the English settings, *Three Shelley Lyrics* and a cycle of five songs from Tennyson's *Maud* both composed in 1891, are sensitive examples of Victorian song at its best; the Verlaine songs, which include 'Il pleure dans mon coeur', are drily elegant; it is left to the four settings of Friedrich Nietzsche to sound a rather more personal note. Deeply felt these songs may be, but too often the feeling is expressed in a borrowed voice.

Of the song cycle from *Maud*, composed with orchestral accompaniment, Delius's great champion Sir Thomas Beecham wrote: 'It is fairly obvious why he chose these particular poems. They are admirably designed for song-writing by a poet, the most musical of his century in England, and the vocal line of them is invariably clear and singable. As an effective background to each of them we have the voice of nature speaking of birds, flowers, the sun, the clouds and the sea, and all this secondary element is illustrated, as it is in *Irmelin*, by the

---

* Sir Thomas Beecham *Frederick Delius* Hutchinson London 1959
† op. cit.

orchestra. . . .'* Elsewhere in his book on Delius, Beecham admits that song-writing was never something essential to Delius, and that 'he seems to have regarded it as a species of relaxation from what was to him the serious interest of his life, the orchestra and any class of composition in which it played a leading part.'†

Two other composers born in the same year as Delius, though hardly of his stature, deserve mention as having produced singable and tuneful ballads and songs which enjoyed a wide popularity in drawing-room and parlour. They are Liza Lehmann and Edward German. Liza Lehmann (1862–1918), of German descent, was in her younger days a successful concert soprano who had sung Schumann *Lieder* to the accompaniment of Clara Schumann. Retiring from performance in her early thirties on the occasion of her marriage, she took up composition and produced a series of song-cycles, by far the most popular of which was *In a Persian Garden*, its texts taken from Fitzgerald's *Rubáiyát of Omar Khayyám*. 'Myself When Young', from this cycle, enjoyed a vogue with baritones and basses which has still not ended, and 'Ah, Moon of My Delight' has remained in the repertoire of popular vocalists of all voice categories. Edward German (1862–1936), too often thought of as the poor man's Sullivan, made his name with operettas such as *Merrie England* and *Tom Jones*, and also composed a number of light and graceful songs, limited in emotional range but agreeably written for the voice.

Arthur Somervell (1863–1937), a composer of a higher order than Lehmann or German, wrote a good many songs, direct in style, intense in expression, and displaying a rare skill and sensitivity in setting the English language. Of his five cycles, Maud (Tennyson), *The Shropshire Lad* (Houseman), *James Lee's Wife* (Browning), *Love in Springtime* (Browning) and *A Broken Arc* (Browning), the finest is *Maud*, despite the fact that 'Come into the garden, Maud' has become a musical as well as a verbal cliché over the years. Somervell's melody always sounds remarkably spontaneous, and the best of his songs possess vigour as well as potent charm. Almost equally fine are the songs of Charles Wood (1866–1926) who edited the folk songs of his native Ireland as well as composing such effective original pieces as 'Ethiopia Saluting the Colours' and 'At the Mid Hour of Night'.

* op. cit.   † op. cit.

In the forefront of those composers most identified with and influenced by the revival of interest in folk song stands Ralph Vaughan Williams (1872–1958). He was an early member of the Folksong Society and an enthusiastic collector of folk tunes, and the folk influence displays itself very early in his songs, for instance in the charming, deservedly well-known 'Linden Lea' (poem by William Barnes), although much in these early songs also stems from Parry. *The House of Life*, a cycle of six sonnets by Dante Gabriel Rossetti, which includes the very familiar 'Silent Noon', in fact owes more to Parry than to the folk spirit, though in its freshness of voice something of the mature composer can also be discerned. Even more individual in tone and forthright in manner are the two sets of *Songs of Travel*, containing between them seven settings of Robert Louis Stevenson. The first of the two sets, consisting of three songs, became the more popular, and understandably so, for 'The Vagabond', 'Bright is the ring of words' and 'The Roadside Fire' are among the composer's most individual and picturesque creations. What they may lack in smoothness of technique, they more than compensate for with their direct unselfconscious accessibility.

Vaughan Williams's art, as revealed in his larger-scale works such as the symphonies, is usually spoken of as being particularly English, with the implication that it does not necessarily travel well. Songs are likely to be even more strongly rooted nationally, and it is true that the spirit, as much as the words, of Vaughan Williams's songs is essentially English, in its forthrightness, its simplicity, its apparent artlessness and ease of communication. Among the more interesting, skilful and assured of the songs are the *Five Mystical Songs* to poems of George Herbert, and the *Three Poems* of Walt Whitman. Although the *Mystical Songs* were composed for baritone, chorus (*ad lib*) and orchestra, they are encountered nowadays, if at all, only in a version for solo voice and piano. The song cycle, *On Wenlock Edge*, to poems from Housman's *A Shropshire Lad*, for voice and piano quintet, is essentially a chamber music work rather than a collection of solo songs. Certainly original and attractive, it does not by any means exactly match the mood, meaning or texture of the poems.

Of the many songs composed by the conductor and pianist Landon Ronald (1873–1938), which proved popular with singers because they were gratefully written for the voice, and possessed an easy charm, 'Down in the Forest' and 'O Lovely Night' have proved the most durable. Gustav Holst (1874–1934) is perhaps not the most exciting of composers, and to some hearers even his songs sound flat and uninviting. Nevertheless, the three sets composed around the turn of the century are not uninteresting in their spare, withdrawn way. These are the four songs of op. 4, the *Six Songs for Baritone* op. 15, three of them settings of Thomas Hardy, and the *Six Songs for Soprano* op. 16. Two other groups virtually complete Holst's song output: *Nine Hymns from the Rig-Veda* translated by Holst, op. 24, and *Twelve Songs*, on poems by Humbert Wolfe, op. 48.

Samuel Coleridge-Taylor (1875–1912), son of an English mother and a father from Sierra Leone, is remembered today as the composer of the once popular oratorio *Song of Hiawatha*, but he also composed a number of songs, including seven *African Romances*. 'Question and Answer' was one of the most frequently heard. Graham Peel (1877–1937), composer of more than 100 songs, the best of them pleasantly tuneful, was especially drawn to A. E. Housman, as, understandably, were most composers of his generation. Peel's setting of 'In summertime on Bredon' was one of the most popular of Housman songs. Similar in style are the songs of Thomas Dunhill (1877–1946), the composer of the operetta 'Tantivy Towers'. Two of Dunhill's Yeats settings, 'The Cloths of Heaven' and 'The Fiddler of Dooney' are particularly attractive in their engagingly unpretentious manner. Henry Balfour Gardiner (1877–1950) is another of the many English composers of this period who, stimulated by the demand on the part of singers and audiences for singable, popular melodies, produced lively and enjoyable songs. So, too, did Rutland Boughton (1878–1960), though his settings of Kipling, Blake, Edward Carpenter and others never achieved a real popularity. The majority of Boughton's songs remain unpublished. Much more successful with the public were the songs of Roger Quilter (1877–1953) whose gift for inventing facile but easily memorized tunes stood him in good stead in his three songs from the Shakespeare plays, composed in 1905. 'O mistress mine' is the most agreeable of them, and has retained its appeal. Quilter later produced more Shakespeare settings, and a great many songs on poems of Dowson, Robert Louis Stevenson, Blake, the Jacobean poets and others. His musical language was conventional, but he made the best possible use of his particular kind of talent, and, in so doing, gave pleasure to a great many people.

The songs of Frank Bridge (1879–1941), one of the most interesting composers of his generation, are perhaps not the most

important element in his *œuvre*, for it is with his orchestral
works and string quartets that he made his greatest impression;
but, in addition to 'Love Went Ariding', a setting of Mary
Coleridge, and a song of rare melodic impulse and buoyancy,
Bridge produced several fine songs, such as 'Go Not, Happy Day'
(Tennyson), 'The Last Invocation' (Walt Whitman) and 'Golden
Hair' (James Joyce). Also attractive are the four early settings
of translations of Heine: 'E'en as a lovely flower', 'Dawn and
Evening', 'The violets blue' and 'All things that we clasp'. A
less considerable composer, Cyril Scott (1879–1970) wrote a
large number of songs, many of which used to be widely admired
for their easy charm. Certainly, taken in small doses they can
be effective, though Scott's musical and emotional range was
not wide, and a dulling sameness emerges from far too many
of his pages. He set his own poems ('Willows', 'Spring Song',
'Evening Melody', 'Oracle' and so on) as well as those of a host
of minor Victorians, Edwardians and Georgians.

Altogether more substantial are the songs of John Ireland
(1879–1962), a composer of rare quality whose best work was
done in the smaller forms of songs and pieces for piano. While
not at all an adherent of any nationalist school of composition,
and not significantly interested in folk song, Ireland yet portrays
in his music an essential Englishness, an instinctive ability to
capture the feeling of English landscape, and, in the songs, a
particularly sensitive response to the language. His setting of
John Masefield's 'Sea Fever' was the only song of Ireland's to
have become really popular in his lifetime, but his large output
contains many songs which are musically its equal or superior,
though perhaps not as forthright and extrovert in expression.
One of Ireland's earliest works of any substance was his song-
cycle, *Songs of a Wayfarer*. Though the title happens to be an
exact translation of Mahler's *Lieder eines Fahrenden Gesellen*,
the texts of Masefield's five songs come from William Blake,
Shakespeare, Rossetti, Dowson and J. V. Blake. In 'Spleen', his
setting of Dowson's 'I was not sorrowful', Ireland already reveals
himself to be a new and individual voice. The three Dowson
and Rossetti songs of *Marigold: Impressions for voice and
pianoforte*, composed in 1913, are particularly attractive, and the
three Arthur Symons songs of 1918–19 ('The Rat', 'Rest' and
'The Adoration') bring an even stronger and more forceful note
into Ireland's music. In the 1920s, Ireland produced some of
his finest songs. Like almost every other composer of his time he

was attracted by the musical possibilities of Housman's lyrics, and in *The Land of Lost Content* (1921) he found fitting musical form and substance for the bitter-sweet flavours of the poet's verses. The five *Thomas Hardy Songs* of 1926 together form a striking cycle whose current neglect by singers is inexplicable. Hardly less remarkable is the beautiful Housman cycle of 1926–7, *We'll to the Woods No More*, three pieces, the third of which, 'Spring Will Not Wait' is unexpectedly, yet, as performance reveals, quite rightly, written for piano alone. Another major cycle, dating from the end of the twenties, is *Songs Sacred and Profane*, uncompromising and deeply felt responses to poems by Alice Meynell, Sylvia Townsend Warner, and Yeats. The *Five Sixteenth Century Poems* of 1938 are more objective in expression. A case could be made out for Ireland as perhaps the finest English song-composer of the 20th-century before the advent of Benjamin Britten.

Of the many composers attracted to the verse of A. E. Housman, one of the most successful in his musical encounters with the poet was George Butterworth (1885–1916) who was killed in action during the First World War. Butterworth, an active member of the Vaughan Williams—Cecil Sharp faction with its intense interest in folk song, was an enthusiastic collector of folk song and dance, and his own songs, especially his Housman settings, reflect this interest very strongly. His output was not large, but there is no doubt that, had he lived longer, he would have made a significant contribution to English song. Butterworth's earliest song is a setting of Shelley's music-inviting 'I fear thy kisses, gentle maiden'. The cycle of six songs from Housman's *A Shropshire Lad* appeared in 1911, as did a single song, 'Requiescat' (poem by Oscar Wilde). In the following year, Butterworth composed his remaining songs, five more Housman poems, including the lovely 'In summertime on Bredon'.

Another casualty of the war was Ivor Gurney (1890–1937), poet as well as composer, for, although he lived until the age of forty-seven, he did so in a condition of shattered physical and mental health due to his wounds, gassing and shell-shock. Gurney's songs are attractive, and the best of them are written in a personal idiom which makes them stand out from much contemporary song. His melodic line, at its most assured, has an almost Schubertian inevitability and ease, and there seems no conflict between his poetic sensitivity and his melodic impulse.

His own melodic gift was too fecund for him to be more than politely interested in the folk song movement. Gurney's songs include settings of the Elizabethans as well as of contemporary poets and of his own verse. 'Captain Stratton's Fancy' (poem by John Masefield) is uncharacteristic, but such songs as 'Last Hours' (John Freeman), 'All night under the moon' (W. W. Gibson) and the lilting 'Down by the Salley Gardens' (Yeats) reveal the quintessential Gurney. His *Five Elizabethan Songs*, originally scored for voice and small orchestra, and later given piano accompaniments, are all of rare beauty, especially John Fletcher's 'Sleep'. Gurney's least impressive songs are those in which, seemingly overawed by the beauties of English poetry, he is content merely to follow the contours of the poem allowing it to dictate rhythm and inflection to the detriment of melodic shape. This, curiously, is a common failing of English 20th-century composers.

Arthur Bliss (b. 1891) has composed a great amount of music for voice, but much of it, in particular the earlier, more experimental work, is in the form of chamber music, such as 'Rout', for soprano and chamber orchestra, its text consisting of isolated syllables devoid of verbal meaning, and 'Madam Noy', a song for soprano, flute, clarinet, bassoon, viola, harp and double bass. Over the years, Bliss's music became more classical in style, and his language more conservative. His songs for voice and piano, even the earlier ones such as *Three Romantic Songs* to poems of Walter de la Mare, composed in 1922, suffer from a certain anonymity of voice, though there are undoubtedly some pleasant pages in *The Ballads of the Four Seasons*, a song-cycle on poems of Li-Po (1923) and *Seven American Poems*, settings of Edna St Vincent Millay and Elinor Wylie (1940).

Herbert Howells (b. 1892) has written songs of rare, gentle charm, mainly on poems of the Elizabethans. A song cycle, *In green ways*, utilizes verse by Shakespeare, James Stephens, Goethe, Skelton and Burkitt Parker. Howells typifies a certain kind of English composer of the first half of the 20th-century, sensitive, quiet, agreeable, but hardly gripping. Arthur Benjamin's talent was livelier than this. Benjamin (1893–1960), an Australian who preferred to live and work in London, had a gift for immediately accessible melody and a skill in instrumentation of which he made excellent use in a number of works of great popular appeal. He was also a distinguished teacher at the Royal College of Music, where his pupils included Benjamin Britten.

Benjamin's wit and attractive lyricism expressed themselves in many musical forms : his songs were not numerous, but the best of them are as good and as important as anything he wrote in the larger forms of opera and the symphony. They include two settings of the Australian poet Hugh McCrae, 'The Moon' and 'The Mouse', a group of three *Greek Poems*, and 'Linstead Market' (traditional). With E. J. Moeran (1894–1950) we are back in the folk song movement, for Moeran, born of an Irish father and an English mother, was profoundly influenced by the folk music of both countries, especially the songs of East Anglia where he grew up, and where he first began to collect folk song. Though he later composed large-scale orchestral and choral works, Moeran's gift was essentially lyric and small-scale, and by far the best of his music is to be found in his many songs. His earliest cycle, *Ludlow Town*, is not among the most successful settings of Housman, for the composer's individuality had not at that time fully asserted itself : *Ludlow Town* has been thought by some critics to sound like John Ireland, who advised and helped his younger colleague at this period of his career. Moeran's finest cycle is undoubtedly the *Seven Poems of James Joyce*, composed in 1929. His other songs include *Four Shakespeare Songs* (1940) and *Six Songs of Seumas O'Sullivan* (1944) as well as a number of arrangements of Norfolk and Suffolk folk songs.

Diametrically opposed, both critically and creatively, to the folk song school, Peter Warlock (1894–1930) found his roots in the music of the Elizabethans and, amongst his contemporaries, Delius. Warlock, whose real name, under which he wrote music criticism, was Philip Heseltine, composed only in the smaller forms. In other words, unlike many composers, he completely understood the nature of his own talent, and never sought to make unsuitable use of it. He wrote a number of short choral works and some pieces for string orchestra, but his greatest interest lay in song. It would be no exaggeration to call Warlock the most remarkable talent in English song since the 17th century. Critics who have written about Heseltine-Warlock usually mention irreconcilable divisions in his nature, and it is true that an apparent manic-depressive personality can be deduced from the songs, some of which are patently manic, others the reverse. Warlock died, it is assumed by his own hand, at the age of thirty-six, leaving behind him 100 songs not unworthy to be compared with the *oeuvre* of Hugo Wolf.

Warlock's general virtues are those of practically every great song composer; a fluent melodic gift, interesting and apposite harmony, a skill and sensitivity in the setting of words to music, and the balancing of the sometimes opposing demands of sense and sound. In Warlock's particular case, the songs tend to divide themselves into those which display an aggressive masculine heartiness and those which reveal a gentler, somewhat melancholic, almost feminine nature. But even to say this is to suggest too crude a division in the composer's nature, and there are many songs, some of them Warlock's finest, which are not easily placed on one or the other side of an imagined dividing line of the mind.

The melancholy element in Warlock's songs reveals itself in the earliest of them, the three songs that make up *Saudades*, written at the age of twenty-two. These settings of Li-Po, Shakespeare and Callimachus were followed, over the next two or three years, by a number of single songs, many of them to Elizabethan or 17th century poems, which established Warlock as a song-composer of originality and an unusually rich melodic gift. The extrovert 'Captain Stratton's Fancy', a setting of John Masefield's poem composed in 1920 has, ironically, remained the most popular Warlock song, along with the lively 'Yarmouth Fair' of four years later. Warlock's masterpiece, and incidentally his most extended composition, is, however, not a song for voice and piano but a song-cycle, *The Curlew* (W. B. Yeats), scored for tenor voice, flute, English horn and string quartet. Among the loveliest of his solo songs are the five which comprise the cycle *Lilligay* composed in 1922, a setting of Arthur Symons's 'Autumn Twilight' which dates from the same year and of which even the self-critical composer himself thought highly, the peaceful 'Contented Lover' (poem by James Mabbe), and, of his settings of contemporary poets, the Bruce Blunt songs, particularly the last song Warlock wrote, 'The Fox'.

The impressive talent of Edmund Rubbra (b. 1901) is revealed to greatest advantage in his symphonies. His feeling for orchestral texture and his highly developed sense of symphonic argument are not qualities ideally suited to the smaller lyrical form of song; nevertheless, Rubbra has composed several songs on Shakespeare (some of the songs from the plays), Shelley, Belloc, Edward Thomas and others, which command respect if not immediate affection. Rather more likeable are the songs of Gerald Finzi (1901–1956). His settings of Thomas Hardy, a poet to whom he returned again and again throughout the years, a poet, too, who is notoriously difficult to set to music, are remarkably successful. Finzi's first Hardy cycle, *A Young Man's Exhortation*, composed in 1933, for tenor, was followed three years later by *Earth and Air and Rain*, ten songs for baritone. In 1949 appeared the finest of the Hardy cycles, the ten songs of *Before and After Summer*. A cycle of five songs from the Shakespeare plays, *Let us Garlands Bring*, composed during the 1940s, is as delightful as the Hardy songs, and makes fewer demands on the listener due to the familiarity of the popular texts. William Walton (b. 1902), despite his melodic resourcefulness and lyrical gifts, has composed very few songs. Two early settings of Swinburne and William Drummond, and three songs on poems of Edith Sitwell virtually exhaust the list of his contributions to the repertoire. His immensely popular *Façade* for speaking-voice and instrumental ensemble makes entertaining use of a number of Edith Sitwell poems, though it apparently shocked some members of its early audiences.

Benjamin Britten (b. 1913), one of this century's geniuses of music, and certainly the finest of living English composers, has written in virtually all forms; clearly, however, he has a special feeling for words, for his greatest and most intensely individual works have been those involving voices, whether in opera (his *Peter Grimes*, *Billy Budd* and *Gloriana* belong to that select list of post-Puccinian operatic masterpieces which includes *Wozzeck*, *Arabella* and *Capriccio*), choral works, cycles for voice and instruments (the *Serenade for tenor, horn and strings* is a work of positively Schubertian stature) or solo song. The composer's long-standing friendship with the distinguished tenor Peter Pears has led to his writing and arranging a number of song-cycles for the tenor voice, just as his admiration for other singers has resulted in such works as the *Songs and Proverbs of William Blake*, for baritone and piano, and *A Charm of Lullabies* for mezzo-soprano and piano.

Britten is the fortunate inheritor of two traditions. From English music and Purcell he derives one aspect of his prodigious genius, and, from the Viennese spirit descending from Mozart through Schubert to Mahler, another. He possesses the most fecund and apparently spontaneous melodic gift of our century, and he has nurtured it well. His music can exude enormous charm, but Britten is not the slave of his own winning personality, and a darker, more forceful voice has asserted itself in many of his works, particularly in the past decade or so. The earliest songs, 'The Birds', a setting of Hilaire Belloc, and *Tit for Tat*, five songs on poems of Walter de la Mare, are childhood and adolescent exercises, though Britten revised and edited *Tit for Tat* for performance as recently as 1969. In his early twenties, at the time of his close friendship with the poet W. H. Auden, he composed several pieces on poems of Auden, including *Our Hunting Fathers*, a cycle for tenor or soprano voice and orchestra, and *On This Island*, for high voice again, this time with piano accompaniment. The five songs of *On This Island* managed to confuse some music critics who appeared to find Auden's poems difficult. One of them, writing several years later in Grove's Dictionary, spoke of 'Auden's skirmishes on the frontiers of unintelligibility which spoil the songs.'* Eric Walter White, able to move with authority in the worlds of both music and poetry, refers more perceptively to the cycle's 'exciting quality of contemporaneity'. 'It was', he continues, 'the product of two young minds thinking along related lines and working to a common purpose, and though it has subsequently been rather overshadowed by the later cycles, it is never likely to lose its special attraction.'† At the same time as *On This Island*, Britten composed his one and only single unattached song, choosing for it Auden's 'Fish in the unruffled lakes'.

For his next cycle, Britten, who has never allowed himself to be confined to the English language alone (in 1939 he had used the prose poems of Arthur Rimbaud in *Les Illuminations* for high voice and strings), turned to the sonnets of Michelangelo and chose seven of the twenty-seven which he set with great panache. The fluid vocal line of these *Seven Sonnets of Michelangelo* for tenor and piano perfectly matches both the style of the poems and the sounds of the Italian language. The cycle was given its first performance in 1942 by the composer and Peter Pears, and most of Britten's music for tenor since then has been composed with the sound of Pears's voice and his special qualities of musicianship in mind. Related in style to the *Michelangelo Sonnets*, though heavier, more sombre in mood, *The Holy Sonnets of John Donne* were composed in 1945 shortly after Britten had returned from a tour of Belsen and other

---

* Frank Howes, in article on Britten in fifth edition of *Grove's Dictionary of Music and Musicians* (Macmillan London 1954)
† Eric Walker White *Benjamin Britten: his Life and Operas* Faber & Faber London 1970

German concentration camps with Yehudi Menuhin, and it is perhaps not too fanciful to imagine that one catches at moments in the cycle an expression of something of the deeply numbing pain of the experience.

The first of three Canticles, a setting of Francis Quarles for tenor and piano, is a work of immediate and lasting appeal. (The second is a vocal duet, and the third is for tenor, horn and piano.) It was followed by *A Charm of Lullabies*, which is indeed charming, as well as skilful in its avoidance of any possible monotony in setting five lullabies for performance together as a cycle. The poems themselves, by Blake, Burns, Robert Greene, Thomas Randolph and John Philip, were chosen for their contrasting qualities. The next cycle, *Winter Words*, consists of eight songs to poems of Thomas Hardy: Britten's music is uncannily Hardyesque in its apparent discursiveness masking a sure sense of form.

Songs from the Chinese for tenor voice and guitar, the poems set in Arthur Waley's English translations, is one of Britten's slighter works. But the *Six Hölderlin Fragments*, set in the original German, is surely one of the greatest of Britten's cycles, though the intensity and the introspection of these *Fragments* militates against their ever achieving the popularity of the more outward-looking works. With *The Songs and Proverbs of William Blake*, Britten returned to the English language to provide an interesting cycle for the German baritone Dietrich Fischer-Dieskau. His last group of songs, to date, is *The Poet's Echo*, settings of Pushkin, in Russian, composed during a visit to the Soviet Union in 1965.

Michael Tippett (b. 1905) is several years older than Britten, and, like him, primarily an opera composer. Unlike Britten, however, he has written very few solo songs. *Boyhood's End*, a short cantata whose text is a prose passage from W. H. Hudson's *Green Mansions*, is a masterly piece of word-setting, while the more conventional sequence of poems by Sidney Keyes and Alun Lewis, *The Heart's Assurance*, is almost equally effective by virtue of Tippett's warm and passionate response to the poems. Peter Pears, for whom both works were composed, has written perceptively, and not uncritically of them.* Of the andante section of *Boyhood's End*, he says: '(it) is one of Tippett's best things, a beautiful vocal weaving around an evocative, slow,

* In his contribution to *Michael Tippett: a Symposium on his Sixtieth Birthday* (edited by Ian Kemp) Faber & Faber London 1965

mirror-like movement ... the subtle colouring of the words through a wide range gives the singer, unaccompanied much of the time, chance after chance to express the finest of verbal nuances.'

If English-language song in the United States of America differs at all significantly from English song, the difference may well lie in the fact that American composers appear to be more open to European continental influence than English composers allow themselves to be. Of course, in a more recently immigrant society, it is hardly surprising that a considerable number of composers are the sons or grandsons of Europeans, and thus more closely linked with the styles and traditions of Europe than are the temperamentally insular British.

Around the turn of the century a number of songs by Reginald De Koven (1859–1920) were highly popular in the United States. De Koven, who studied at Oxford and then pursued a career on the continent, was a composer of operas, some of them bordering on operetta, others in more serious vein. His 400 or more songs are evidence of a facile melodic gift and great industriousness; curiously the only composition by De Koven that is encountered at all nowadays is the ballad 'Oh Promise Me', which comes from his light opera *Robin Hood*, produced in Chicago in 1890. Still much in demand at weddings, 'Oh promise me' was in fact composed earlier than 1890 as a separate song, and inserted into the *Robin Hood* score at a late stage of rehearsals.

Edward MacDowell (1861–1908), by temperament a 19th-century German romantic, pursued his musical studies in France and Germany, and then lived in Germany for a time before returning to his native America. A fine pianist, most of his best music was composed for the piano, but some of his forty-two songs also reveal a fresh lyrical impulse that keeps them in the repertoires of American singers. Many of them are settings of poems by the composer himself, but the attractive set of *Six Love Songs* composed in 1890 makes use of poems by W. H. Gardner. Less highly regarded than MacDowell is Amy Mary Beach (1867–1944), known as Mrs H. H. Beach, though she possessed an enviable melodic gift which she employed in a number of pleasant, undemanding ballads, such as 'Ah love, but a day'. More considerably gifted than either, Charles Ives

(1874–1954), a curious compound of primitive and experiment-
alist, composed in most forms, producing a number of songs in
a mixture of individual styles. As the fifth edition of Grove
says tartly of him, as a song writer he 'will probably remain an
"interesting historical figure" until singers learn to negotiate his
most empirical vocalism with ease—and accompanists become
proficient with the helpful wooden sticks that cover large chord-
clusters on the keyboard.'

Largely taught in the United States, though he also studied
for some months with Elgar, John Alden Carpenter (1876–1951)
was one of the most interesting and inventive American composers of his time. His symphonic and ballet music shows an
easy mastery of orchestral technique and an instinctive sense of
form. The latter quality is also in evidence in his songs. Some
enterprising concert singer ought to examine Carpenter's
Watercolours, a Chinese song suite for mezzo-soprano and
chamber orchestra, composed in 1918. Richard Hagemann
(1882–1970), composer and conductor, was born in Holland,
but travelled to New York in his early twenties as accompanist
to Yvette Guilbert and decided to stay in the United States.
For many years he conducted at the Metropolitan Opera, and
later made appearances in films, usually portraying a conductor
or pianist. Of his many songs to English texts, most of them
sentimental but attractive ballads, 'Do not go, my love' is
probably the best known.

Charles Tomlinson Griffes (1884–1920), who studied in Berlin
under Humperdinck, composed some graceful, though perhaps
no more than palely interesting songs, to German and English
texts. His settings of Lenau and Heine sound curiously like
Debussy, but the *Five Poems of Ancient China and Japan*,
written on five- and six-note scales, are more individual and
arresting. Of Griffes's German settings, that of Geibel's 'Wohl
lag ich einst in Gram und Schmerz' (no. 5 of the five *German
Songs* of 1909–10) is musically the most substantial. Doyen of
living American composers, Virgil Thomson (b. 1896) studied in
Paris with Nadia Boulanger, and later came into contact with
the French group of Les Six, with Satie and with the expatriate
American writer Gertrude Stein, all of whom contributed their
influence on his thought and his music. It is hardly surprising,
therefore, that Thomson's songs should include so many settings
of the French language. At their best, his songs are refreshingly
free from staleness and mannerism, their structure clear and firm,

their language unpretentious, if perhaps a trifle impersonal. Two Gertrude Stein songs of the 1920s and 'Commentaire sur Saint Jérome' (Marquis de Sade) are among the most arresting of Thomson's earlier songs, and his engaging setting of Kenneth Koch's 'Let's Take a Walk' (1959) stands out from his more recent essays. Born in the same year as Virgil Thomson, Roger Sessions (b. 1896) lacks his contemporary's exuberance and facility. Sessions composes slowly, and his list of works is not large. It includes a few songs which are highly regarded by American music critics. Another composer of the same generation whose songs have been admired is Roy Harris (b. 1898), a classical traditionalist with a distinctive American voice.

Probably the most important living American composer is Aaron Copland (b. 1900), a Boulanger pupil whose creative personality is somewhat schizophrenic, alternating between a Stravinsky-influenced angular terseness and a relaxed extrovert expansiveness. Copland's songs, most of them in the latter style, include a splendid cycle, *Twelve Poems of Emily Dickinson*, composed in 1949–50, as well as affectionately arranged folk songs and revivalist hymn tunes. Symphonic and ballet music, however, make up the larger part of Copland's *oeuvre*. Samuel Barber (b. 1910), on the other hand, has a greater involvement in vocal music, and is himself a baritone. Romantic by temperament, and conservative in musical language and technique, he has written a number of highly attractive songs to texts by such poets as James Stephens, A. E. Housman, James Joyce, Gerard Manley Hopkins and W. B. Yeats. Barber's most famous vocal composition, if one excepts the opera *Anthony and Cleopatra* which was commissioned to open the new Metropolitan Opera in 1965, is 'Dover Beach', a setting of Matthew Arnold composed in 1931 for voice and string quartet. The cycle, *Hermit Songs*, excellent songs on texts by mediaeval Irish monks, was first performed in 1953 by the soprano Leontyne Price, with the composer accompanying.

David Diamond (b. 1915) lacks any incisiveness of creative personality, though his lyrical style is certainly accomplished. His not very numerous vocal works include a somewhat unusual cycle of nine songs, *L'Ame de Debussy*, their texts taken from Debussy's letters. Lukas Foss (b. 1922) was born in Berlin, and arrived in the United States in his teens. His music, too, lacks any strongly defined character, though he is a fluent melodist. Foss has written some quite attractive songs, as has another foreign-born American of the same generation, Ernest Gold (b. 1921 in Vienna). He is an accomplished composer of music for films, including *Exodus, Judgment at Nuremberg* and *On the Beach*, and his songs include a romantic cycle, *Songs of love and parting*, written in 1961–2.

Ned Rorem (b. 1923), one of the best living American song composers, perhaps because he tends to specialize in song, writes in a musical language that is direct, communicative, personal and engaging. He concentrates on setting contemporary American poets, which he does with conspicuous success, in songs that are neither drearily arcane nor mechanically popular in style. In this genre he is almost an American equivalent of Benjamin Britten.

The songs of Leonard Bernstein (b. 1918) include two determinedly smart cycles, *I hate music* (1943) and *La Bonne Cuisine*, settings of French recipes (1949). Bernstein is mentioned here, however, for his contributions to popular song, through 'show-biz' concoctions such as *West Side Story*. The Broadway musical, decadent offspring of Viennese operetta, descends from Strauss, Lehár and Stolz, through such European-Americans as Victor Herbert (born in Dublin; 1859–1924), Sigmund Romberg (born in Hungary; 1887–1951) and Rudolf Friml (Prague; 1879–1972) to the native-born Cole Porter (1893–1964), Irving Berlin (b. 1888), Jerome Kern (1885–1945), George Gershwin (1898–1937) and Duke Ellington (1899–1974). The musical has produced a number of delightful tunes, modern American counterparts of those 18th century English songs written for the pleasure gardens in London.

EPILOGUE

In song, as in all other musical forms, the gap between the good and the popular has now widened to the point where the two concepts have taken up opposing positions. The music critically most admired today is really liked by the fewest people, so it is not surprising that concert singers in the main continue to draw the bulk of the regularly performed repertoire from the great periods of the past when the gap, if it existed, was hardly noticeable. There seems something childlike, in any case, in today's widely postulated proposition that the *Zeitgeist* must be so directly, uncompromisingly and consciously reflected in its art. The great creators of the past—Shakespeare, Goethe, Jane Austen, Dostoevsky, Beethoven—would have been amused or bemused by such a suggestion, however much and however obviously their times affected their own temperaments and thus, indirectly, their work. Song, in particular, is and should be instinctive, untortuous, and in the deepest sense natural. It will continue to flourish only if it keeps a certain distance from the more intellectualized art forms. Song is, by definition, tuneful. Though tunes are fewer on the ground now than they were fifty and a hundred years ago, the real singers, both creators and performers, will continue to know how and where to find what tunes there are.

SELECTIVE BIBLIOGRAPHY

SELECTIVE BIBLIOGRAPHY

Bach, A. B. *The Art Ballad* (Edinburgh, 1890)
Brown, M. J. E. *Schubert Songs* (London, 1967)
Capell, R. *Schubert's Songs* (London, 1928)
Friedländer, M. *Brahms's Lieder* (Oxford, 1929)
Jefferson, A. *The Lieder of Richard Strauss* (London, 1971)
Lehmann, L. *Eighteen Song Cycles* (London, 1971)
      More Than Singing (London, 1946)
Moore, G. *Singer and Accompanist* (London, 1953)
Noske, F. *French Song from Berlioz to Duparc* (New York, 1970)
Plunket Greene, H. *Interpretation in Song* (London, 1911)
Porter, E. G. *Schubert's Song Technique* (London, 1961)
Sams, E. *The Songs of Hugo Wolf* (London, 1961)
Schumann, E. *German Song* (London, 1948)
Stevens, D. (ed.) *A History of Song* (London, 1961)
Warlock, P. *The English Ayre* (Oxford, 1926)
Walsh, S. *The Lieder of Schumann* (London, 1971)
Young, P. M. *The Story of Song* (London, 1956)

INDEX OF COMPOSERS AND POETS

INDEX OF COMPOSERS AND POETS

INDEX OF SONG TITLES

INDEX OF SONG TITLES

There has never been a truly comprehensive survey of concert song. Charles Osborne has succeeded in bringing into one volume descriptions of all the more important *Lieder, mélodies,* Russian and English songs from the seventeenth century to the present day.

It is all too easy to think of the territory as a mountain expanse dominated by the Germanic peaks: Schubert, Schumann, Brahms, Wolf and Strauss. Mr Osborne certainly gives due weight to the awe-inspiring output of these five, but his aerial view reveals other summits just as impressive in their way: there is the French *massif,* for example, including Duparc, Bizet, Fauré, Ravel, Debussy, Poulenc; the major Russian chain of Glinka, Borodin, Balakirev, Tchaikovsky and Mussorgsky; the twin English towers of Warlock and Britten.

There are gentler outcrops too—composers whose songs rarely reach the heights, but who always repay exploration and who are given full consideration by Mr Osborne: Mendelssohn, for example, Jensen, Loewe, Chausson, Medtner, Busoni, Turina, Stanford, John Ireland . . . And finally there are the major composers whom we associate with large-scale achievements, often to the detriment of some very fine songs: Mozart, Beethoven, Liszt; Dvořák; Bellini, Donizetti and Verdi; Chopin; Grieg; Sibelius; Szymanowski. These are the heartlands of song, but Mr Osborne also delves into much little-known material, commenting helpfully throughout.

The book could well prove itself to be an essential work of reference for singers, and those wishing to extend and vary their repertoire will find it a splendid treasure-chest. Mr Osborne is a trustworthy guide: he can save hours of research by pinpointing the highlights of a composer's